Creoles of Color of the Gulf South

Creoles of Color
of the Gulf South

Edited by James H. Dormon

The University of Tennessee Press / Knoxville

Library of Congress Cataloging-in-Publication Data

Creoles of color of the Gulf South / edited by James H. Dormon.—1st
ed.
    p. cm.
  Includes bibliographical references and index.
  ISBN 0-87049-916-5 (cloth : alk. paper).
  ISBN 0-87049-917-3 (pbk. : alk. paper)
  1. Creoles—Louisiana. 2. Creoles—Gulf States. 3. Louisiana—Social
life and customs. 4. Gulf States—Social life and customs.
  I. Dormon, James H.
F390.C87C74 1996
976.3'00496073—dc20   95-4432
                                            CIP

To the memory of Ulysses S. Ricard Jr.

Contents

Illustrations

Preface

Among the myriad metamorphoses wrought by the contact of Old World and New World cultures, none exceeded in significance the actual creation of new peoples. The human biological and cultural results of the "Columbian Exchange" included as a primary consequence the genetically (and culturally) mixed populations that followed in the wake of the European invasion of the Americas. At virtually every point of large-scale contact between the indigenous populations and the European newcomers the process appears to have been inevitable. Beginning with the creation of the vast mestizo population of what became Latin America, followed by the smaller (but no less significant) métis population of French Canada, and on a much smaller scale the variety of genetically mixed peoples resulting from the arrival of the British, Dutch, German, and other colonizers and colonists, new sorts of people with special destinies came to be among the great variety of new "Americans." The advent of the African appearance in the New World, largely the result of the great Atlantic slave trade, brought yet another dimension to the creation of new peoples through the process of creolization in the Caribbean and the Americas. Among these peoples, of course, was the group that appeared in Louisiana and along the Gulf Coastal Plain in the eighteenth century, whose descendants in the nineteenth century came to be called "Creoles of Color."

It is perhaps significant in this context that the term "Creole" claims an etymology deriving from the Latin *creare*—"to beget" or "create." New World Creoles were indeed "created" as the byproducts of the European colonial process as augmented by the slave trade, and such Creoles came to play out their own roles in the colonial ventures of the various European colonial powers. But any discussion of Creoles and creolization must begin with the clear understanding that the term has been used historically in an enormous variety of ways and has taken on a protean quality that can lead to great confusion in the absence of clarification. While it is not my intention to provide an elaborate comment on the historical uses of the term (this would require a book in itself), a few general etymological and definitional observations are in order.

While the earliest usages of the term "Creole" are still debatable, it is generally accepted that the term appeared first in Portuguese as *crioulo,* meaning a New World slave of African descent. By the seventeenth century the term had come to be applied more generally to persons (and sometimes to *products*) native to the colonies and, more particularly, to the French colonies, including ultimately Louisiana (Hall 1992: 157–58; Tregle 1992: 137–38). In Louisiana throughout the colonial period (1699–1803), Creole (in Spanish, *criollo*) referred in a general sense to persons born in the colony of either African or European descent, or to any miscegen (i.e., a product of miscegenation), including African and Native American mixtures, termed Grifs. The most common colonial usage, however, was as a reference to persons born into slavery in a given colony, differentiating such Creole slaves from slaves born elsewhere (Hall 1992: 157).

In the later eighteenth century, and more especially in the nineteenth, "Creole" took on variant meanings depending largely on the situation and the identity and circumstances of the speaker employing the term. As a means of differentiating themselves from the foreign-born, and especially the Anglo-Americans, native Louisianians (black, white, and mixed) began referring to themselves as Creoles. This terminology held throughout the antebellum period, though by the 1820s one group of such Creoles began to distinguish themselves from all others. The growing community of Afro-European miscegens who were descended from colonial free persons of color and who occupied a special, intermediate place in the racial and social order of antebellum Louisiana and the Gulf port cities began referring to themselves as "Creoles of Color."[1]

It is this meaning that prevails with at least *some* degree of consistency in the work at hand. It should be understood, however, that the continuing evolution of the term's usage renders a perfect consistency of usage impossible. Such terminologies, like ethnic groups themselves, are never static, unchanging, immutable realities. It would be impossible to impose any definition on either the group or its descriptive terminology that would be consistently applicable throughout time and historical circumstance. Any such effort would in itself distort reality. In my conclusion to this book I will return to conceptual and definitional matters, but largely in an effort to analyze the ways in which the group has defined *itself* (and designated itself) in the second half of the twentieth century. Thus shifting usage of the term continues in process.

It is of course these self-proclaimed "Creoles of Color" that constitute the subject of this collection of essays. In recent years the scholarship pertaining to the group has grown substantially (and substantively). In part as a result of the availability of painstakingly compiled data bases and quantitative methodology and in part as a reflection of a more generalized interest in ethnic cultures, scholars have produced major works addressed to the understanding of this altogether unique population (e.g., Hirsch and Logsdon 1992). A recent workshop on Gulf South data bases held in New Orleans, for example, pointed to the kinds of computer-based research material now available that have added immeasurably to the detailed investigation of the social history of the Gulf region. Specific sessions offered discussions of data-based material on such topics as notarial records (covering probate, sale, and emancipation records pertaining to Gulf slaves), sacramental records (including birth, baptismal, and death records), censuses, shipwrecks, and cartography. Notably, the participants in the workshop (all members of the Gulf Coast Historical Database Group) included four of the contributors to this collection, all of whom have utilized such material in their work.

As the complex history of the Gulf Creoles of Color emerges, some particulars of their story take on a recognizable pattern, parts of which this collection attempts to delineate. The process whereby the Gulf Creoles came into being looks back into the French colonial period and continues as a process well into the antebellum years. As genetic intermixture, acculturation (broadly, "creolization"), and the expansion in numbers of the free persons of color (the *gens de couleur libre*) interacted over time and place, the people calling themselves Creoles of Color emerged by the second quarter of the nineteenth century as a distinctive, self-aware ethnic community.

In the New Orleans area (where the process commenced), in the Mississippi River settlements northwest of New Orleans, in Spanish Mobile and Pensacola and their environs, in the prairie region of what is now southwest Louisiana, in the Cane River/Isle Brevelle community of Natchitoches Parish, and in a variety of smaller enclaves, identifiable communities of Creoles of Color emerged to claim (in Virginia Gould's terminology) "the middle ground" between slaves and free blacks, on the one hand, and the dominant whites, on the other. Persistent in their determination to preserve their status, the members of this group maintained their ethnic identity even after the Civil War, Reconstruction, and Jim Crow segregation denied them their special legal and social privileges. And while the value attachments to their ethnic identity shifted notably over the decades of the twentieth century, the fact of their special historical circumstances provided the ego-serving emotional need to maintain their ethnic community.

Such, then, are the broad contours of their story. The essays forming the body of this collection deal with specifics and particulars of certain aspects of that story.

The social-historical fundamentals are treated in a series of four essays opening the collection. Kimberly Hanger treats the process whereby the ancestors of the Gulf Creoles came to assume their special status, largely during the Spanish colonial period in New Orleans and the contiguous countryside. (Although this collection focuses on Creole communities *outside* New Orleans, the origins of the ethnic group necessitate careful consideration of circumstances prevailing in the New Orleans area during the late colonial period in order to comprehend the provenance of the group). Virginia Gould takes the emergent Creoles into the Gulf ports of Mobile and Pensacola and provides a discussion of the emergence of a self-conscious ethnic group determined to hold on to its identity and its status. Loren Schweninger ranges more broadly through the Gulf region in treating socioeconomic developments into the post–Civil War period. And Carl Brasseaux concentrates on the bayou and prairie regions of Louisiana and east Texas in his treatment of the Prairie Creoles from the late eighteenth century to the late nineteenth.

Specific features of what might be termed Gulf Creole culture are the topic of the next series of essays by, in turn, an anthropological folklorist (Nick Spitzer, on aspects of Creole folklore, focusing on the Creole Mardi Gras in a single Louisiana community), a second folklorist (Barry Jean Ancelet, on the music of the Prairie Creoles), and a cultural linguist (Albert Valdman, on Creole language and linguistics).[2] Finally, my own essay on twentieth-century developments (historical and cultural) concludes the collection, endeavoring (as noted) to re-address matters of definition and conception and to treat ethnic group maintenance among the Louisiana Creoles. I also attempt to pull together some of the major themes developed in the earlier essays.

As is likely inevitable in collections of this sort, there is an element of eclecticism in the editorial selection of content. Moreover, there is considerable diversity in the approaches of the contributors. Such is also inevitable in any transdisciplinary scholarship. Eight different authors representing four disciplines and five specializations are likely to proceed in rather different directions and address rather different concerns. As overall editor, I have made these selections with such considerations fully in mind. But I have also endeavored to provide an element of logical organization and consistency even in view of eclecticism. Thus, while the first half of the collection appropriately focuses on eighteenth- and nineteenth-century historical developments, anthropological and folkloristic concerns based in the methodologies of those disciplines bring key aspects of the Creole experience to the late twentieth century. And, lest these comments appear overly defensive, let it be said from the outset that I consider eclecticism in this collection to be a strength rather than a weakness.

Nonetheless, even a cursory glance at the coverage afforded in these pages reveals some major omissions in the overall ethnohistory of the Gulf Creoles. By design, New Orleans after 1803 receives only slight consideration. The same is true of the important Cane River/Isle Brevelle region, where a most notable Creole community has existed from the late eighteenth century to the present. The reason for these omissions is simple: In both cases, earlier scholarship has treated them seriously and, on balance, well (Anthony 1978; Domínguez 1986; Gehman 1994; Haskins 1975; Hirsch and Logsdon 1992; Mills 1977; Rankin 1978; Woods 1972, 1989). This collection is designed to fill in some of the existing gaps— that is, to consider areas *not* given great attention prior to this time—and especially to consider to the Creole experience *outside* New Orleans and the Cane River country.

Yet another major gap in the collection has a different and altogether lamentable provenance. The River Parish Creoles of Color were to have been covered in an essay undertaken by Ulysses S. Ricard Jr., formerly of the Amistad Research Center in New Orleans. His untimely death on October 7, 1993, terminated that project. The loss of this fine young scholar, himself a New Orleans Creole and a lifelong student of the history and culture of the Creoles of Color, has left a major gap in Creole scholarship. It is a gap not likely to be filled, and surely not to be filled with work reflecting the care and insight that Ulysses brought to the subject. It is entirely appropriate that this volume be dedicated to his memory.

Any scholar undertaking to cover the River Parish Creoles, however, will be well served by Gwendolyn Hall's analysis of colonial Pointe Coupee in her award-winning 1992 book, *Africans in Colonial Louisiana: The Development of Afro-Creole Culture in the Eighteenth Century.* Her work on this area is likely to be definitive, and her book must be the beginning point for anyone seeking to understand the enormous complexity of ethno-racial developments in early Louisiana. Ricard's notes and data, to be made available to scholars at the Amistad collection, will likely plot the course for those seeking to pursue this fascinating dimension of the Creole story. In the meantime, let the essays in the collection at hand speak to other aspects of that story as they address their own specific topic areas.

As regards the larger significance of the Creole of Color experience, one last introductory comment seems in order. The ethnohistorical experience of the Gulf Creoles provides a notable (and neglected) dimension of the history of the African-American population or, perhaps more accurately, of a genetically and culturally mixed population (a definitively *Creole* population) that was and is a part of the American ethnic mosaic. Until recently, scholars (of both the multicultural and monocultural persuasions) have generally accepted a racial classificatory system that omitted any place for marginal peoples existing *between* the primary racial classifications in the United States. The Creoles of Color not only made their place in the "middle ground"; they also sought their very identity there. In a period in which America is still apparently obsessed with racial concerns, even as interracial social contacts grow ever more commonplace (and increasingly accepted) and as interracial families increase in number, the experience of the Gulf Creoles may well stand as the primary historical example of a mixed population that endured not despite but rather because of its marginality. Recent scholarship patently points to that pervasive interest and concern with matters of race and miscegenation in America today (Davis 1991; Root 1992; Russell, Wilson, and Hall 1992; Webster 1992). And the Gulf Creoles have even found their way into the popular press, as is evidenced by the recent appearance of a major article detailing their paradoxical history in the pages of the New York *Village Voice* (Wood 1994). Surely the experience of the Creoles of Color provides an essential ethnohistorical perspective to this ongoing national obsession with race and racial dynamics in the history of the United States and, indeed, in the Western world. This collection constitutes a collective effort to fill in some of the hitherto missing pieces of that story.

Notes

1. This usage came to be accepted (albeit at times reluctantly) by the white population, and the usage persisted even when in the postbellum years the genetically European (i.e., white) families descending from Creole ancestors claimed the label "Creole" as exclusively their own (Domínguez 1986; Tregle 1992: 138–40).
2. Professor Valdman's essay on creole linguistics treats language from the perspective of a specialist in creolization and suggests an apparent paradox: Most Creoles of Color did not speak Creole as a primary language. But it is clear that they were familiar with the dialect, and most of them did speak it on occasion, albeit selectively. It was also central to the language environment in which they lived and was thus clearly a major part of their culture.

References

Anthony, Arthé A. 1978. "The Negro Creole Community of New Orleans, 1880–1920: An Oral History." Ph.D. diss. University of California, Irvine.

Davis, F. James. 1991. *Who Is Black? One Nation's Definition.* University Park, Pa.: Penn State Univ. Press.

Domínguez, Virginia. 1986. *White by Definition: Social Classification in Creole Louisiana.* New Brunswick, N.J.: Rutgers Univ. Press.

Gehman, Mary. 1994. *The Free People of Color of New Orleans: An Introduction.* New Orleans: Margaret Media, Inc.

Haskins, James. 1975. *Creoles of Color in New Orleans.* New York: Crowell.

Hall, Gwendolyn Midlo. 1992. *Africans in Colonial Louisiana: The Development of Afro-Creole Culture in the Eighteenth Century.* Baton Rouge: Louisiana State Univ. Press.

Hirsch, Arnold R., and Joseph Logsdon. 1992. *Creole New Orleans: Race and Americanization.* Baton Rouge: Louisiana State Univ. Press.

Mills, Gary B. 1977. *The Forgotten People: Cane River's Creoles of Color.* Baton Rouge: Louisiana State Univ. Press.

Rankin, David. 1977–78. "The Impact of the Civil War on the Free Colored Community of New Orleans." *Perspectives in American History* 11: 379–416.

Root, Maria P., ed. 1992. *Racially Mixed People in America.* Newbury Park, Calif.: Sage Publications.

Russell, Kathy, Midge Wilson, and Ronald Hall. 1992. *The Color Complex: The Politics of Skin Color among African Americans.* New York: Doubleday Anchor Books.

Tregle, Joseph G. 1992. "Creoles and Americans." In Hirsch and Logsdon, 1992: 131–85.

Webster, Yehudi. 1992. *The Racialization of America.* New York: St. Martin Press.

Wood, Joe. 1994. "Escape from Blackness: Once Upon a Time in Creole America." *Village Voice* 29 (49) (Dec. 6, 1994): 25–29.

Woods, Sr. Frances Jerome. 1972. *Marginality and Identity: A Colored Creole Family Through Ten Generations.* Baton Rouge: Louisiana State Univ. Press.

———. 1989. *Value Retention Among Young Creoles: Attitudes and Commitment of Contemporary Youth.* Mellen Studies in Sociology, vol. 5. Lewiston, N.Y.: Edwin Mellen Press.

ONE

Kimberly S. Hanger

Origins of New Orleans's Free Creoles of Color

The origins of antebellum New Orleans's large, influential, and proper-tied free black population, unique to the United States South, can be found in the city's colonial era. Although free blacks lived in Louisiana from almost its beginning under French rule (1699–1769), it was during the Spanish regime (1769–1803) that demographic, economic, political, and military conditions meshed with cultural and legal traditions to favor the growth and persistence of a substantial group of free people of color (table 1.1). In the latter part of the eighteenth century, the free black population grew not only in numbers, but some members gained also in afflu-ence, acquiring property, military titles, and status as *vecinos* (landed citi-zens) in society. Interpersonal relations in this small community on Spain's northern frontier ameliorated prejudice, facilitated familiarity among persons of all races, nationalities, and classes, and enabled indi-viduals to advance, always within acceptable limits, on their own merit or with the aid of kin and patronage connections. Only when Louisiana's plantation system matured and slavery intensified with profitable sugar and cotton cultivation in the initial years of American rule did officials and planters together restrict manumissions and free black activities.

This chapter looks at the forebears of New Orleans's Creoles of Color, at all free persons of African descent. Although free blacks had special privileges and rights, as did other racial, status, and occupational groups within Spanish corporate society, they cannot be viewed as one monolithic group. Some maintained associations and cultural identity more closely with slave society, especially those who were newly freed or whose spouses or relatives remained enslaved. Second-generation free blacks or those with white relatives or greater wealth tended to associate more frequently with white society. Before the United States Congress abolished the external slave trade to Louisiana in 1804, free blacks and slaves entered the colony willingly or by force from Africa, Europe, and throughout the Americas (Hall 1992). Once the slave trade was cut off, however, more and more Louisiana blacks were native born (Creoles).

Table 1.1

Colonial New Orleans Population, Year by Racial/Status Group

	Whites	Blacks		Indian	
Year		Slaves	Free Blacks	Slaves	Total
1721	278	173[a]		21	472
1726	793	78		30	901
1732	626	258		9	893
1771	1,803	1,227	97		3,127
1777	1,736	1,151	315		3,203
1788	2,370	2,131	820		5,321
1791	2,386	1,789	862		5,037
1805	3,551	3,105	1,566		8,222

SOURCES:1721: Jay K. Ditchy, trans., "Early Census Tables of Louisiana," *Louisiana Historical Quarterly* 13 (2) (Apr. 1930): 214-20; 1726: Daniel H. Usner Jr. *Indians Settlers and Slaves in a Frontier Exchange Economy: The Lower Mississippi Valley Before 1783* (Chapel Hill: University of North Carolina Press for the Institute of Early American Culture, 1992), 48–49; 1732: Charles R. Maduell, comp. and trans., *The Census Tables for the French Colony of Louisiana from 1699 through 1732* (Baltimore: Johns Hopkins University Press, 1972), 75. 1771: Lawrence Kinnaird, *Spain in the Mississippi Valley, 1765-1794*, 3 vols. (Washington, D.C.: Government Printing Office, 1946-1949), 2: 196; 1777: AGI-PC 2351, 12 May 1777; 1788: AGI-PC 1425, 1788; 1791: Census of the City of New Orleans, 6 Nov. 1791, New Orleans Public Library; 1805: Matthew Flannery, comp., *New Orleans in 1805: A Directory and a Census* (New Orleans: Pelican Gallery, 1936).
[a]First three sources do not distinguish between slaves and free blacks.

Many of those blacks identified as Creoles of Color in the nineteenth century had parents or grandparents of various ethnic makeup who gained their freedom in Louisiana during the Spanish regime of the eighteenth century.[1]

Indeed, it was during the three and a half decades of actual Spanish rule in Louisiana (1769–1803) that free persons of African descent in New Orleans made their greatest advances in terms of demographics, privileges, responsibilities, and social standing. In desperate need of allies and laborers, Spanish authorities fostered the growth and protection of a free black population, primarily for their own ends rather than for the benefit of people of color. Not all slaves sought freedom, a state that free persons of color and whites often experienced differently, but those who did yearn for liberty were more likely to attain it under Spain's dominion than under that of France or the United States. African Americans astutely availed themselves of conditions present in Spanish New Orleans not only to gain freedom, but also to attain decent living standards and to advance their social status or at least that of their children (Hanger 1991).

The various legal avenues to freedom available to and pursued by persons of African descent are surveyed using such primary source materials as notarial registers, census and tax records, court proceedings, and sacramental records. Although free blacks initiated and expanded their numbers and influence primarily through manumission during the Spanish period, natural increase and immigration also played a part in the group's demographic growth.[2] Methods deemed illegal by the dominant white society, such as revolt and escape, have been investigated by other scholars (Andreu Ocaríz 1977; Din 1980; Hall 1992; Holmes 1970; Kerr 1993) and are not included here. While most of the data is drawn from New Orleans, several of the free and slave people of color involved lived on farms and plantations outside the city and came to New Orleans to transact legal business. Some lived in the city but held property in its hinterlands, and others moved from the city to the countryside and vice versa. Contact between New Orleans free people of color and their country kin and friends was frequent and enduring. Thus, this essay addresses the development of a group of people who lived both in and outside New Orleans.

The Setting: Colonial New Orleans

Founded in 1718 on the site of a long-established Native American portage point where the Mississippi River comes closest to the shores of Lake Pontchartrain, New Orleans was Louisiana's principal urban center and port. The furs, hides, timber, and agricultural products of the Mississippi Valley region flowed through the city en route to the West Indies, the North American colonies/states, New Spain, and occasionally Europe. New Orleans also served as the entrepôt for slaves and various goods, such as flour and cloth, that colonials could not supply or manufacture themselves. France held Louisiana and its capital city of New Orleans from 1699 to 1763, when it ceded the colony to Spain under provisions of the Treaty of Paris in that year. Spain did not actually take control of Louisiana until 1769 and governed it until 1803.

Under French and Spanish rule Louisiana's value was mainly strategic. Both Bourbon monarchies viewed Louisiana as useful primarily

within the context of larger geopolitical considerations: neither wanted
Britain to seize it. Although Spain, like France, considered Louisiana an
economic burden, the Spanish crown hoped to utilize it as a protective
barrier between mineral-rich New Spain and Britain's increasingly aggres-
sive North American colonies. Spain thus actively endeavored to attract settlers and slaves to the region, not only to defend it but also to balance the
somewhat hostile French population remaining in Louisiana and to promote agricultural and commercial growth (Wall 1990; Weber 1992).

The Slave Trade to Louisiana

Wholesale importation of slaves from Africa to Louisiana began in 1719,
when ships commissioned by John Law's Company of the Indies deposited five hundred Guinea slaves on the banks of the Mississippi. These
slaves, along with indentured servants, salt and tobacco smugglers, debt-
ors, soldier-farmers, and colonists who immigrated of their own volition,
labored to construct the new colonial capital and produce crops for subsistence and export. Although Indian enslavement continued well into
the Spanish period, Native Americans never met Louisiana's labor de-
mands; one French governor, the Sieur de Bienville, even proposed to
Saint-Domingue officials an exchange of three of his Indian slaves for
two of their African slaves (Usner 1979). He and other officials and settlers could not convince slave traders to send the number of bondpersons
needed to exploit colonial resources to their full potential, primarily because in economic terms Louisiana was one of the least significant colonies in both the French and Spanish imperial systems (Hall 1992).

The traffic in slaves to Louisiana did not really take off until the
last three decades of the eighteenth century, when the colony was "re-
Africanized," following its initial importation of Africans between 1719
and 1731. Traders brought slaves to Louisiana directly from Africa,
mainly from Senegal and the Bight of Benin (Fiehrer 1979; Hall 1992).
During the 1780s Spain and its governors in Louisiana also encouraged
merchants to import African and Creole slaves from the West Indies. A
royal *cédula* (decree) of 1782 admitted slaves from the French West
Indies duty-free. Two years later another order modified that *cédula*, al-
lowing certain slaves to enter duty-free but charging a 6 percent duty on
other bondpersons. A liberal decree of 1789 granted freedom to black
slaves who had fled from alien lands and sought sanctuary in Louisiana.

In light of the Saint-Domingue revolt that erupted in 1791 and Louisianians' fears that black slaves from the French islands would inspire
their own slaves to rebel, Spanish Governor François-Louis Hector, Baron

de Carondelet et Noyelles, banned slave imports from the West Indies. Carondelet lifted restrictions in 1793, but re-instituted them in June 1795, to last for the duration of the Franco-Spanish war. Even though the war ended one month later, the rebellion in Saint-Domingue continued; Carondelet issued a new proclamation forbidding the entrance of any black slaves, even those coming directly from Africa, into the colony. Although Louisianians continued to smuggle slaves in order to meet their rising labor needs, local authorities did not again sanction the foreign slave trade until 1800 (Lachance 1979).

Emergence of the Free Black Population

The first recorded emancipation of an African slave in Louisiana was that of Louis Congo, who obtained his freedom by accepting a position as colonial executioner in the early 1720s. From the very beginning of New Orleans's history, free people of color resided in the city, but their exact numbers were unknown. French census takers did not indicate whether persons of African descent were slave or free; they consolidated free blacks with either hired hands or black slaves (table 1.1). The 1721 census of New Orleans enumerated 145 white males, 65 white women, 38 children, 29 white servants, 172 blacks, and 21 Indian slaves. By 1726 New Orleans's black population had risen to 300, but it dropped to 258 by 1732 (28.9 percent of the total population). Only when Spain effectively took over Louisiana in 1769 did census takers begin to distinguish between free blacks and slaves and between *pardos* (light-skinned blacks) and *morenos* (dark-skinned blacks). Spanish figures, however, were no more accurate than those of the French era, and the Spanish census takers usually undercounted free persons of color. For example, a count of 97 free persons of color in 1771 was ridiculously low, given that militia rosters for 1770 list 61 free *pardos* and 238 free *morenos* between the ages of fifteen and 45 living within four leagues (twelve land miles) of New Orleans (Archivo General de Indias, Papeles Procedentes de Cuba [hereafter abbreviated as AGI-PC], 188-A).

It was during the Spanish era of colonial rule that the New Orleans free black population grew by leaps and bounds, in relation to both the free and nonwhite populations as well as to the total populations (tables 1.1 and 1.2). Free blacks made up only 7.1 percent of the city's African-American population in 1769, but rose to a high of 33.5 percent by 1805. In contrast to demographic trends found for many Spanish-American regions at the beginning of the nineteenth century, free nonwhites never outnumbered slaves in New Orleans, but they nevertheless made up a

Table 1.2

Proportion of Free People of Color in the Total, Free, and Non-White
Populations, New Orleans, 1771–1805

Year	% of Total Population	N	% of Free Population	N	% of Non-White Population	N
1771	3.1	3127	5.1	1900	7.3	1324
1777	9.8	3202	15.4	2051	21.5	1466
1788	15.4	5321	25.7	3190	27.8	2951
1791	17.1	5037	26.5	3248	32.5	2651
1805	19.0	8222	30.6	5117	33.5	4671

SOURCES: 1771: Lawrence Kinnaird, *Spain in the Mississippi Valley, 1765-1794*, 3 vols.
(Washington, D.C.: Government Printing Office, 1946-1949), 2: 196; 1777: AGI-PC
2351, 12 May 1777; 1788: AGI-PC 1425, 1788; 1791: Census of the City of New Orleans, 6 Nov. 1791, New Orleans Public Library; 1805: Matthew Flannery, comp., *New
Orleans in 1805: A Directory and a Census* (New Orleans: Pelican Gallery, 1936).

substantial proportion of the nonwhite population (Klein 1986). The number of free blacks in the total population expanded sixteenfold over the
Spanish period. Immigration of Saint-Domingue refugees, manumission,
and natural increase fueled this growth well into the antebellum era
(Domínguez 1986; Lachance 1988).

In Louisiana, as in many areas of Spanish America, the crown fostered the growth of a free black population in order to fill middle-sector
economic roles in society (as artisans, petty traders, farmers), to defend
the colony from external and internal foes, and to give African slaves an
officially approved safety valve. Spanish policymakers envisioned a society in which Africans would seek their freedom through legal channels—compensating their masters for property lost by means of service,
money, or material goods—rather than by running away or rising in revolt.
In turn, slaves would look to the Spanish government to *"rescatarnos de
la esclavitud"* (rescue us from slavery) and subsequently protect their
rights and privileges as freedmen (Klein 1986).

With this vision in mind, Spain, upon acquiring Louisiana from
France, made colonial laws conform to those prevailing throughout the
empire. For the governing of slaves and free blacks, Spanish Louisiana
codes primarily drew upon provisions of *Las siete partidas* and the

Recopilación de leyes de los reinos de las Indias, and they also were influenced by the French *code noir* that had been issued for the French West Indies in 1685 and introduced in Louisiana in 1724.[3] Although the *code noir* imposed harsh penalties upon erring slaves and, in the words of Herbert Klein, "proved to be one of the more oppressive slave codes in the Americas" (Klein 1986: 195), it gave free blacks full legal rights to citizenship, ironically after providing unequal punishments and restricting their behavior in preceding articles of the code. Local regulations, however, frequently impinged upon these rights, denying free blacks legal equality with white citizens (Baade 1983; Hall 1972).

In keeping with its aim of encouraging growth of a free black population in Louisiana, the Spanish crown implemented a practice common in its American colonies and known as *coartación:* the right of slaves to purchase their freedom for a specified sum of money agreed upon by their masters or arbitrated in the courts. Louisiana's *code noir* had permitted masters over the age of twenty-five to manumit their slaves, with prior consent from the superior council (the French colonial governing body). Spanish regulations, however, did not require official permission for masters to free their slaves and even allowed slaves to initiate manumission proceedings on their own behalf. Under Spanish law slaves did not have to depend upon the generosity of masters to attain freedom; rather, slaves relied on their own efforts and on the aid of a favorable legal system. Louisiana slaves and parties arguing on their behalf recognized support from Spanish officials for "a cause so recommended by the law as that of liberty."[4] Research in city records for the Spanish era confirms the "direct causal connection between the Spanish Luisiana judicial practice of *coartación* and the emergence of a numerous and socially significant community of free *gens de couleur*" noted by scholar Hans Baade (1983: 47–48).

Avenues to Freedom: General Observations

During the period when Spain ruled New Orleans, black slaves utilized both familiar and new, more effective methods guaranteed by Spanish law and practice to attain the status of free person of color. The process of manumission is grouped into two broad categories: 1) proceedings instituted by the slave's master (voluntary), and 2) those initiated by someone other than the slave's master (by the slave or by third-party purchase). Unconditional manumissions granted *inter vivos* (while the donor was still living) or by testament and manumissions conditioned upon additional service constitute further divisions within the first category; amicable purchase and forced issuance of a *carta de libertad* in front of the

Table 1.3
Type of Manumission by Year and Gender, New Orleans, 1771–1803

Years	Inter Vivos Male	Inter Vivos Female	Will Male	Will Female	Conditional Male	Conditional Female	Total Category One	Self-Purchase Male	Self-Purchase Female	Third Party Male	Third Party Female	Self-Purchase Tribunal Male	Self-Purchase Tribunal Female	Third Party Tribunal Male	Third Party Tribunal Female	Total Category Two
1771–1773 (N-164)	26 15.9[a] 20.2[b] 26.8[c]	71 43.3 55.0 73.2	10 6.1 7.8 41.7	14 8.5 10.9 58.3	1 0.6 0.8 12.5	7 4.3 5.4 87.5	129 78.7 100.1[d]	3 1.8 8.6 14.3	18 11.0 51.4 85.7	7 4.3 20.0 70.0	3 1.8 8.6 30.3	0 0.0 0.0	3 1.8 8.6 100.0	0 0.0 0.0 0.0	1 0.6 2.9 100.0	35 21.3 100.1[d]
1781–1783 (N-233)	23 9.9[a] 19.2[b] 31.9[c]	49 21.0 40.8 68.1	13 5.6 10.8 34.2	25 10.7 20.8 65.8	5 2.1 4.2 50.0	5 2.1 4.2 50.0	120 51.4 100.0	20 8.6 17.7 33.9	39 16.7 34.5 66.1	7 3.0 6.2 29.2	17 7.3 15.0 70.8	8 3.4 7.1 53.3	7 3.0 6.2 46.7	6 2.6 5.3 40.0	9 3.9 8.0 60.0	113 48.5 100.0
1791–1793 (N-269)	24 8.9[a] 17.6[b] 31.6[c]	52 19.3 38.2 68.4	22 8.2 16.2 40.7	32 11.9 23.5 59.3	1 0.4 0.7 16.7	5 1.9 3.7 83.3	136 50.6 99.9[d]	6 2.2 4.5 15.4	33 12.3 24.8 84.6	29 10.8 21.8 49.2	30 11.2 22.6 50.8	6 2.2 4.5 35.3	11 4.1 8.3 64.7	11 4.1 8.3 61.1	7 2.6 5.3 38.9	133 49.4 100.1[d]
1801–1803 (N-322)	31 9.6[a] 24.6[b] 36.5[c]	54 16.8 42.9 63.5	16 5.0 12.7 50.0	16 5.0 12.7 50.0	1 0.3 0.8 11.1	8 2.5 6.3 88.9	126 39.1 100.0	34 10.6 17.3 46.6	39 12.1 19.9 53.4	51 15.8 26.0 46.4	59 18.3 30.1 53.6	0 0.0 0.0 0.0	4 1.2 2.0 100.0	3 0.9 1.5 33.3	6 1.9 3.1 66.7	196 60.9 99.9[d]
TOTAL (N-988)	104 10.5[a] 20.4[b] 31.5[c]	226 22.9 44.2 68.5	61 6.2 11.9 41.2	87 8.8 17.0 58.8	8 0.8 1.6 24.2	25 2.5 4.9 75.8	511 51.7 100.0	63 6.4 13.2 32.8	129 13.1 27.0 67.2	94 9.5 19.7 46.3	109 11.0 22.9 53.7	14 1.4 2.9 35.9	25 2.5 5.2 64.1	20 2.0 4.2 46.5	23 2.3 4.8 53.5	477 48.3 99.9[d]

NOTES: [a] % of total N for given years; [b] % of total in category; [c] % of male/female in Type; [d] % of male/female in Type; [e] error due to rounding.
SOURCES: Acts of: Juan Bautista Garíc, vols. 2-4, Jan. 1771–Dec. 1773; Andrés Almonester y Roxas, Jan. 1771–Dec. 1773, Jan. 1781–Apr. 1782; Rafael Perdomo, Apr.–Dec. 1782 and vols. 1-2, Jan.–Dec. 1783; Leonardo Mazange, vols. 3-7 (1), Jan. 1781–Apr. 1783; Fernando Rodríguez, vols. 7 (2), 1, Apr.–Dec. 1783; Francisco Broutin, vols. 7, 15, 25, Jan. 1791–Dec. 1793; Pedro Pedesclaux, vols. 12-19, Jan. 1791–Dec. 1793 and vols. 38-45, Jan. 1801–Dec. 1803; Carlos Ximénez, vols. 1-5, Jan. 1791–Dec. 1793 and vols. 17-19, Jan. 1801–Nov. 1803; Narciso Broutin, vols. 3-6, Jan. 1801–Dec. 1803. Orleans Parish Notarial Archives, New Orleans, La.

governor's tribunal (either by the slave, a relative, or a friend) comprise finer distinctions within the second category.

Between 1771 and 1803 an increasing percentage of slaves attained freedom by way of their own or a third-party's initiative, while a declining proportion had to rely on their masters' generosity (table 1.3).[5] During this period, when Spain controlled the judicial system, proceedings instituted by persons other than the slave owner gradually came to predominate, rising from one-fifth of all manumission cases in the early 1770s to three-fifths in the early 1800s. For the sample years as a whole, the number of category 1 and category 2 manumissions was about even. More slaves entered the free population with the passing of each three-year period—doubling from the beginning to the end of the Spanish era—but obviously not at a rate that could entirely account for the marked increase in New Orleans's free black residents.[6] Nevertheless, as more and more slaves attained freedom, they gave birth to free children and thereby contributed to natural growth.

The text of several Spanish documents indicated that slaves and free persons acting in the interest of slaves recognized and acted upon the privileges extended to them by Spain.[7] In all likelihood, as the Spanish period advanced New Orleans slaves and interests acting on their behalf gained greater awareness that allowed them to take advantage of the privileges Spain's judicial system offered. With the exception of the last decade, the number of cases brought before governors' and *alcaldes'* (magistrate and member of the cabildo, or town council) tribunals rose dramatically during the era under study. Like Africans in other colonial regions, slaves in New Orleans often had to struggle to secure their rights. Slave and master frequently haggled over the purchase price: in the absence of a written contract the slave encountered difficulties proving the existence of an agreement; many slaves sought protection through the legal system, sometimes without success; and, if written in a will, provisions for self-purchase could be disputed by heirs.

Within every avenue to freedom, females outnumbered males roughly two to one (figure 1.1) for an overall sex ratio of fifty-eight males for every one hundred females. This ratio paralleled the sex ratio for New Orleans free blacks but was lower than that for the city's slaves, whose sex ratio hovered around eighty-two and rose to ninety-five in 1805 (refer to table 1.1). Thus, compared to their proportion of the total New Orleans slave population, bondwomen secured freedom more frequently than did bondmen. These findings correspond favorably with those of James Thomas McGowan for New Orleans and of other scholars for urban centers throughout Spanish America. After analyzing notarial records for New Orleans from 1770 to 1803, McGowan noted that "three times as many women (123) as men (41) between the ages of 20 and 49 purchased their freedom" (1976: 202). This trend was attributed in part to the fact that female slaves could more readily acquire the necessary funds by selling services and goods and by begging. In addition, females, deemed less valuable than males, were able to collect their purchase price in a shorter time span, and masters were more willing to part with them than with male slaves. More important, female slaves outnumbered male slaves in urban areas like New Orleans where self-purchase was more common (Cohen and Greene 1972; Klein 1986).

In New Orleans and elsewhere in the Americas, voluntary manumission practices tended to favor *pardos,* especially children, whereas *morenos* primarily benefited from the practice of self-purchase to achieve free status, and they frequently acted on it.[8] In fact, for those slaves in New Orleans who purchased freedom directly through the master or indirectly

Fig. 1.1. Type of manumission by gender, New Orleans, 1771–1803. From Orleans Parish Notarial Archives, New Orleans, Louisiana.

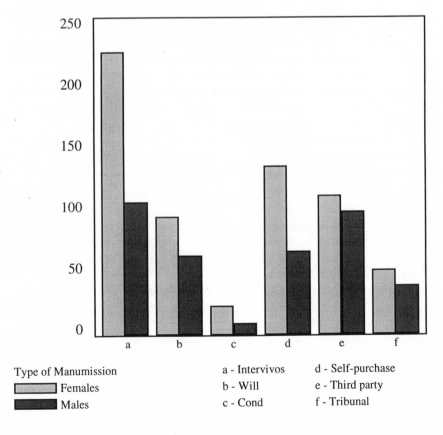

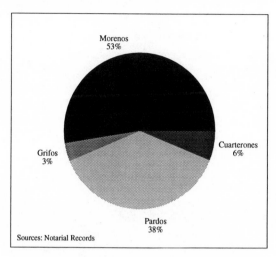

Fig. 1.2. Phenotype of slaves manumitted, New
Orleans, 1771–1803. From Orleans Parish Notarial
Archives, New Orleans, Louisiana.

through the tribunal, the ratio of dark-skinned (*moreno* and *grifo*) to light-skinned (*pardo* and *cuarterón*) was three to two. Overall, *morenos* made up 53 percent of all slaves manumitted (figure 1.2). Due to the failure, however, of many emancipation records to indicate the phenotype of slave children manumitted along with their mothers (for whom skin color was usually provided), the number of *pardos* in the sample is most likely artificially low.

To accumulate the funds needed to purchase one's freedom often required many years of labor and saving, and *coartado* slaves were on the average older than other manumitted slaves. Male and female slaves in their productive adult years (from about age twenty to forty) most commonly possessed the resources, such as skills and physical strength, needed to buy their liberty. Then again, masters were more reluctant to part with their prime slaves, forcing them to turn to tribunals for redress.

With each passing decade the average value of slaves manumitted by exchange of money or goods rose (figure 1.3). This increase was especially noticeable from newborn slaves to those aged forty-nine. As the age of slaves increased, the value of males surpassed that of females; in general, the value disparity was greatest among slaves in their forties. No matter what the age, however, purchase of a *carta* represented a major investment for the slave or a third-party white, free black, or other slave. In Louisiana the price of freedom increased during the Spanish period, and it rose even higher in the antebellum era as officials closed

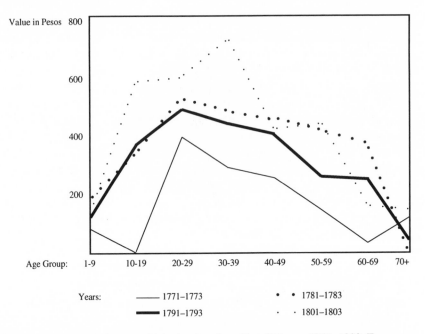

Fig. 1.3. Mean value of slaves purchasing freedom, New Orleans, 1771–1803. From Orleans Parish Notarial Archives, New Orleans, Louisiana.

the foreign slave trade and restricted opportunities for manumission. Many people of color and even some whites labored long years and used most of their scarce resources to free themselves, consorts, friends, or kin, indicating the premium they placed on freedom. Although material conditions were often the same for slaves and free blacks living in an urban environment, there was at least a perceived difference between bondage and liberty.

Types and Examples of Manumission

Inter Vivos *Manumission*

The most common type of legal path to freedom, manumission granted *graciosamente* (gratis) by the master during his or her lifetime, comprised one-third of the total 988 sample cases and almost two-thirds of voluntary (category 1) cases found for the era of Spanish rule. In many instances slaveholders liberated adult women and their children, or even more complex kin units, without compensation to themselves. Slaveholders commonly manumitted these female-headed families for good and loyal services and for the love and care they had shown the master, without any allusion to informal sexual relationships or common-law unions. In some cases, however, such relationships can be deduced. For example, on July 31, 1773, Raymundo Gaillard manumitted his *parda* slave Marion, forty-seven years old, along with her six children, all *cuarterones* Constanza (thirteen), Margarita (eleven), Adelaida (nine), Raymundo (at seven the only son, probably named after his father), Helena (five), and Bacilia (eighteen months) (Almonester y Roxas [July 31, 1773] Orleans Parish Notarial Archives, New Orleans, Louisiana, 188 [hereafter cited by notary's last name, volume, date, and folio(s), and abbreviated as Notarial]). In 1775 these same children received a donation of property from Gaillard (Garic 6 [Oct. 7, 1775]: 240, Notarial) and, according to the 1778 census of New Orleans, the *parda libre* Marion, her eight children, and one slave woman lived with Gaillard, a cooper. When she wrote her will in 1802, Marion Dubreuil (also known as Brion) identified herself as a *parda libre,* a native of New Orleans, and natural daughter of Juana, a deceased *morena libre.* She also listed her eight surviving natural children, five by Gaillard and three older ones by the now dead *moreno libre* Bautista. Among her belongings was a plot of land on the corner of Dumaine and Bourbon Streets on which Don Raymundo had built her a house. Her codicil dated six months later added two more children mistakenly omitted from her will: Bautista and María Luison, father unidentified (Pedesclaux 41 [June 16, 1802]: 445, 42 [Dec. 20, 1802]: 923, Notarial).

White and free black slaveholders who manumitted slave women and their children the same or the next day after purchasing them most likely were united in consensual unions. Occasionally slaveholders admitted paternity when freeing their slaves *inter vivos.* When Carlos Begin manumitted the *pardito* Carlos in 1793, he recognized the slave as his natural son by the *morena* María, also Begin's slave and a native of the African nation of "Essar." At Carlos's baptism the next day, Begin "recognized the child as his own." Copies of the *carta de libertad* and baptismal record were included in court proceedings instituted by the *pardito*'s guardian and godfather when Begin died in May 1794 and named his one-year-old son his only heir (Pedesclaux 19 [Oct. 30, 1793]: 904, Notarial; Books of Black Baptisms, Spanish Period, Archives of the Archdiocese of New Orleans, New Orleans, Louisiana [hereafter abbreviated as BB] 5: 350; Spanish Judicial Records, Louisiana State Museum Historical Center, New Orleans, Louisiana [hereafter abbreviated as SJR] 1794051901).

In one unusual and complicated case a half brother and sister—the *moreno libre* Luis Maxent and the *parda libre* Margarita Duplanty, wife of the white Don Roque Fantoni—agreed to manumit a slave they had both inherited from their mother, a *morena libre.* The slave was Luis Maxent's three-and-a-half-year-old son by another of his mother's slaves, the *morena* Mariana. In addition, Maxent conceded to sell his interest in the slave Mariana to his sister. Mariana went to Havana where Duplanty and her husband resided, while the young child stayed in New Orleans with his father (Ximénez 1 [1791]: 497, Notarial). Like many whites and free blacks, Maxent cared about his child, but showed no interest, except monetary, in the mother.

Free people of color, as well as whites, manumitted slave kin and property by *inter vivos* donation (Hanger 1991). In 1793 the *moreno libre* Enrique Samba issued *cartas* to his *morena* slave and her daughter at the end of nine years of service (Ximénez 5 [1793]: 649, Notarial). In addition to holding slaves as property, free blacks purchased and freed siblings, children, grandchildren, and godchildren. For elderly free persons of color, in particular, the sums required to buy and manumit slave kin took long years to accumulate; they could afford to invest in little else. In some instances free blacks had to purchase relatives and friends on credit and could not free them until after repaying the debt. For unexplained reasons, one *pardo libre,* Juan Medes, bought his *grifo* son Luis but did not manumit him until twenty years later (Pedesclaux 43 [1803]: 221, Notarial).

Although not as frequently as children, elderly slaves were also manumitted voluntarily without conditions and during the master's lifetime. When liberating older slaves, few slaveholders provided for their future care, or at least the records do not indicate that they did. Some slaveholders donated items to them at a later date, and, as seen below, masters who liberated slaves in their wills also tended to bequeath them goods, although such goods were not given exclusively or even primarily to elderly bondpersons. A typical *inter vivos* case was that of the emancipation of Catin, an eighty-year-old *morena,* whom Don Pedro Deverges and his wife, Doña Catalina Dupard, manumitted in 1775 without any allowance for her impending needs (Garic 6 [1775]: 274, Notarial). A slave for her entire life, Catin—and other elderly freed persons like her—at age eighty could not hope to provide for herself other than by begging, stealing, or relying on friends and relatives.

Manumission by Testament

In addition to manumitting slaves unconditionally during their lifetimes, slaveholders wrote provisions into their wills for the eventual liberation of beloved servants. Time lapses between writing of the last testament and actual death, and thus freedom for the designated slave, could span a few days or several years. Masters seldom granted *cartas* to all their slaves en masse. In their wills they selectively conferred liberty gratis to a favored few, allowed others to purchase their freedom, and relegated the majority to continued bondage.

As with *inter vivos* donations of liberty, masters who freed slaves in their wills occasionally admitted paternity. In 1802 Don Juan Bautista Nicollet denied paternity of one person of color while acknowledging fatherhood of another. In his will Nicollet emphatically revoked, denied, and declared null and void a note written in Spanish that he was forced to sign on his deathbed in which he recognized Magdalena Chauvin as his natural daughter. He claimed that the note was signed under duress and totally false. Nicollet, however, *did* recognize as his natural child his slave named Luis Nicollet, provided for his son's manumission, and gave him two thousand pesos (the monetary unit upon which the United States dollar was based and equivalent in value to the dollar at the time). Nicollet ordered his testamentary executor to administer the donated money until Luis reached majority age and also to care for and educate Luis. In other articles Nicollet issued a *carta* for his slave Magdalena and gave her two thousand pesos and donated smaller sums to his slaves who remained in bondage, including one of his slave godchildren (N. Broutin 4 [1802]: 463, Notarial).

Like Nicollet, slaveholders freeing their slaves by testament some-times donated goods to these slaves or provided for their care in other ways. One unusual testament combined provisions for a slave's welfare and paid labor along with compensation for the heirs. On June 11, 1776, Francisco Gauvin composed his will, in which he specified that his heirs were to pay his *morena* slave Rosa, eighteen years of age, seventeen reales (eight reales to one peso) per month and supply her with food and clothing for a period of ten years. The heirs were to free her at the end of the ten years in exchange for her accumulated wages. Gauvin died two days after making his will (Almonester y Roxas [1776]: 434, Notarial).

Free persons of color also wrote wills in which they freed slaves. Simón, a *grifo libre*, liberated his *morena* slave María, sixteen, whom he had raised in his house as a daughter, and he appointed his grandfather, the *moreno libre* Alexandro, as guardian of María. Simón also named her his only heir to property that included twelve cows, seven horses, and two arpents of land four leagues upriver from New Orleans in the district of Tchoupitoulas (Almonester y Roxas [1779]: 462, Notarial). The *morena libre* Magdalena Naneta, alias Lecler, ordered her executor to free two of her three slaves at her death and to purchase the freedom of her slave husband at his estimated worth (Mazange 6 [1782]: 833, Notarial).

Conditional Manumission

New Orleans slave owners frequently emancipated their slaves voluntarily, including very young and old ones, but with the condition that the freed person continue to serve his or her former master or heirs for a number of years or for the rest of the master's life (Hanger 1991). While working for their masters, former slaves in some instances were treated as free persons: they were able to sue and be sued, buy and sell property, and make contracts. At other times masters stipulated that these nominally free persons continue to serve them as slaves, and if they did not, the promise of freedom could be revoked. For example, Don Cecilio Odoardo, lawyer of the royal *audiencia* of Santo Domingo and lieutenant governor of Louisiana, manumitted the two *parda* daughters—Feliciana, seven, and Margarita, five—of his *parda* slave Margarita with the condition that for the rest of his days they remain in his house and labor for his family and accompany him on journeys when his duty to the king called. In addition, if the slave Margarita caused Odoardo any problems, the act of manumission for her daughters was to be declared null and void (Garic 5 [1774]: 245 Notarial). A more generous master was Don Pedro Rousseau, royal naval officer, captain, and commander of the Spanish ship *Galveston*. In October 1782 he manumitted his twenty-four-year-old *parda* slave named Pelagia contingent upon six years further service, but one year later he canceled that obligation and ratified her status of freedom (Mazange 6 [1782]: 872, Notarial; Rodríguez, 7(2) [1783]: 791, Notarial).

There were a few cases from the Spanish era in which masters liberated their slaves *graciosamente,* only to have the former slaves turn around and obligate themselves to serve their former owners for a period of time. Apparently not all slaves welcomed the uncertainties of freedom and preferred the security of familiar surroundings and relationships. On July 16, 1778, Doña Elizabeth de Montault Dauterive unconditionally manumitted her nineteen-year-old *cuarterona* Felicidad, daughter of Dauterive's other slave, Margarita, a *mestiza*. Moved by this generous act, the next day Felicidad voluntarily signed a note of obligation to Dauterive that stated she would labor four more years (Almonester y Roxas [1778]: 312, Notarial). This case also indicates that persons of Indian ancestry were still being held as slaves in Louisiana, even though in 1769 Governor Alejandro O'Reilly had declared Indian slavery illegal in the colony. In 1772 Luisa, a twenty-one-year-old *morena libre,* also obligated herself to serve her former master, the wholesale merchant Don Gerónimo La Chiapella, who had freed her two months prior. Luisa stated that she acted voluntarily in recognition of the great benefits her former master had given her by freeing her *graciosamente* and that she gave him, or his widow if he should die, complete dominion over her as if she were a slave. Although the obligation was to last four years, La Chiapella canceled it in 1773 (Almonester y Roxas: 96, 199, 267, Notarial). Perhaps these newly freed women truly wanted to remunerate their former owners for generous acts, lacked the resources, skills, and kin networks needed to survive as free persons, or wished to retain benefits stemming from ties of patronage to influential whites.[9] Many ex-slaves, domestics in particular, continued to serve former masters, but few labored without monetary compensation.

Self-Purchase

During the Spanish period of rule, a rising proportion of slaves in New Orleans acquired liberty through self-purchase, either directly from the master or indirectly by the governor's tribunal (refer to table 1.3). As noted above, this process of self-purchase was known as *coartación*, "a peculiarly Spanish custom which slowly worked itself into law" in Cuba (Knight 1970: 130). A slave could pay for him or herself by installments or in one lump sum, and if the slave were sold, the credit amassed toward self-purchase would be transferred to the new owner. The master issued a *carta de libertad* either when the entire sum had been paid or when a certain amount of it had been received. In the latter scenario the ex-slave repaid his or her former master with part of any salary earned as a free person (Klein 1986).

A common practice throughout Spanish and Portuguese America and an occasional one in the French and British colonies, *coartación* had become formalized into law in Cuba by the eighteenth century, and, when Louisiana came under Cuba's jurisdiction, *coartación* was implemented there, too. Slaves presented their purchase price either with earnings gained by their own efforts or money supplied by relatives or friends. In accordance with French colonial custom, most slaves, especially urban slaves, were allowed some free time during which they sold their services or grew crops to sell; the Spanish continued and legalized this custom. Slaves began to realize that their "aspirations for liberty rested on the administration of justice by the Spanish in the colony" and that the institution of self-purchase "expressed the Spanish recognition (1) that slavery was not the natural condition of men; (2) that slaves had a right to aspire to freedom; and (3) that masters had a right to just return for their property" (McGowan 1976, 194). The *coartación* also recognized the slave's property rights (Baade 1983).

Cases from the New Orleans notarial records reveal that officials acting for Spain implemented, adjudicated, and enforced the right of slaves to self-purchase through gradual payment in Louisiana. Slaves bought

their liberty in large or small increments, though most slaveholders required complete restitution before issuing a *carta*. For example, Don
Fernando Alzar manumitted his *morena* slave Julia, age thirty-eight,
whom he had purchased *"coartada"* three and a half years earlier, when
she compensated him the sum he had paid for her (Pedesclaux 40 [1802]:
127, Notarial). In another case a testamentary executor promised to free
Clemencia, a twenty-six-year-old *morena* from Guinea, if she paid four
hundred pesos over a three-year period (F. Broutin 7 [1791]: 357, Notarial).

Other masters granted *cartas* to slaves who had satisfied only part of
their purchase price, with a promise to complete the transaction at a later
date. In 1791 Don Francisco Carrière and his wife, Doña Julia de la
Brosse, manumitted their *moreno* slave Michaut for one thousand pesos.
At the time Michaut had already deposited two installments of five hundred and one hundred pesos with his owners, and he swore to pay the
remaining four hundred pesos at a rate of five pesos per month (F. Broutin
7 [1791]: 253, Notarial).

Spanish law in Louisiana, as in Cuba, also guaranteed the slave's
right to transfer a promise of freedom and sums paid when another party
purchased or inherited the slave. In 1802 José Montegut sold his forty-
year-old male slave, an accomplished shoemaker, to the *pardo libre*
Agustín Bins, also a shoemaker. Montegut had promised the slave his
freedom for 700 pesos, and the slave had already contributed 350 pesos.
Thus, when Montegut sold the slave to Bins, he did so for 350 pesos and
on condition that Bins free the slave upon payment of that amount
(Pedesclaux 42 [1802]: 842). When Don Santiago Hursol purchased the
parda Juana in 1775, he did so with the express obligation and condition
to allow the *parda* to work and pay for what remained of her self-purchase price. By June 1779 Juana, now nineteen years old, had "turned
over 250 pesos to Hursol, and he issued her *carta*" (Almonester y Roxas
[1779]: 361, Notarial).

Most slaves, however, bought their *cartas* with a one-time payment.
Upon request, masters commonly allowed slaves to purchase themselves
and sometimes even an entire slave family. María Luisa, the thirty-two-
year-old *parda* slave of Don Jácabo Dubreuil, second lieutenant of the
Battalion of the Plaza de Armas, requested from her master her *carta*
and that of her four children: Noël (seven), Joseph (five), Miguel (two
and a half), and Francisca (three months). She paid Dubreuil 500 pesos
for their freedom (Almonester y Roxas [1772]: 251, Notarial). In this
case—and there were many others like it—María Luisa purchased herself and then acted as a third party to buy the *cartas* of her children. A
more complex kin group purchase involved the fifty-three-year-old

morena Magdalena, who bought her own liberty for 350 pesos and within the next few days purchased *cartas* for her twenty-year-old son, Francisco (300 pesos), twenty-three-year-old daughter, Lileta (350 pesos), and Lileta's two young sons, Francisco and Carlos (150 pesos each) (Ximénez 2 [1792]: 229, 231, 234, 235, 237, Notarial).

Even elderly slaves frequently had to pay for liberty. The sums these slaves paid were usually nominal, but they nevertheless attested to years of sacrifice and toil. Their resources and physical strength expended for the gain of their owners, elderly freedpersons faced a dismal future unless they had kin or patrons to assist them. One of the oldest slaves to purchase her freedom was the *morena* Magnón. She was ninety-six years old when she paid thirty pesos to Nicolás Sampana to liberate her in 1775 (Almonester y Roxas [1775]: 140, Notarial).

In one unusual case a slave gave to her master another slave in exchange for her freedom. Doña Luisa Dutisne manumitted Carlota, a sixty-year-old *morena,* when Carlota presented Dutisne a young *moreno* slave named Telemaco, who was ten or eleven years of age (Garic 4 [1773]: 88, Notarial). Although the practice of substituting one slave for another in order to obtain freedom was rare in New Orleans, it was customary in other parts of the Americas. Slave artisans or retailers in particular possessed the means to purchase freshly arrived Africans, teach these *"bozales"* their craft, and acculturate newcomers in the process. Skilled slaves then exchanged the newly trained slaves for their own freedom. Masters, in turn, received young, skilled, *ladino* (an African who had been "seasoned") slaves to replace older bondpersons. The New Orleans slave Carlota probably engaged in much the same process.

Third-Party Purchases

A relative or friend often paid the price of a slave's freedom; indeed, because some documents did not specifically state the source of funds, financial aid from kin and acquaintances was probably more common than the numbers in table 1.3 indicate. Whites, free blacks, and slaves requested masters to free certain bondpersons and supplied the money to pay for them. Nicolás de Allo paid 250 pesos to the wholesale merchant Don Claudio Francisco Girod for the *carta de libertad* of José, the six-month-old *pardito* son of Girod's *morena* slave Theresa. Although he did not state it publicly, Allo most likely was José's father (Pedesclaux 38 [1801]: 288, Notarial). White fathers who admitted their paternity included Don Honorato Orao, *padre natural* of the *pardito* Martín, eight years old and the son of a *morena* slave named Adelaida. In 1803 Orao paid 400 pesos to Don Santiago Larcher for Martín's *carta* (Pedesclaux 45 [1803]: 881, Notarial).

Interested parties found children less expensive to manumit while they were still in the womb. A father who purchased the *carta* of an unborn slave paid only twenty-five pesos, and several white men risked that sum in order to take advantage of a bargain in freeing their pending offspring. Such a venture entailed some gambling because the child could be stillborn or die soon after birth. One white man, José Gilly, attempted to reduce elements of risk by paying the expenses of a midwife and renting the pregnant slave, Leonor, at ten pesos per month until she delivered the baby. Gilly, however, assured Leonor's owner, the *parda libre* Francisca Robert, that Leonor could continue to serve Robert as long as she did not overwork her (Pedesclaux 39 [1801]: 569, Notarial).

Free persons of color also purchased *cartas* for slave kin. After soliciting Don Joseph Villar on many occasions, the *parda libre* Marion finally convinced him to liberate her son Janvier, a nineteen-year-old Creole (here meaning born in the Americas) *pardo,* for four hundred pesos and her daughter Luisa, alias Mimi, a Creole *grifa* about twenty years of age, for two hundred pesos (Garic 9 [1778]: 595, Notarial). In addition to paying with cash, free people of color also exchanged their services for the freedom of loved ones. The free *pardo* Estevan contracted with Don Francisco Langlois in 1792 to serve for five years in whatever capacity Langlois desired. In return, Langlois granted Estevan the favor of freeing his mother, the *parda* Tonton, valued at four hundred pesos. Langlois also promised to maintain, feed, and care for Estevan if he became ill (Pedesclaux 15 [1792]: 487, Notarial).

Like whites and free blacks, slaves paid masters to issue *cartas* for friends and relatives, but most likely such purchases involved much greater personal and material sacrifices. When slaves used scarce resources to manumit others, they placed a desire to liberate fellow bondpersons above their own freedom in true acts of compassion, consideration, and selflessness. Examples include the *parda* slave Margarita, who gave Don Juan Bautista Senet two hundred pesos to manumit her *cuarterón* son Pedro, two years of age (Garic 10 [1779]: 78, Notarial).

Free persons of color sometimes stipulated in their testaments that funds from their estates be used to purchase *cartas* for slave relatives and friends. Before sailing for Havana in 1770, the *parda libre* Margarita wrote her will; she requested that her executor sell her house and land on Royal Street and use the proceeds to purchase the freedom of her mother, Genoveva, a *morena* belonging to a Monsieur Andry. Should Genoveva die before the will was executed, Margarita instructed her executor to purchase the *carta* of her brother Luis, a *moreno* slave of Don Gilberto Antonio de San Maxent. What money remained was to be given to either Genoveva or Luis for their daily expenses (SJR 1770030101).

When the *parda libre* María Francisca Riche wrote her will in 1791, she listed among her possessions a house, a slave, and various household effects. She ordered her executor to take proceeds from the sale of some of her goods and purchase *cartas* for her brother Pedro and her sister María Francisca, both slaves of Don Luis Agustín Meillon. In turn, these siblings were to use what funds remained to free María Francisca's two slave daughters. Two and a half years later Peter purchased his freedom for 550 pesos and María Francisca bought hers for 100 pesos; both went before a tribunal to force Meillon to free them (Pedesclaux 12: 47, 17: 474, 18: 562, Notarial). Why the above parties choose to wait until their deaths in order to purchase kin and friends is not clear.

Manumission before a Tribunal

When a master refused offers of money in exchange for a slave's freedom, the slave, a relative, or a friend could petition in front of a tribunal to demand issuance of a *carta de libertad* at the slave's estimated worth. Knowledgeable slave appraisers *(tasadores)* took into consideration "circumstances of the times," skills, physical condition, age, and gender when making their assessments. Although most *tasadores* were fair and could agree on one value, occasionally the slave-appointed appraiser came up with a low figure, while the master's representative estimated high. In these cases a court-appointed *tasador* usually settled the dispute with an evaluation somewhere in the middle of the two extremes.

Examples of slaves petitioning for a just appraisal included a *parda* named Catalina, thirty-three, who in June 1773 requested that the tribunal issue *cartas* for her and her daughter Felicidad, five years old, for their price of estimation. Catalina and Felicidad, along with Catalina's other two young children, were slaves of the estate of Don Juan Bautista Destrehan. After five months of disputed appraisals the parties involved finally agreed on a price of 320 pesos for both Catalina and her daughter (Almonester y Roxas [1773]: 287, Notarial). Insufficient funds also delayed settlement of petitions for manumission. A *morena* slave of Don Juan Bautista Mercier, Francisca, requested her freedom from the *tribunal de la Real Justicia* (court of royal justice) in June 1791. Appraised at 550 pesos, Francisca could not pay that amount. More than two years later she again appeared before the tribunal with the required money, demanding to purchase her *carta* (Pedesclaux 18 [1791]: 629, Notarial).[11]

Most third parties who petitioned tribunals for a slave's freedom were free blacks. Siblings, parents, children, and other relatives often made these requests. When the *moreno libre* Juan Bautista convinced a tribunal to manumit his sister Constanza, he agreed that both he and Constanza would support and feed her two-year-old son, Francisco, who remained a slave of Don Luis Declouet (N. Broutin 3 [1801]: 126, Notarial). Another free man of color, the *cuarterón* Juan Bautista Cholán, asked a tribunal to free his natural daughter María. Both María and her *morena* mother belonged to the estate of Don Francisco Chauvin Delery. Because María was now over three years old, Cholán argued that she could live apart from her mother, and the court agreed. It granted María's carta for 200 pesos, 119 pesos and 2 reales of which the estate already owed Cholán for wood. Like many males, Cholán made no attempt to free his slave consort (Ximénez 2 [1792]: 213, Notarial).

New Orleans slaves followed several avenues to freedom during the era of Spanish rule in Louisiana. Although for the period as a whole the majority of slaves continued to receive liberty by way of acts instituted by the master, as they had under French rule, a rising and ultimately predominant proportion of manumissions were initiated by the slaves themselves. The slave or an outside party purchased freedom directly from willing masters and indirectly from more reluctant owners through the governor's tribunal. Spanish administrators in Louisiana implemented this custom of *coartación,* a practice that had evolved into law in response to adaptations in slave systems throughout the Iberian colonies. The system of self-purchase "required the full-scale recognition of the slave's right to personal property and to the making of contracts," a recognition French administrators and colonials had refused to make (Klein 1986: 194–95).

    Coartación offered advantages to slaveholders, slaves, *and* the Spanish government, and all three groups acted according to their interests. The crown benefited from a growing free population of color that tended to accept its middle status in a three-tiered society, aspired to attain the privileges of white colonials, and supplied the colony with skilled laborers and militia forces. Although they pushed the limits of the law to their advantage, free blacks in New Orleans, like their counterparts throughout the Spanish empire, rarely tried to overthrow the dominant society. *Coartación* gave them a legitimate safety valve. In addition, *coartación* provided slave owners with incentives that encouraged slaves to work more productively, reduced their provisioning costs, and compensated owners at the slaves' estimated fair value. Legal manumission also acted as an effective form of social control by offering liberty to obedient bondpersons and denying it to rebellious ones. In turn, the system facilitated slave efforts to acquire the necessary cash or goods with which to purchase their freedom independent of the master's will (Karasch 1987; Klein 1986). Like Africans throughout the Americas, New Orleans blacks "worked the system" to take advantage of opportunities presented them in their efforts to attain freedom and improve their status and their children's status.

Although free persons of color consistently experienced exploitation and prejudice in a hierarchical society such as prevailed in New Orleans, the continuous, intensifying, and expensive struggles undertaken by many slaves to attain freedom attested to their appreciation of liberty as something desirable. A few cases discussed above and undoubtedly some others not yet identified indicate that not all slaves aspired to free status or viewed such status as advantageous. In an urban setting such as New Orleans, slave artisans and traders, in particular, moved about, transacted business, and socialized much the same as free persons of color. Their ability to do so, however, could be taken away from them at any time at the whim of their owners; persons legally manumitted at least exercised a greater measure of control over their lives. As in Cuba and Brazil, free blacks in New Orleans grew in numbers (from 97 in 1771 to 1,566 in 1805) and in status during Iberian rule, both in response to laws and cultural attitudes and to such material factors as demographics and economic activities. Antebellum Louisiana's large free population of color, unique in the United States South, traced its roots to the Spanish regime, when slaves could attain freedom with greater ease than at any other time in the state's history.

Notes

1. Throughout this work I use the inclusive somatic terms "free black" and "free person of color" to encompass anyone of African descent; that is, any free non-white person whether he or she be pure African, part white, or part Native American. The exclusive terms *pardo* (light-skinned) and *moreno* (dark-skinned)—preferred by contemporary free blacks over *mulato* and *negro*—are utilized to distinguish elements within the nonwhite population. Occasional references delineate further between *grifo*—offspring of a *pardo(a)* and a *morena(o),* and in some cases of a *pardo(a)* and an *india(o)*—*cuarterón*—offspring of a *pardo(a)* and a white—and *mestizo*—usually the offspring of a white and an Amerindian but in New Orleans sometimes meaning the offspring of a *pardo(a)* or *moreno(a)* and an *india(o).*

   The term Creole of Color was not used in Louisiana during the Spanish period and acquired its distinct meaning in the nineteenth and twentieth centuries. Colonial documents sometimes refer to a person, usually someone of African ancestry, as a "creole of Jamaica," "creole of Martinique," "creole of Louisiana," etc., meaning a native of that particular place. Throughout the New World, creole was applied to anyone of European or African ancestry born in the Americas.

2. Although numbers of free immigrants, white or black, were not recorded in any systematic manner during the Spanish colonial period, scattered references in the

documents can be found to free blacks entering Louisiana from Europe, the Anglo colonies (later the U.S.), central America, Mexico, and the Caribbean. Following the 1791 outbreak of revolution in Saint-Domingue, increasing numbers of free blacks immigrated from that island, although not in near the numbers of the 1809 and 1810 influx.

Calculation of natural increase (births over deaths) is almost impossible given the unreliability of data from censuses, which undercounted free blacks and women, and sacramental records, which only included individuals who were baptized and buried by church officials. The number of funerals for African Americans was especially low, probably because they or their masters were unwilling to pay the minimal one-and-a-half-peso fee for burial; a decent funeral cost at least eight pesos (see Records of the Diocese of Louisiana and the Floridas, roll 2). An idea of the incongruous nature of the records can be gained by looking at those for 1788–91. It is surmised that few free blacks immigrated to New Orleans during this period that predated the Haitian Revolution, and thus what growth there was would be due to natural increase and manumission. A rough calculation of births and deaths compiled from the sacramental registers indicates a net growth of 97 free blacks between 1788 and 1791 (301 births minus 204 deaths). However, the number of free blacks in New Orleans only increased by 42 during the same time period. And these figures do no include at least 100 manumissions during the period. Very likely the census figures are wrong and are undercounting a much greater increase in the free black population, and/or the number of burials are too low.

Further analysis of primary sources is needed before a relatively accurate assessment of the causes of growth in New Orleans's free black population can be made. This author's general feeling is that manumission was the major contributor to free black growth during the Spanish period.

3. The *Siete partidas, Recopilación de leyes* (Compilation of the Laws of the Kingdoms of the Indies), and *code noir* codified slave law, the first two for the Spanish kingdom and the third for the French colonies. Based on Roman law, the *Siete partidas* were compiled in the thirteenth century by Alfonso X of Castile and applied to many aspects of the social order, including slavery. The Spanish crown collected many laws issued over the years for its colonies in the New World and compiled them into the *Recopilación de leyes* in 1681. The *code noir* represented the first French attempt to compile a slave code for its colonies (Klein 1986: 190–96).

4. For example, see Court Proceedings of Francisco Broutin 11 [Mar. 17, 1792]: 74–100, Notarial. Traditional and even some recent works claim that Spanish administrators continued application of the French *code noir* after assuming control of Louisiana. Gilbert C. Din (1980) asserts that the Code of O'Reilly incorporated the *code noir* with only a few alterations, an interpretation initiated by Judge François-Xavier Martin's *History of Louisiana* (1827). A more thorough examination of primary sources, however, definitively shows that "such a radical 'Francophile' view of the legal history of the Spanish Luisiana [Baade's purposefully unique spelling of Louisiana] cannot, however, still be maintained today" and that "the judicial authorities of Spanish Luisiana routinely applied Spanish rather than French law between 1770 and 1803" (Baade 1983: 43). My own research in notarial and judicial documents confirms Baade's findings. The slaves and their representatives repeatedly stated their recognition of a change in slave law and those laws that governed freedmen (Hanger 1991).

5. Statistical data presented in this essay are drawn from a sample of notarial acts for three years in each decade of Spanish rule: 1771–1773, 1781–1783, 1791–1793, 1801–1803. Even though Spain took actual possession of Louisiana late in 1769, 1771 was the first year in which complete records for at least two notaries were available and in which there were cases dealing with free persons of color; 1803 was the last year of Spanish control over the judicial system. These comprise the beginning and ending years of the sample, and the other year groups were chosen to maintain consistency and to register change over each decade.

6. Analysis of cases from a sampling of three years in each decade does not permit an exact calculation of what proportion of the growth rate among free blacks was attributable to manumission (as opposed to immigration and reproduction).

7. Both white and free black masters and their slaves recognized differences between French and Spanish law and attitudes. When Don Francisco Raquet purchased the *parda* Francisca from Mr. Leches in September 1769, he promised her freedom after six years of service. The sale and promise were made by an informal note *(papel simple)* according to the ancient customs of the colony. In 1772 Raquet recorded the promise of freedom before a notary. He stated that under the previous rule slaves were considered movable property or chattel *(bienes muebles)*, and there was no need to have a notary record transactions dealing with slaves. Raquet wanted to register a formal document with the authorities of the new dominion (Almonester y Roxas [1772]: 35, Notarial). The free *morena* Angela Perret also noted a change in the status of slaves. The ancient custom of treating slaves as chattel no longer prevailed, and now even free persons of color could manumit their slaves without seeking special permission from the government. She thus sought a formal recording of the freedom she bestowed upon her daughter and two grandchildren (Almonester y Roxas [1772]: 165, Notarial). Another slave, the *moreno* Juan Bely, referred to his right to petition the tribunal for liberty against the wishes of a reluctant slaveholder. Bely asserted that he had continually requested the widow and testamentary executor of his late master (Don David Ross) to issue him a *carta* at the price of his estimated worth. For this reason he exercised rights conceded him by the Spanish crown according to royal decree in order to name an estimator *("En cuya virtud usando del derecho que S.M. por Real Cedula me concede, nombro por mi tasador Don Fernando Alzar")*. The court appointed Don Josef de Toca as Bely's *defensor,* and Ross's estate named its estimator. Unfortunately, the record ended at this point (Court Proceedings of N. Broutin 60 [1803]: 1495–1501, Notarial).

8. Klein generalizes for Latin America that "among those who purchased their freedom there was an even distribution of women and men" (1986: 228), but in Spanish New Orleans female self-purchasers greatly exceeded males. In addition to various explanations for the preponderance of females in the free black population offered in the previous paragraph, another factor might be that the lucrative tasks of street and shop vendor, seamstress, and cook were usually performed by female slaves. While these occupations offered opportunities to accumulate funds even after paying the master a stipulated sum, talents associated with them usually did not raise the slave's value, unlike artisan skills. Also, the more populous free black females often left their possessions to other females, slave and free, when they died.

9. Karasch, for example, found that in Rio ex-slaves who "had antagonized former owners and had been thrust into their new lives without patron or profession" faced a bleak struggle just to survive. Indeed, "since so many freedpersons were

women, many continued to work as servants for their previous owners and so maintained old patterns of dependency. . . . By continuing dependent relationships with her former owner, a freedwoman seldom experienced a change in her living conditions and personal security, since her former owner would serve as her protector," not always an adverse situation. On the other hand, "for slaves who had been given their freedom gratuitously and turned out of their owner's house, life was quite difficult," especially without kin or friends to lend support (1987: 362–64).

10. One such place was Rio de Janeiro, Brazil. During the first half of the nineteenth century supplies of slaves were plentiful and prices low in Rio, and slaves frequently owned other slaves. Karasch has found that masters of trusted skilled and managerial slaves "permitted them to acquire property for their own use, including land and other slaves, and eventually to earn their freedom by buying themselves" (Karasch 1987, 211, 243).

11. Some valuations were so high that slaves never did purchase their freedom. One such slave was named María. In 1803 the *moreno libre* Juan Pedro appeared before the court to demand the *carta* of his daughter, a twelve-year-old *morena* slave of Doña Isabel Proffit. When both appraisers valued María at 700 pesos, Juan Pedro protested that she was not worth more than 350 pesos; 700 pesos was an enormous sum, and he could not pay it. Thus, the court denied María her *carta* and made Juan Pedro pay 17 pesos in court costs (Court Proceedings of N. Broutin 58 [1803]: 781–90).

References

Andreu Ocaríz, Juan José. 1977. *Movimientos rebeldes de los esclavos negros durante el dominio español en Luisiana.* Zaragoza: Cuaderos de Filosofia y Letras.

Archivo General de Indias, Papeles Procedentes de Cuba, Seville, Spain. Abbreviated as AGI-PC, followed by record number.

Baade, Hans W. 1983. "The Law of Slavery in Spanish Luisiana, 1769-1803." In *Louisiana's Legal Heritage,* ed. Edward F. Haas. 43–86. Pensacola: Perdido Bay Press, for the Louisiana State Museum.

Books of Black Baptisms, Spanish Period, Archives of the Archdiocese of New Orleans, New Orleans, Louisiana. Abbreviated as BB.

Cohen, David W., and Jack P. Greene, eds. 1972. *Neither Slave nor Free: The Freedmen of African Descent in the Slave Societies of the New World.* Baltimore: Johns Hopkins Univ. Press.

Din, Gilbert C. 1980. "*Cimarrones* and the San Malo Band in Spanish Louisiana." *Louisiana History* 21: 237–62.

Domínguez, Virginia R. 1986. *White by Definition: Social Classification in Creole Louisiana.* New Brunswick, N.J.: Rutgers Univ. Press.

Fiehrer, Thomas Marc. 1979. "The African Presence in Colonial Louisiana: An Essay on the Continuity of Caribbean Culture." In *Louisiana's Black Heritage,* ed. Robert R. Macdonald, John R. Kemp, and Edward F. Haas. 3–31. New Orleans: The Louisiana State Museum.

Hall, Gwendolyn Midlo. "Saint Domingue." 1972. In *Neither Slave nor Free: The Freedmen of African Descent in the Slave Societies of the New World,* David W. Cohen and Jack P. Greene, eds. 172–92. Baltimore: Johns Hopkins Univ. Press.

————. 1992. *Africans in Colonial Louisiana: The Development of Afro-Creole Culture in the Eighteenth Century.* Baton Rouge: Louisiana State Univ. Press.

Hanger, Kimberly S. 1991. *"Personas de varias clases y colores:* Free People of Color in Spanish New Orleans, 1769–1803." Ph.D. diss., Univ. of Florida.

Holmes, Jack D. L. 1970. "The Abortive Slave Revolt at Pointe Coupée, Louisiana, 1795." *Louisiana History* 11: 341–62.

Karasch, Mary C. 1987. *Slave Life in Rio de Janeiro, 1808–1850.* Princeton: Princeton Univ. Press.

Kerr, Derek N. 1993. *Petty Felony, Slave Defiance, and Frontier Villainy: Crime and Criminal Justice in Spanish Louisiana, 1770–1803.* New York: Garland Publishing.

Klein, Herbert S. 1986. *African Slavery in Latin America and the Caribbean.* New York: Oxford Univ. Press.

Knight, Franklin W. 1970. *Slave Society in Cuba During the Nineteenth Century.* Madison: Univ. of Wisconsin Press.

Lachance, Paul F. 1979. "Politics of Fear: French Louisianians and the Slave Trade, 1786–1809." *Plantation Society in the Americas* 1: 162–97.

————. 1988. "The 1809 Immigration of Saint-Domingue Refugees to New Orleans: Reception, Integration, and Impact." *Louisiana History* 29: 109–41.

McGowan, James Thomas. 1976. "Creation of a Slave Society: Louisiana Plantations in the Eighteenth Century." Ph.D. diss., Univ. of Rochester.

Orleans Parish Notarial Archives, New Orleans, Louisiana. Cited by notary's last name, date, volume, and folio(s), and abbreviated as Notarial.

Records of the Diocese of Louisiana and the Floridas. On microfilm in various repositories, including the Historic New Orleans Collection.

Spanish Judicial Records, Louisiana State Museum Historical Center, New Orleans, Louisiana. Abbreviated as SJR.

Usner, Daniel H., Jr. 1979. "From African Captivity to American Slavery: The Introduction of Black Laborers to Colonial Louisiana." *Louisiana History* 20: 25–48.

Wall, Bennett H., ed. 1990. *Louisiana: A History.* 2nd ed. Arlington Heights, Ill.: Forum Press.

Weber, David. 1992. *The Spanish Frontier in North America.* New Haven: Yale Univ. Press.

TWO

Virginia Meacham Gould

The Free Creoles of Color of the Antebellum Gulf Ports of Mobile and Pensacola: A Struggle for the Middle Ground

More than fifty years ago scholars began to explore the interpenetration of the cultures and peoples of the New World. Melville Herskovits first described the phenomenon of acculturation in an article published in 1925 (Herskovits 1925). Then, in the 1930s, Gilberto Freyre published a pivotal book, *Casa-Grande e Senzala* in which he described the diverse inhabitants of early Brazil, how they mingled and intermingled, absorbed and were absorbed into a new people with a unique culture (Freyre 1933). Despite the creative work of Herskovits and Freyre, however, it was not until the 1960s and 1970s that scholars began to explore diligently the phenomenon of acculturation. In a groundbreaking work published in 1967, Magnus Mörner explored the emergence of one segment of the new people of the Americas, those who were racially mixed. Edward Brathwaite followed his predecessors with a book in which he examined the process of creolization, or the formation of the new, or Creole, culture in Jamaica (Brathwaite 1971). More recently, Richard White and Gwendolyn Hall published works on the development of the new cultures and people in the territories held by the French in North America. White wrote of the peoples of the Great Lakes (White 1991) while Hall examined those of Louisiana (Hall 1992).[1]

All of these scholars, and many more, discarded the belief that the white, master class culturally dominated or even obliterated the native peoples and slaves of their regions. Instead, they discovered that the exploited and dominated peoples of the New World—people who were once thought to be culturally extinguished—were, in fact, exerting considerable influence on the dominant population. Instead of one culturally dominant group influencing another, the process was one in which inhabitants from different cultural backgrounds came together, albeit unevenly, to form new, distinctive peoples and cultures. That process of mutual influence has now been described in many regions of the New World. Certainly, a new culture and people evolved in the region that bordered the northern Gulf of Mexico. There, as much recent scholarship has demonstrated, colonial frontier conditions encouraged the emergence of a new Creole culture different from those brought to the region by the African, Native American, and European inhabitants (Hall 1992; Usner 1992; Tregle 1992).

The free Creoles of Color of Mobile and Pensacola serve particularly well as a representation of creolization. They, better than any other segment of the Creole population, symbolize the meeting of the white Europeans, Native Americans, and African slaves. As the product of that meeting, or interchange, the free Creoles of Color were not black, white, or red; neither slave nor free. Instead, they were the natural expression of the socially flexible world that evolved around them, the visible representation of the evolutionary process of creolization. The world that fostered them, however, changed as the colonial years unfolded into those of the antebellum period. Conditions that had been supportive during the colonial era disappeared as the antebellum period progressed, compelling the free Creoles of Color to adopt defensive mechanisms in order to protect their identities and their status.

The origins of the free Creoles of Color of Mobile and Pensacola can be traced to the political and economic turmoil that dominated the region during the colonial period. By the end of the seventeenth century, Spain, France, and Britain were actively vying for the region that bordered the Gulf. Spain was the first to place a settlement in the region with an outpost at Pensacola in 1698. The French soon followed with a settlement at Biloxi in 1699. That settlement did not prove as successful as the French had hoped, however, so they moved their capital to Mobile in 1702. Yet, even as Spain established its claim over Florida and France claimed Louisiana, the geopolitical struggle over the region did not end. The colonies, along with their outpost settlements, were bartered back and forth between the Spanish, the French, and the English throughout the eighteenth and early nineteenth centuries (Hamilton 1910).

While the colonial powers competed for the vast region that bordered the Gulf, their settlers were left to struggle for survival (Usner 1992). Believing that a plantation economy was the only one feasible in the otherwise inhospitable environment, settlers demanded the importation of African slaves (McGowan 1976). Slaves had accompanied the first Spanish and French settlers into the region. Evidence of the earliest slaves can be found in the sacramental records of the Cathedral of the Immaculate Conception in Mobile. One of the early documents is the baptism of Jean Baptiste on June 11, 1707. Jean Baptiste was a seven-year-old "Negre" slave of Jean Baptiste Le Moyne de Bienville. Jean Baptiste was more than likely not born in Louisiana. Two other slaves belonging to Bienville were baptized in 1707: three-year-old Joseph and the newborn Antoine Jacemin. Antoine Jacemin's mother was an unnamed slave of Bienville's. Her father, François Jacemin, was a slave of Captain Chateauguay's. Those early slaves in Mobile and Pensacola, however, were few in number and had accompanied their masters only as personal servants.[2]

The importation of slaves for the purpose of plantation agriculture did not occur until after 1719 when thousands of slaves began to be transported directly from Africa. Between 1719 and 1731, 22 ships carried 5,761 slaves to Louisiana from Juda (Whydah), Cabinda (Angola), and Senegal. After 1731, only one other ship landed slaves in French Louisiana. That was the *St. Ursin,* which debarked 190 slaves in 1743 from Senegal. Yet, despite this rapid deployment of African slaves into the region, plantation agriculture was a failure. At various times, planters based their hopes on the production of indigo, sugarcane, tobacco, and rice. But none of the crops proved consistently successful, and the settlers were forced to rely on subsistence farming, the abundance of natural resources, and trade with the Indians in order to survive. With few other resources, settlers, slaves, and free people of color participated in face-to-face networks of exchange with the local Indians and with one another. Subsistence farming and trade in clay, lumber, and deer hides, not plantation slavery, dominated the economy of the region (Coker and Watson 1986; Hall 1992, 58–60; Usner 1992).

The failure of plantation agriculture and thus the economy had a definitive effect on the social relations of the population. Unable to establish economic and political dominance, colonial planters and merchants never fully subjugated their slaves. Relations between slaves and their owners remained a constant struggle over who was in control. Slaves pressed their owners for autonomy and, within certain parameters, managed to exercise some control over their daily lives. Tied to owners who could not consistently provide basic provisions, slaves negotiated the right to cultivate their own plots of land and use Sundays for worship, rest, or marketing. Many did not even live with their owners. It was not unusual for slaves in colonial Mobile and Pensacola to provide food, clothing, and housing for themselves and their families. Given the opportunity, slaves negotiated for as much self-reliance as possible (McGowan 1976: 97–161). Slaves in Louisiana, Antoine LePage DuPratz recognized in 1734, frequently preferred to take care of their own needs (DuPratz 1763).

Numerous slaves attained their freedom during the politically and economically unstable colonial period. Many avenues of freedom existed for them. Some simply escaped, blending into the Indian population or forming small communities of maroons in the swamps around the ports.

Most slaves who were freed, however, purchased their own freedom or were legally freed by their masters or mistresses in return for outstanding or faithful service. The first evidence of a freed slave is in the baptism records of the Cathedral of the Immaculate Conception. On July 26, 1715, Janneton, the former slave of "Mr. Charlie," brought her infant son, Michel, to the Church to be baptized by the priest. In the record, Janneton declared that her son's father was a French soldier named La Terrier. Since Janneton was freed before the birth of her son, he was born a free person.[3]

Slave women, like Janneton, and their offspring often found freedom in their relations with free men. The records do not say, but it is more than likely that Janneton's freedom was purchased by La Terrier. After all, it would have been economically astute of La Terrier to purchase Janneton's freedom before the birth of their child and perhaps the birth of other children. Certainly it was not always the case, but ample documentation exists in the records to suggest that it was the tradition for free white men and free men of color to purchase and free the slave women with whom they cohabited. If they could not or did not free the women before they had children, they often freed them along with their children (Gould 1991; Nordmann 1990).

For example, Jean Chastang of Mobile cohabited with and then freed a family slave, Louison, with whom he fathered ten children. Chastang acknowledged one of his children in the baptismal records of the Cathedral of the Immaculate Conception. He also acknowledged the others and his liaison with their mother, Louison, in his will. In that document, he bequeathed to his "beloved friend and companion, Louison, a free negro woman, who has resided with me for twenty years past and has been my sole attendant in health and particularly in sickness, my entire estate and dwellings." Louison's alliance with Jean would not have been acceptable to all slave women. But some tolerated, even encouraged, such liaisons. After all, cohabitation could be an avenue out of slavery for the women and for their children.[4]

An analysis of Mobile's census and sacramental records suggests that less than 1 percent of the population before 1763, or during the period that the French ruled the region, were recorded as free people of color. That extremely low number could be the consequence of the efforts of French administrators to protect slave women from sexual exploitation. If found guilty of entering into concubinage with one of his slave women, a master could be forced to forfeit her. Further, if a soldier was found guilty of sexually exploiting a slave woman, he could be imprisoned or even sentenced to death. In order to reinforce the act, administrators accepted the testimony of slave women. Another reason that so few free people of color appear in the early records has been suggested by the recent research completed by Gwendolyn Hall in settlements in Louisiana. Hall finds that there were numerous free people of color in Louisiana who did not show up in the census records as free people of color. Instead, according to her preliminary findings, they were recorded as white (Hall 1992). One explanation for that practice could be that local officials hoped to demonstrate a larger white population to the Crown than actually existed.[5]

The baptismal records between 1763 and 1781, or during the period that the British administered the port, are incomplete so it is not possible to analyze them with any consistency. The sacramental records for the entire British period consist of only a few pages, which suggests that either many of the records were lost or that the Catholic population of Mobile did not have a priest for long periods of time. The few extant records do suggest, however, that the freed population was either growing at a much faster rate than in earlier years or that the British were more careful about recording race. Clearly, many more free people of color appear in the records than during the earlier French period. Only further demographic study of the population, now underway, will more closely determine the nature of the early population.[6]

The baptismal records that span the period from 1781 through 1812, or that period during which the Spanish administered Mobile, reflect a significantly larger number of free people of color than that found during the earlier French years. Certainly, the Spanish were more careful about racial classification. It was only after their priests began to administer the churches that the sacramental records of the white population were recorded in separate books from those of the slave, free people of color, and Native Americans. The *Baptisma Nigrorum,* or the book in which the baptisms for the slaves and free people of color were recorded between 1790 and 1801, includes approximately 130 baptisms of the infants of slaves. Approximately 60 infants of free people of color were also baptized during that time.[7]

The large number of free people of color that inhabited the ports by the later Spanish period reflected the political, economic, and social realities that existed in the region. The Spanish administrators who arrived to govern the ports realized that they were feared and disdained by the region's Anglo and French inhabitants. Some of those inhabitants left when the Spanish captured the ports, but others chose to stay, with neither group looking kindly upon their Spanish administrators. Yet, neither did the Spanish administrators look kindly upon the mostly French and Anglo inhabitants they were supposed to govern. The Spanish, who had not forgotten that a revolt had been staged against them in New Orleans in 1768, attempted to dilute the power of the white planter and merchant class by forging an alliance with the free people of color (McGowan 1976: 217–393).

The Spanish attitude toward the free people of color of Mobile and Pensacola was not unique. Spanish officials throughout Latin America and the Caribbean depended on free people of color to support their policies. In order to provide skilled labor, the Spanish traditionally enlarged their base of support by guaranteeing the growth of the free colored population. The Spanish implemented two policies soon after they captured Mobile and Pensacola in the early 1780s. First, they enacted a policy that allowed slaveholders to free their slaves through a simple act recorded by a notary. The other policy was the Spanish custom of *coartaciôn,* which gave slaves the right to purchase their own freedom. The policy was important even though only a few slaves were able to purchase their freedom because it demonstrated in concrete terms the Spanish attitude that slavery was an unfortunate but temporary condition that could be overcome. (Baade 1983: 43–86; Fiehrer 1979: 3–31).

By 1787, just seven years after Spanish administration began, Mobile's free people of color numbered 88. That number may seem small, but only 425 whites could be found there at the same time. In that year, approximately 20 percent of the free population was comprised of free people of color. By 1805, after 25 years of Spanish occupation, the number of free people of color in Mobile had increased to 205, a number that represented approximately 30 percent of the free population. The free colored population in Pensacola exceeded the growth of that segment of the population in Mobile. Between 1784 and 1820, it grew from 27 to 252. That increase was nearly tenfold. Thus, by 1820, the free people of color in Pensacola represented 36 percent of the free population.[8]

A comparison of the growth of the slave, white, and free colored populations in both Mobile and Pensacola demonstrates the point. In Pensacola between 1784 and 1820, the white population declined from 381 to 349, the slave population grew from 184 to 227, an increase of 23 percent, and the free colored population climbed from 28 to 56, an increase of 100 percent. By 1805, the number of free people of color had doubled again to 116. That number amounted to an increase of 107 percent. The 1820 census reported another large increase. In that year, the population was counted at 184; it had increased by 59 percent.[9]

The growth of the population of free people of color in Mobile also outstripped that of the white and slave population. An analysis of the 1787 Spanish census of Mobile indicates that there were 441 whites in the port in that year. In 1805, that number had grown to 675. The white population had experienced a 53 percent increase. The number of slaves actually decreased during those years. In 1787, there were 725 slaves in the port, but only 612 in 1805, a 16 percent decrease. The number of free people of color increased the most dramatically. There were 64 free people of color in Mobile in 1787. By 1805 their numbers had grown to 250. That number amounts to an increase of 291 percent.[10]

The large number of free people of color in Mobile and Pensacola represented the interpenetration of the black slave, Native American, and free white populations. Many other New World slave systems—for instance, the one that evolved in the American South—were more successful in preserving the social order that separated slavery from freedom, black from white. The inhabitants of Mobile and Pensacola, however, did not exist in a world in which a strict interpretation of race and class ordered the population. Instead, their world was fraught with economic uncertainty, a reality that served to knit them together, despite their diversity. Yet, within that world, where ability and adaptability outweighed considerations of color and class, racial mixing was tolerated and even encouraged (Gould 1991; Hall 1992; Nordmann 1990; Shelley 1971; Usner 1992).

Interracial liaisons were also abetted by the demographic imbalance of the population. In Mobile in 1805, the sex ratio of the white population was 76. In other words, there were 383 white males in a community that claimed only 292 white females. The sex ratio for free people of color was reversed. Although not as unbalanced as that of the white population, that of the free people of color was 104.9. According to that number, there were almost 105 females for every 100 males. In 1784, Pensacola's white population had a sex ratio of 68.7. That of the free colored was 170. The census taken at the end of the Spanish period, in 1820, included 248 white males and only 200 white females, a sex-ratio of 81. The sex ratio of the free people of color in Pensacola in that year was 273. That is, there were 151 females and 101 males.[11]

Notwithstanding necessity, many of the inhabitants of Mobile and Pensacola preferred interracial liaisons. Nowhere else, wrote C. C. Robin, was racial "tolerance more extended." Continuing his discussion of the practice, Robin added that it appeared to him that white men often preferred to form liaisons with slave and free women of color. It was the "cohabitation of whites with women of color more than anything else that contributes to the multiplication of colored people at a higher rate than that of the whites." Many of the inhabitants, according to Robin, "form alliances with these colored women and have children of them." The tradition, he continued, extended to the rural region, where "the Creoles prefer to live with these women rather than give to a white woman the title of spouse." The extraordinary growth of the racially mixed population of free people of color supports Robin's observation (Robin 1966: 249–50).

Certainly, racial mixing was a common practice in Mobile and Pensacola. The first recorded descendant of a white inhabitant and an African slave woman was Michel, the son of Janneton and the French soldier La Terrier. Michel was baptized in 1715, a full four years before African slaves were being imported in large numbers into the colony. A close look at the Pensacola census of 1820 demonstrates just how common the relations between white men and slave and free women of color were. Data from that census suggest that of the 179 households in the city in that year, 42 included free women of color who were openly cohabiting with white men. It is more difficult, but not impossible, to surmise that slave women were cohabiting with whites. Thus, they are excluded from this count, which suggests that more than 20 percent of the households contained racially diverse cohabitants.[12]

By the end of the colonial period, the large population of racially mixed free people of color in Mobile and Pensacola had begun to formulate a cohesive community that extended across the Gulf Coast. The 1820 Spanish census of Pensacola demonstrates the point. In that year, the census taker reported that the majority of the free people of color, or 141, had been born in Pensacola. However, approximately one-half that many, or more than 70, listed their birthplace as Louisiana. Many of those from Mobile and New Orleans had moved to Pensacola as the governance changed from French to British and then to Spanish. The entire population of Pensacola grew from 650 in 1802 to 1,398 in 1805, a rate of increase of 215 percent. William Coker and Douglas Inglis astutely point out in their analysis of the census of Pensacola of 1805 that the migration from Louisiana was so great that it would not have been unusual for people to have slept in the streets (Coker and Inglis 1980). Furthermore, a large number of those who immigrated were free people of color. The census of 1802 lists 74 free people of color in residence. By 1805, there were 197. During those years, the population of free people of color grew by 266 percent.[13]

Several of the prominent free Creoles of Color of Mobile and Pensacola were originally from New Orleans. One Mobilian who claimed New Orleans as his birthplace was Regis Bernody. Bernody was born in New Orleans in 1760, but moved to Mobile after the Spanish took possession of the city in 1780. After moving to Mobile, Bernody became a prosperous businessman and the head of a large and influential family. Another native of New Orleans who moved to Mobile and then Pensacola was Euphrosine Hinard. Hinard was born in New Orleans in 1776. The natural but illegitimate daughter of Don Francisco Hinard, a white man, and Mariana Grondel, a free woman of color, Euphrosine was plaçeed to Don Nicolas Maria Vidal, the *auditor de guerra* of Spanish Louisiana in 1790 when she was fourteen years old. During the time that Hinard cohabited with Vidal, she bore him two daughters, Maria de la Merced and Carolina. After she left New Orleans, Hinard lived in Mobile for several years and then moved to Pensacola where she became a prosperous businesswoman. Another free Creole of Color who left New Orleans for Pensacola was Salvatore Ruby, a free mulatto who was born in New Orleans in 1765. Ruby served with distinction in one of the free colored Spanish militia units in New Orleans until 1816, when he was appointed the commanding officer of the Company of Urban Black and Mulatto Militia Unit in Pensacola (Holmes 1970: 61–62). Most of those who moved to Mobile and Pensacola had relatives and friends scattered across the region.[14]

Even though it appears that free people of color began to formulate a cohesive community during the colonial years, it does not appear that they recognized themselves as a distinct community of *Creoles of Color* until after the region had been ceded to the United States. That is not to suggest that none of the inhabitants were identified as Creoles but, rather, that during the eighteenth century, Creole did not connote a cultural identity. Instead, colonial inhabitants and lay and religious administrators employed the term *creole* to designate the origin of anyone—black, white, or racially mixed (but not Native American)—born in the New World.

Creole was originally derived from the Portuguese term *criola,* which was meant to identity slaves born in the New World. But by the eighteenth century, the term *creole* implied anyone of European or African descent born in the New World (Hall 1992). During the early formative years on the Gulf Coast, *creole of this Colony* was used interchangeably with the designation *native of this Colony* (Domínguez 1986). The first time the term *creole* appears in the records is in the baptismal entry for Jean Baptiste Alexandre, which is dated July 11, 1734. The record states that Jean Baptiste, born May 10, 1734, was the son of Jean Baptiste Alexandre and Françoise Hypolite Bodin, both *creoles* of the said parish.[15]

While Jean Baptiste Alexandre was the first person to be termed a Creole in the records, he was evidently not the first person of European descent born in Louisiana. The identity of that person is obscure. The first person recorded in the baptismal records of the mission at Mobile was Jean François, son of Jean LeCan and Magdelaine Robert of France. Jean François was born October 4, 1704, in Mobile and baptized a few days later. However, the death certificate of Robert Talon, recorded May 24, 1745, describes him as the "first *creole of the colony.*" Furthermore, a baptism recorded January 5, 1719, describes Robert Talon as the father of Jeanne, born that day to Jeanne Praux, the legitimate wife of Robert Talon. That record strongly suggests that Talon was born before 1704 and thus was the first *creole of the colony* as he was described at his death. Even though we will never be certain whether it was Talon or LeCan who was the first person born in the colony to European parents, it is clear their identity as *creoles* only denoted place of birth, not cultural or racial heritage.[16]

It was only later, during the nineteenth century, that *creole* began to imply a cultural identity that transcended race and class. The shift in the meaning of the term *creole* from identification of place of birth to cultural identity occurred as economic and political change began to threaten the social relations and status of the original inhabitants, or *ancienne population*. The members of the *ancienne population* thought of themselves as having their origins in the region; a condition, in their opinion, that made them superior to those who were from elsewhere (Tregle 1992). That distinction became more and more important as the social, economic, and political change that accompanied the nineteenth century increasingly threatened them (Domínguez 1986).

In Mobile and Pensacola, the initial threats to the *ancienne population* occurred as planters began to find success in the large-scale production of cotton. The French were the first to grow cotton successfully, but it was the British who recognized its potential. Bernard Roman, a traveler who wrote of his adventures as he journeyed through east and west Florida in the 1770s, reported on the ease of growing the crop. "Cotton," he wrote, "will grow in any soil, even the most meager and barren sand we can find." The British traveler also noted, however, that the intensive labor necessary for the separation of seed from the fiber made the large-scale production of the plant unfeasible. It was not until the invention of the cotton gin and the opening of the fertile territory north of the ports from the United States that the region's plantation economy boomed (Amos 1985; Roman 1775: 139–71).

The prosperity of plantation agriculture changed relations between planters and their slaves. As soon as plantation agriculture became profitable, planters pressed the territorial councils in Alabama and Florida for more stringent slave codes (Duval 1839; Toulmin 1823). For instance, soon after it was convened in 1824, the Legislative Council of Territorial Florida began to limit the activities of slaves. Under the new laws of Florida, slaves were prohibited from carrying firearms, prohibited from working for themselves on Sundays, and prohibited from trading between themselves without consent from their owners or overseers. By 1828, slaves could not be sold between one person and another, except under certain conditions, and they could not leave the bounds of the plantation without a written pass. Laws were also instituted that prescribed the death penalty for any slave maiming or intending to kill a white person. Slaves found guilty of felonies not punishable by death could be legally lashed with a whip, burned with a hot iron, or have their ears nailed to a post. Slave codes enacted in Alabama followed the same pattern (Aiken 1833; Duval 1839; Toulmin 1823).[17]

The territorial councils of Alabama and Florida increasingly viewed free people of color with suspicion and devised laws to halt the growth of their population. The private acts of manumission allowed under Spanish law were prohibited in Mobile and Pensacola soon after the region was ceded to the Americans (Duval 1839; Toulmin 1823). According to the laws that were passed by each territorial government, masters could neither legally manumit their slaves nor allow them to purchase their freedom without official permission from either the court or the legislature. Age limits were soon added to the restrictions on manumission, and then freed slaves were ordered to leave their respective states (Clay 1843; Duval 1839; Toulmin 1823). By 1860, lawmakers in Alabama and Florida had enacted laws that completely prohibited manumission. Slaveholders, like slaveholders in the rest of the South, considered free people of color a danger to the institution of slavery and thus sought to eliminate them.[18]

A shift in migration patterns also reinforced the consolidation of the social system of slavery. Throughout the eighteenth and early nineteenth centuries, migrants from the Western world regularly moved into and out of the region. A glance at the census records of Mobile and Pensacola that include place of origin reveals the diverse nature of the population. The 1820 census of Pensacola is a good example. In that year, the census taker found inhabitants in Pensacola from Spain, France, Africa, Mexico, Italy, Morocco, Germany, Canada, Portugal, Great Britain, the Caribbean, the Canary Islands, and the United States. Mobile's population was as diverse as that of Pensacola.[19]

In 1822, Lt. George McCall, stationed in Pensacola with the United States Fourth Infantry, wrote a letter home describing the international diversity of the residents he found in the little port. His letter describes the scene he observed while standing at the corner of the town plaza one bright Sabbath morning. There was a "motley multitude of grave and gay, aged and young," he wrote, "wending their way towards the house of worship." The first person, according to McCall, "was an elderly Spanish lady, whose thick veil descends in ample folds about her person." The woman, McCall noted, was followed "at a respectful distance, by a neatly-dressed slave, carrying her chair and cushion; the first of these articles being inverted in such a way that the bottom rests on the gay cotton handkerchief with which the girl's head is decorated, and the back descending behind, leaves one hand free for salutation, which the other clasps the cushion." After the slave came a group of young men, loitering indolently along. Next there was an old Frenchman, "all complaisance, bowing to all he meets." Finally came the "feminine, black-eyed, naive young Creole, whose air and carriage are as striking and attractive as her dress is simple and modest." As McCall unwittingly suggests, the diverse inhabitants of the region had learned to exist comfortably side by side (McCall 1868: 16).

Nineteenth-century migration patterns changed radically from those of the eighteenth century, and those changes challenged the identity and status of the region's inhabitants. The nineteenth century brought a group of settlers into the region whose very presence affronted the "original" inhabitants, who deemed themselves the *ancienne population.* Overwhelmingly, nineteenth-century migrants were Americans who, in search of their fortunes, had begun to move across the Appalachians, down the Mississippi River, and across the Gulf when the region was ceded to the United States. Between 1805 and 1860, Mobile's population grew from 2,677 to 29,258. Pensacola's population also grew. There were 695 people, excluding slaves, living in Pensacola in 1820. By 1850, the population had grown to 2,164. Since Pensacola's soil was too sandy to support plantation agriculture and it did not have the system of waterways that fed Mobile's port, its population grew more slowly.[20]

Despite its slower growth, Pensacola, like Mobile, attracted numerous Americans who soon outnumbered and culturally threatened the *ancienne population.* Joseph Tregle has outlined the process that led to the recognition of a specific cultural identity by the *ancienne population* of New Orleans. Tregle asserts that, for several decades at the beginning of the nineteenth century, white Americans and Creoles engaged in a battle for control of New Orleans's society, with each group struggling to "mold the whole to its particular design." Issues dividing the factions ran so deep, he argues, "that those involved in the contest not unreasonably thought of themselves as engaged in a struggle for the very soul of the community." It was during that process, as described by Tregle, that the *ancienne population* recognized the threats posed by the Americans and asserted privilege in the only way they could: by claiming that their origin in the soil naturally endowed them with a native identity that was superior. It was the identification of native origin with status that the *ancienne population* translated into a cultural identity (Tregle 1992: 131–85).

In Mobile and Pensacola the timing and scale of the struggle for control was different from that in New Orleans since the *ancienne populations* of Mobile and Pensacola were much more quickly overwhelmed by Americans. Yet, in both ports the reaction to the struggle was much the same. "Creole," which had previously indicated place of origin, was reinterpreted as *Creole,* which connoted the culturally cohesive population of black, white, and racially mixed free people who were tied to the region through heritage and culture.

Americans and the white, black, and racially mixed Creoles in Mobile and Pensacola feared and resented one another. Commentators who wrote of the region rarely failed to note the divisiveness between the Americans and Creoles—of no matter what race or condition. Each group frowned on the behavior of the other. The Duke of Saxe-Weimar-Eisenach commented on the enmity between the two groups in his description of New Orleans. "The aversion of the French Creoles to the Americans," he wrote, "is notable" (Saxe-Weimar-Eisenach 1827). George McCall, the American lieutenant stationed in Pensacola, described the Creoles and Creoles of Color as indolent and self-indulgent (McCall 1868: 16).

Creoles and Americans had little in common. They preferred different foods, different architecture, and different neighborhoods. They worshiped in different churches. Overwhelmingly, the *ancienne population* clung to its Catholicism; the Americans to their Protestantism. Each refused to speak the other's language. Americans stubbornly spoke only English; the Creoles only French, Spanish, or the local creole dialect. Harriett Martineau noted that language was a key factor in separating the two groups. In her commentary, she wrote that the division between the Americans and the Creoles was "visible even in the drawing room." The French complained, she wrote, that the "Americans will not speak French, will not meet their neighbors even half way in accommodation of speech" (Martineau 1838: 271). The commissioners appointed to govern Mobile during the territorial period recognized the language barrier and published all laws and regulations in English and in French (Toulmin 1823).

Pride of language divided the old from the new residents. The probate records of Jane Landry, a free Creole woman of color of Mobile County demonstrate how jealously the original inhabitants protected their language and their identities. In an attempt to settle Landry's estate, the probate court of Mobile County heard testimony about her identity from several of her neighbors. One of her neighbors, an American, testified that he had known Jane Landry before her death, but that he had not known her well. Landry, according to her neighbor, ran a small general store that served her neighborhood. But she was never friendly to him or to her other American neighbors. She refused to speak anything but French, the American testified, even though everyone knew that she was fluent in English.[21]

Pride of language was different in Pensacola. There, even though a large part of the population was French, it was not the predominant language spoken in the port. George McCall noted in a letter home to his family that all "three languages (English, Spanish, French) are spoken respectively by the representatives of the three nations, but if I except the English, the Spanish is probably more spoken in society, and is more or less understood by all." Pensacola's preference for the Spanish language was just one expression of its Spanish heritage (McCall 1868: 14).

Threatened by being overwhelmed by Americans and American ways, the *ancienne population* of Mobile and Pensacola recognized the similarity of their interests and culture in response to the other, American culture. White, black, and racially mixed Creoles identified with one another across race and class. McCall captures this process of acculturation and identification in another of his letters in which he described the *ancienne population* as fragmented and yet cohesive. The inhabitants who made up the town, he noticed, had "successively passed under the domination of Spain, France, and England," and consequently there was a great diversity in the population. Yet, at the same time, McCall wrote that the locals formed "something like a distinct provincial character; their prominent traits wearing a coloring peculiarly their own, the effect of climate, mode of life, and other decidedly local causes." As McCall suggests, the cultural evolution of the original population that inhabited the region was a dynamic process in which diverse groups had come together and begun to share a common style. Indeed, he believed that the population was so acculturated that there was a "strange similarity in the appearance of individuals, and in their habits and manners" and that much of their similarity was "the natural result of a mingling of races . . ." (McCall 1868: 13–14).

Black, white, and racially mixed Creoles recognized that they shared a unique culture that had evolved over generations of mutual experience. They realized that their identities were knit together by kinship, common interest, and culture. The death notice of John Rigo of Pensacola demonstrates the relations between the white Creoles and the free Creoles of Color. "The deceased being a native of Pensacola, being a quadroon and a descendant of one of the earliest settlers. John Rigo enjoyed the respect and confidence of all who knew him and the confidence was made manifest on more than one occasion by his elevation to places of public trust" (Barr and Hargis 1938).

Free Creoles of Color took pride in the heritage they shared with the white Creoles and fostered their relations with them. Sacramental records for both ports demonstrate that Creoles of Color often chose whites to serve as the godparents to their children. Often the whites who served as godparents were related to their racially mixed godchildren. In Mobile, for instance, the white Hilaire Dubroca served as the godfather to Josephine Dubroca. Josephine Dubroca was the racially mixed daughter of Hilaire

Dubroca's brother, Maximillian, and his free Creole of Color cohabitant, Euphrosine Andry. Sometimes a white neighbor would be asked to serve as a godparent. For instance, the *mulata* Maria Ruby had four of her children confirmed in Pensacola in 1798 and in every case a white *Creole* served as sponsor or godparent. Francisco Navarro served as the *padrino* of her son Pedro. Don Ygnacio Courville served as the *padrino* for her sons Francisco Benigno and Luis Zeferino, and Doña Adelaida Dutillet was the *madrina* of Maria Ruby's daughter, Maria de la Encarnaçion.[22]

Written and unwritten commitments between the racially mixed and white *Creoles* became especially important as the Americans that migrated into the region brought different attitudes about race with them. The social system of slavery that evolved in the South was based on presumptions about race that were similar to those of the Gulf Coast region. Assumptions in the South, however, were adhered to more literally. Even as the inhabitants of the Gulf Coast found themselves in a world in which racial classification could be overlooked, most slaveholders in the southern colonies reinforced a rigid racist hierarchy. Racial mixing was taboo in the Anglo-American colonies. Certainly, miscegenation occurred there, but it remained hidden from view. Racially mixed slave children were nearly always denied by their white fathers, who knew that their reputations would be ruined if the truth were known. Few of those children were recognized or freed (Berlin 1974; Johnson and Roark 1984).

The discreet identities of the free Creoles of Color became increasingly important after the region was ceded to the United States. The Louisiana Purchase Treaty of 1803 and the Adams-Onis Treaty of 1819 guaranteed the rights of citizenship to the *ancienne population*. While the language of the treaty was meant to protect the entire population that Spain left behind, it was only the free Creoles of Color who were forced to rely on its guarantees. For instance, a law was enacted in Alabama in 1822 that prohibited "any free negro or mulatto, either directly or indirectly, to retain any kind of spirituous liquours within this state." The same act provided, however, that the prohibition should not affect those "free negro, mulatto, or other persons, who, by the treaty between the United States and Spain, became citizens of the United States, or the descendants of any such person." In 1828, a law was enacted by the territorial council in Florida that prohibited free people of color from owning weapons without first obtaining a license from the justice of the peace. The law specifically exempted the free Creoles of Color of Pensacola from the restrictions (Clay 1843; Duval 1839; Toulmin 1823).

Recognizing that their status depended on their separation from slaves and other free people of color who had few rights, the free Creoles of Color of Mobile and Pensacola sought to protect and maintain their distinctiveness. One way in which they protected their individual and group identity was through endogamous marriage. The early sacramental records of St. Michael's Church in Pensacola are not presently available to scholars, but the marriage records of the Cathedral of the Immaculate Conception in Mobile are relatively complete. By the nineteenth century, according to those records, the Creoles of Color were exclusively marrying other Creoles of Color. Between 1830 and 1836, fifteen marriages of free Creoles of Color were performed at the Cathedral of the Immaculate Conception. All of the marriages were between established members of the Creole of Color community. For instance, Maximillian Dubroca married Annette Bernody in May 1831, and in June 1831 Louise Chastang married Bazile Dubroca. Then, in April 1834, Nesin Dubroca married Britanie Bernody. As an institution that was central to the identities of the free Creoles of Color, the Catholic Church reinforced endogamous marriage patterns by mandating that its parishioners marry inside the Church. Catholics, who for the most part dominated the original population, followed the mandate by only marrying Catholics. Restricted by law from marrying outside their legal status and determined to protect their identities, the free Creoles married other free Creoles.[23]

Baptismal records suggest that even when free Creoles of Color eschewed marriage, they overwhelmingly cohabited in their own group. A few women chose to live with white men, most of whom appear to have been Creoles. There is little evidence in either Mobile or Pensacola, however, that free Creoles of Color cohabited with free blacks or with slaves. For instance, after the region was ceded to the United States and Anglo-Americans began to overwhelm the *ancienne population,* free Creoles of Color began to act exclusively as godparents to the children of other Creoles of Color. In Mobile in May 1812, two free Creoles of Color, Jose Astien and Catalina Don Juan, served as the godparents to Juan Baptiste, the infant of Fermin Trenier and Basilio Padillo. In June 1812, Isabel and Edwardo Colin, free Creoles of Color, served as the godparents of Margarita, the infant of Margarita Chastang and Augustin Colin.[24]

Besides family ties, free Creoles of Color protected their identities and status through the formation of exclusive organizations. The only extant records for these organizations are those for Mobile, but the records in Mobile mention associated organizations in New Orleans and Pensacola. The free Creole of Color associations in Mobile included the Creole Fire Department, the Creole Social Club, and the ladies auxiliary of the Creole Social Club. The Creole Fire Department was officially founded in the 1820s as one of the fire companies in Mobile. It was an exclusive, by-invitation-only association that held regular weekly meetings that were often attended by the local priest. The Creole firemen marched in local parades. They organized balls, picnics, and other social functions to raise money for their company and their equipment. The Creole Social Club and its ladies auxiliary also held weekly meetings. Their main purpose was to provide insurance for their members. Any member who got sick could appeal to the organization for living expenses, or for burial expenses when necessary. Each organizations remained active throughout the nineteenth century, and each offered its members protection against hardship and the increasing racism that was closing in around them.[25]

Education also separated free Creoles of Color from slaves and other free people of color. Soon after the legislative councils in Alabama and Florida were established, they instituted laws that forbade anyone from teaching free people of color to read or write (Duval 1839; Toulmin 1823). Consequently, most free people of color in Alabama and Florida were illiterate. Free Creoles of Color in Mobile and Pensacola, however, were educated along with white Creoles by the Catholic Church. Furthermore, in 1833, the legislature of the state of Alabama officially recognized the unique status of the Creoles of Color when it passed an act that was more than a tacit acknowledgment of the unique status of that segment of the population. In that act, the legislature directed the mayor and aldermen of the city of Mobile to authorize and license teachers to educate the children of the free Creoles of Color (Clay 1843).

Alabama's lawmakers clearly intended for only those children who were the "descendants of those persons who were residents of the said city and counties, at the time the treaty was made between the French republic and the United States of America, in April 1803" to be educated. The act stipulated that other children of free people of color were not to be educated by the city. In order to assure that only Creole children were educated, the law further stated that "none of the colored children shall be so taught or instructed, until they shall first have the permission of the said mayor and alderman of the city of Mobile and they shall have recorded the names of such children in a book to be kept by them for that purpose." If such a list was kept, it has not survived (Toulmin 1823).

Despite the treaties and their own extraordinary efforts, the free Creoles of Mobile and Pensacola began losing status, and they feared for their freedom during the final decades before the War between the States. During the 1840s and 1850s, the legislatures of Alabama and Florida reversed their earlier actions and began enacting restrictive laws aimed at free people of color that did not specifically exclude the Creoles of Color. For instance, in the 1840s Alabama and Florida enacted guardianship laws that mandated that free people of color had to enlist white men to act as their guardians, had to have their guardians sign certificates of guardianship, and had to register the certificates with the court. The guardianship laws were intended to prohibit free people of color from buying or sell-ing property without the written permission of their guardians. That re-striction was hauntingly similar to the restrictions that forbade slaves from buying or selling property without the permission of their owners. The penalty for buying or selling property without first securing a guardian's permission was a fine.

In 1848, a Florida guardianship law specified that all free Negroes and mulattoes over twelve years of age who failed to secure a guardian were subject to a fine of not less than ten dollars. If the fine was not paid, the judge of the probate court was authorized to commit the of-fender to jail until the fine and all of the court proceedings were paid. There is no evidence in either Mobile or Pensacola that the guardianship laws of the 1840s were honored. But the laws passed in the 1850s were enforced. A new law was passed in Alabama in 1851–52 that provided that the county judges of probate were given authority to appoint guard-ians for free people of color. Another in Florida in 1856 provided one punishment for the free people of color who did not have a guardian and another for anyone doing business with them. In that law, any free Ne-groes and mulattoes over twelve years of age who failed to appoint a guardian as provided by the law of 1848 were subject to a fine of not less than ten dollars. If the fine was not paid, the judge of the probate court was authorized to jail the offender until the fine and proceedings were paid. Further, anyone who bought or sold to a free Negro or mu-latto in Florida without the written permission of his or her guardian would be fined between one hundred dollars and five hundred dollars.[26]

One woman who experienced the humiliation of the legislation was Euphrosine Hinard, the free woman of color who had been plaçeed to Don Nicolas Vidal before his death. Hinard was an astute business-woman, respected by her black and white neighbors. Throughout her life-time, she had freely and successfully participated in the economic activities of her community. Records in New Orleans, Mobile, and Pensacola trace her economic activities, but her business acumen was especially known in Pensacola, where she owned a brickyard and speculated in real estate and slaves. Hinard's relations with her neighbors changed, however, in 1857 when she was forced by law to choose a white male guardian, Zanon Souchet, in order to continue conducting her business activities. The document stated that Souchet consented to Hinard's "buying from and selling to any person or persons any real, personal, or chattel property in the county aforesaid for the term of twelve months from date."

White Creoles in Mobile and Pensacola could no longer protect their racially mixed kin from the restrictive laws that were aimed at them. All they could do was to offer to serve as their guardians. A list of guardians in Pensacola demonstrates that the white males who acted as guardians of the free Creoles of Color were white Creoles. The list also demonstrates the kinship that existed between the white Creoles and the free Creoles of Color. For instance, Francisco Collins acted as the guardian of Joseph and Mary Ann Collins and Sebastian Barrios served as the guardian of Fernando and Severino Barrios. Yet, even though most guardians appear to have been kin to those whom they protected, accepting any guardian would have been anathema to the free Creoles of Color.[27]

Recognizing that their world was becoming increasingly restricted by the attitudes and laws that sought to consolidate the social system of slavery, many of the free Creoles of Color decided to leave their homes for ports in Spanish America, the Caribbean, or France. White Creoles in Mobile urged the free Creoles of Color to migrate to Haiti. Reports indicate that two groups migrated there shortly before 1850 (White, 1: 33). In 1857, two ships left Pensacola for Tampico, with many of the free Creoles of Color aboard. On April 4, 1857, an article appeared in the *Pensacola Gazette* that expressed the sentiments of the white kin and neighbors that the Creoles of Color left behind as they sailed away on the schooner *Pinta.* "The Exodus—On Tuesday last, thirty five free colored persons took their departure from this city for Tampico, and in a few days, the balance who are still remaining will also leave for the same place. It was a painful sight to see them parting from their friends and their native country to seek homes in a foreign land. They take with them the sympathy of all our citizens on account of the causes which have led them to leave us, and also their best wishes for their future happiness and prosperity in their new home."[28] The schooner *William,* which left Pensacola in August of the same year for Tampico, is believed to have carried the remainder of those who chose to flee. Evidence of the impact of the migration from Pensacola can be found in the state's census records. A census taken in 1855 demonstrates that there were 351 free people of color living there in that year. The next census, taken in 1860, includes only 153 free people of color.[29]

Even though many of Pensacola's residents expressed sympathy in the *Pensacola Gazette,* the Creoles of Color were bitter. They were angry that the status and safety that they had inherited as the descendants of a new world order were being denied them. Indeed, by the final years of the antebellum period, they lived in fear that they would lose the little freedom that remained to them. One woman expressed the sentiments of the entire group as they were fleeing Pensacola. As the schooner *Pinta* sailed away from the dock, the mother of Athalie Gagnet tossed a rock into the bay and was reputed to have said, "O, little rock, when you come back up again, I'll come back to Pensacola" (Barr and Hargis 1938).

Despite intolerable conditions, some of the Creoles of Color of Mobile and Pensacola stayed on, relying on their unique identities, their ties to the white Creoles, and group cohesiveness for protection. Others who had migrated elsewhere returned to the region after the Civil War. Evidence of their return is in the cemeteries, where tombstones record the foreign birthplaces of many members of their families. The war years and their aftermath released them from threats of re-enslavement, but emancipation brought them new challenges. The extreme racism and Jim Crow laws of the latter part of the nineteenth century more completely segregated the Creoles of Color from their white kin and neighbors. But, at the same time, the free Creoles of Color distanced themselves from the large numbers of freed blacks in their communities. Yet, even though their exclusivity brought them harsh criticism from the black community during the late nineteenth century and the twentieth, most continued to define themselves outside the dominant black community that surrounded them.

Notes

1. Some of the material appearing herein appeared in a preliminary and variant form in the *Gulf Coast Historical Review* 9 (1) (Fall 1993): 26–46.
2. Baptismal record dated June 11, 1707, Archives of the Cathedral of the Immaculate Conception, First Book of Baptisms, Mobile, Alabama. Hereafter the dates given for the records of the Cathedral of the Immaculate Conception will be cited as CIC.
3. Baptismal record, July 26, 1715, First Book of Baptisms, CIC.
4. Will Book 2: 22–23, and 112, Mobile County Records, Mobile County Courthouse, Mobile, Alabama. Chastang acknowledged his daughter in her baptism records, *Baptisma Nigrorum,* 1781–1805, CIC.
5. *Edit servant de Reglement pour la Gouvernement et l'Administration de la Justice, Police, Discipline et le Commerce des Esclaves Nègres, dans le Province de la Louisiane, 3 Moreau de Saint Méry 88, Louisiana Historical Society Publications* 75–90 (1908). For the recorded racial composition of the early population, see the first Book of Baptisms, CIC.
6. First Book of Baptism, CIC.
7. *Baptisma Nigrorum,* CIC.
8. *General de la Jurisdiction de la Mobila del Primero de Enereo del Año 1787, Legaho 206,* records of the Spanish period, Mississippi State Archives, Jackson Mississippi; *Census de Mobila, Septembre 12, 1805, legajo 142,* records of the Spanish period, Mississippi Territorial Archives, Jackson Mississippi; *Padrón General de le Plaza de Panzacola, 1820,* Archivo General de Indias, Papeles Procedentes de Cuba, Seville, Spain (hereafter abbreviated as AGI-PC), legaho 1944. The census has been translated and compiled in Coker and Inglis 1980.
9. *Padrón General de le Plaza de Panzacola, 1784,* AGI-PC, legaho 36. The 1784 census is translated and compiled by Coker and Inglis 1980. *Padrón General de Oeste Floride, 1805,* AGI-PC, legaho 142 B. *Padrón de Panzacola, 1820.* The 1805 and 1820 censuses was translated and compiled by Coker and Inglis 1980.

10. *General de Mobila, 1787; Census de Mobila, 1805.*
11. *Census de Mobila, 1805; Padrón de Panzacola, 1784; Padrón de Panzacola, 1820.*
12. Baptismal record, July 26, 1715, CIC; *Padrón de Panzacola, 1820.*
13. *Padrón de le Plaza de Panzacola, 1802,* AGI-PC, legajo 59. The 1802 census has been published in Coker and Inglis 1980 and in McGovern 1972; *Padrón de Oeste Floride, 1805.*
14. Bernody Probate Records, the Probate Court of Mobile County, Ala.; The will of Don Nicolas Maria Vidal, New Orleans Parish Notarial Archives; The property records of Euphrosine Hinard are included in a collection under her name in the Archives of the Escambia County Courthouse, Escambia County, Florida. The term *plaçeed* is a French one and connoted, in Louisiana, the placement of free women of color with white men. Since the inhabitants of Louisiana were forbidden to marry across racial lines, the term was used to suggest the common quasi-official interracial relationships that replaced marriage.
15. Baptismal record, July 11, 1734, CIC.
16. Baptismal records, Oct. 10, 1704; June 11, 1707; July 11, 1734; and May 24, 1745, CIC.
17. The Acts of the General Assembly of Florida for the antebellum period are housed at the office of the secretary of state, Tallahassee, Florida; the laws for Alabama are housed at the Alabama Department of Archives and History, Montgomery, Alabama.
18. Acts of the General Assembly of Alabama; Acts of the General Assembly of Florida.
19. *Padrón de Panzacola, 1820.*
20. *Census de Mobila, 1805; Population of the United States in 1860* (Washington, D.C.: Government Printing Office, 1864); *Seventh Census of the United States: 1850* (Washington, D.C.: Robert Armstrong, 1853).
21. Landry probate records, Probate Court of Mobile County.
22. *Baptisma Nigrorum,* Jan. 15, 1804; CIC; Confirmations conferred in the plaza of Pensacola, The seventh day of May, to the following by the Most Reverend Señor Don Luis Peñalver y Cardenas, First Worthy Bishop of this Diocese, in the present year of 1798.
23. Marriage records, May 1831, June 1831, Apr. 1834, CIC.
24. Baptismal records, May 1812 and June 1812, CIC.
25. The records of the Creole Fire Department and the Creole Social Club and its auxiliary are housed at the Mobile Museum.
26. Acts of Assembly of Florida; Acts of the Assembly of Alabama.
27. Archives of the Escambia County Courthouse.
28. *Pensacola Gazette,* Apr. 4, 1857.
29. *Pensacola Gazette,* Aug. 1857; Florida State Census, 1855; *Population of the United States in 1860.*

References

Aiken, John G. 1823. *Digest of the Laws of Alabama.* Montgomery, Ala.
Amos, Harriet E. 1985. *Cotton City: Urban Development in Antebellum Mobile.* Tuscaloosa: Univ. of Alabama Press.
Baade, Hans W. 1983. "The Law of Slavery in Spanish Luisiana, 1769–1803." In Edward F. Haas, ed., *Louisiana's Legal Heritage.* New Orleans: Louisiana State Museum.

Barr, Ruth B., and Hargis, Modeste. 1938. "The Voluntary Exile of the Free Negroes of Pensacola." *Florida Historical Quarterly* 17: 1–14.

Berlin, Ira. 1974. *Slaves without Masters: The Free Negro in the Antebellum South.* New York: Oxford Univ. Press.

Brathwaite, Edward. 1971. *The Development of Creole Society in Jamaica.* Oxford: Clarendon Press.

Clay, C. C. 1843. *A Digest of the Laws of the State of Alabama: Containing All the Statutes of a Public and General Nature, in Force at the Close of the Session of the General Assembly, in February, 1843.* Tuscaloosa.

Coker, William S., and G. Douglas Inglis. 1980. *The Spanish Censuses of Pensacola, 1784–1820.* Pensacola: Perdido Bay Press.

Coker, William S., and Thomas D. Watson. 1986. *Indian Traders of the Southeastern Spanish Borderlands: Panton, Leslie & Company and John Forbes & Company, 1783–1847.* Gainesville: Univ. Presses of Florida.

Domínguez, Virginia R. 1986. *White by Definition: Social Classification in Creole Louisiana.* New Brunswick, N.J.: Rutgers Univ. Press.

DuPratz, LePage. 1763. *History of Louisiana.* 2 Vols. London.

Duval, John P. 1839. *A Compilation of the Public Acts of the Legislative Council of the Territory of Florida, Passed Prior to 1840.* Tallahassee.

Fiehrer, Thomas Marc. 1979. "The African Presence in Colonial Louisiana: An Essay on the Continuity of Caribbean Culture." In Robert R. McDonald, John R. Demp, and Edward F. Hass, eds. *Louisiana's Black Heritage.* New Orleans: The Louisiana State Museum

Freyre, Gilberto. 1933. *Casa-Grande e Senzala.* Josè Olympio. Trans. and reprinted in 1946 as *The Masters and the Slaves.* New York: Alfred A. Knopf.

Gould, Virginia Meacham. 1991. "In Full Enjoyment of Their Liberty: The Free Women of Color of the Gulf Ports of New Orleans, Mobile, and Pensacola, 1769–1860." Ph.D. diss., Emory Univ.

Hall, Gwendolyn Midlo. 1992. *Africans in Colonial Louisiana: The Development of Afro-Creole Culture in the Eighteenth Century.* Baton Rouge: Louisiana State Univ. Press.

Hamilton, Peter J. 1910. *Colonial Mobile: An Historical Study Largely From Original Sources, of the Alabama–Tombigbee Basin and the Old South West From the Discovery of the Spiritu Santo in 1519 until the Demolition of Fort Charlotte in 1821.* Boston: Houghton Mifflin.

Herskovits, Melville J. 1925. "The Dilemma of Social Pattern." *The Survey Graphic* 6.

Hamilton, Peter J. 1977. *Old Mobile: Fort Louis De La Louisiane 1702–1711.* Tuscaloosa: Univ. of Alabama Press.

Holmes, Jack D. L. 1970. *Pensacola Settlers, 1781–1821.* Pensacola: Pensacola Historical Restoration and Preservation Commission.

Holmes, Jack D. L. 1983. "Do It! Don't Do It!: Spanish Laws on Sex and Marriage." In Edward R. Haas, ed. *Louisiana's Legal Heritage.* Pensacola: Perdido Bay Press.

Johnson, Michael P., and James L. Roark. 1984. *Black Masters: A Free Family of Color in the Old South.* New York: W. W. Norton.

Martineau, Harriett. 1838. *Retrospect of Western Travel.* Vol. II. London: Saunders and Otley.

McCall, Major General George A. 1974. *Letters From The Frontiers.* A facsimile reproduction of the 1868 edition. Gainesville: Univ. Presses of Florida.

McGovern, James R., ed. 1972. *Colonial Pensacola.* Pensacola: Pensacola-Escambia County Development Commission.

McGowan, James Thomas. 1976. "Creation of a Slave Society." Ph.D. diss., Rochester Univ.

Mörner, Magnus. 1976. *Race Mixture in the History of Latin America.* Boston: Little Brown and Company.

Nordmann, Christopher. 1990. "The Free Negroes in Mobile County, Alabama." Ph.D. diss., Univ. of Alabama.

Pickett, Albert James. 1896. *History of Alabama; And Incidentally of Georgia and Mississippi, From the Earliest Period.* Sheffield, Ala.: Robert C. Randolph.

Robin, C. C. 1966. *Voyage to Louisiana, 1803–1805.* Trans. and abridged by Stuart O. Landry. New Orleans: Pelican Publishing Co.

Roman, Bernard. 1775. *A Concise Natural History of East and West Florida.* New York: R. Atkins.

Saxe-Weimar-Eisenach, Bernard. 1827. *Travels through America during the Years 1825–1826.* Philadelphia: Carey, Lea, and Carey.

Shelley, Dian. 1971. "The Effects of Increasing Racism on the Creole Colored in the Three Gulf Cities Between 1803 and 1860." M.A. thesis, Univ. of West Florida.

Toulmin, Harry. 1823. *A Digest of the Laws of the State of Alabama Containing Restrictions and Resolutions in Force at the End of the General Assembly in January, 1823.* New York: Ginn and Curtis.

Tregle, Joseph, Jr. 1992. "Creoles and Americans." In Arnold Hirsch and Joseph Logsden, eds. *Creoles of New Orleans: Race and Americanization.* Baton Rouge: Louisiana State Univ. Press.

Usner, Daniel H. 1992. *Indians, Settlers, and Slaves in a Frontier Exchange Economy: The Lower Mississippi Valley Before 1783.* Chapel Hill: Univ. of North Carolina Press.

Weber, David J. 1992. *The Spanish Frontier in North America.* New Haven: Yale Univ. Press.

White, Richard. 1991. *The Middle Ground, Indians, Empires, and Republicans in the Great Lakes Region, 1650–1815.* Cambridge: Cambridge Univ. Press.

THREE

Loren Schweninger

Socioeconomic Dynamics among the Gulf Creole Populations: The Antebellum and Civil War Years

In the past generation, scholars have produced a substantial literature about free people of color in the Gulf region. During the 1970s, Laura Foner, Ira Berlin, John Blassingame, Gary Mills, Herbert Sterkx, David Rankin, among others, focused attention on the unique values and attitudes of free colored people, often mulattoes, who lived in a three-tiered society not unlike slave societies in the Caribbean and South America (Berlin 1974, 1976; Blassingame, 1973; Foner 1970; Mills 1977; Rankin 1974, 1977–78; Sterkx 1972). More recently, David Whitten, Gwendolyn Midlo Hall, Joseph Logsdon, Caryn Cossé Bell, and Christopher Nordmann added investigations of sugar planter Andrew Durnford, Francophone Africans in New Orleans, and free blacks in Mobile to show how the region, as part of the French and Spanish empires, boasted an unusual blend of cultural, economic, and legal traditions (Hall 1992; Logsdon and Bell 1992; Nordman 1990; Whitten 1981). In all, these and other authors have significantly expanded our understanding of free African Americans in the region.

Much of this literature, however, focuses on free blacks rather than on Creoles of Color, highlights New Orleans, and either ends or begins with the Civil War. In addition, although books and articles examine specific locations, districts, parishes, individuals, and clans, few scholars have systematically analyzed the cultural and economic changes that occurred among colored Creoles before and after the war outside of the Crescent City. How were the attitudes and values of the group shaped by economic circumstances? And how did these change over time? This essay examines the attitudes, values, and changing economic status of colored Creoles beyond the Crescent City during the middle decades of the nineteenth century. It seeks to understand the relationship between culture and economic standing, and to compare the free colored Creole population of the Gulf with various groups of free African Americans in the southern states before and after the Civil War (Hirsch and Logsdon 1992: 189, 195).

The origins of this group stretched back to the Spanish, French, and territorial periods, when immigrants from Europe and the Caribbean, unable to find suitable partners in areas where men largely outnumbered women, took slaves and free blacks as their companions.[1] In the Florida Territory, Spanish men often lived with mulatto or black women, treated their mulatto children as their own, had them baptized in the Catholic Church, and provided them with economic security. On the west side of Pensacola, for example, Antonio Collins cohabited with mulatto Ellen Boudain, Dr. Juan Ruby with mulatto Maria Carolotta Thompson, John Sunday with his slave Ginny and their mulatto son, John Jr., and John Pons with his mulatto mistress, Maria Rosaria. Members of the Pons family, one of the most prominent colored Creole clans in Florida, engaged in various business activities and claimed descent from two Spanish military officers (Thomas 1911: 336; Sutton 1990).

In Alabama, various colored Creole families and clans emerged during the early nineteenth century in the same manner. The wills of various Spanish and French inhabitants of Mobile reveal how white men provided for their colored partners and mulatto children. "I give and bequeath unto Claire Paddille the quartronne Woman who lives with me and who is the mother of my Children," John Chavanna wrote in 1820, "all the property both real and personal of which I may die possessed." About the same time, Daniel Juzan provided for his two families, one white, one black. To his "Children of Color"—Delphine, Dalcour, Camine, Marselett, and Merone—he gave one thousand dollars. Hilaire Dubroca bequeathed the bulk of his estate to Isabelle, "a coloured woman who has lived with me for many years," and to his mixed-blood children, Bazille, Louise, Arsene, Cephire, and Arthur. Dr. Jean Chastang, the Mobile surgeon who served as a medical consultant at the Spanish fort of San Esteban de Tombecbe, also provided for his mulatto children, Zeno and Basil Chastang (Amos 1985: 90; Holmes 1975: 10–11; Nordmann 1990: 1–33).[2]

Similar interracial family backgrounds existed among free persons of color in Louisiana: the Durnford, Oliver, and Reggio families in Plaquemines; the Ponis family in St. John the Baptist; the Honores and Decuirs in Pointe Coupée Parish; the Donattos and Meullions in St. Landry Parish. Members of the Metoyer, Coincoin, Conant, Rocques, Morin, LeCourt, Rachal, Dupre, and Sarpy families in Natchitoches Parish were often related by blood or marriage. One colored Creole clan originated when the white French settler Claude Thomas Pierre Metoyer took slave Marie Thereze Coincoin as his mistress. They had ten children, seven of whom lived (Mills 1977: 74–76; Schweninger 1990: 101; Sterkx 1972: 204–7).[3]

The relatively high economic station of these early colored Creole clans derived largely from white men bequeathing land, property, and slaves to their partners or mulatto children. Typical in this regard was Jean Chastang of Washington County, Mississippi Territory (Alabama's first county), who bequeathed his "beloved worthy friend and companion Louison," a free woman of color who had lived with him for twenty years, all the lands and tenements on which he lived, ten cows and calves, two bulls and two horses, silverware, beds, bedding, furniture, and a slave family consisting of a father, mother, and two children. When she died, he said, his estate should be passed on to their ten children and a "female Mulatto named Francoise" to enjoy in equal proportions, including "the natural increase" of the slave property. To ensure that the emancipation papers of the slave born Louison, signed under Spanish rule in 1780, would remain valid under United States law, Chastang reiterated that Louison and her children "were fully and completely free and emancipated, to all intents and purposes whatsoever."[4]

During the 1830s and 1840s, the children and grandchildren of early immigrants from the Caribbean, France, and Spain improved their economic position through intermarriage and by assisting one another in various financial matters. Often literate and clustered in small communities from Florida to Alabama and various Louisiana parishes, they maintained tightly knit clans, socialized with one another, married within their groups, and supported one another in the acquisition of land and slaves. A generation after Jean Chastang wrote his will, for example, various family members had intermarried with the Andre, Bazile, Collins, Lorent, and Dubroca families, the most prosperous colored Creole families in Alabama (King and Barlow 1985: 3, 27, 31).

Not an insignificant proportion of colored Creoles outside of New Orleans were slave owners. Although precise statistics are not available, the areas of the Gulf region where colored Creoles lived in greatest numbers were also sections with the highest density of free black slave owners. In Florida in 1830, fourteen of the fifteen free persons of color who owned slaves were residents of Escambia and St. John's Counties, which included the cities of Pensacola and St. Augustine and their colored Creole populations. Among African-American slave owners in Alabama in the same year, exactly half (24 of 48) were residents of Mobile County, including seven members of the Chastang clan. Among the 130 free black slave owners in seven rural Louisiana sugar and cotton parishes (Iberville, Natchitoches, Point Coupée, St. John the Baptist, St. Landry, St. Martin, and West Baton Rouge), 43 Creoles of Color owned a total of 1,327 slaves, or nearly one-fifth of all black-owned slaves in the Lower South. While the proportion of colored Creoles who owned slaves in Florida,

Alabama, and Louisiana was probably not as high as the approximately one-third among white families in the region, slaveholding was nonetheless widespread within most clans (Schweninger 1990: 104–5; Stampp 1956: 30; Woodson 1924: 1, 3, 6–9).

This was particularly true, as historian Gary Mills has shown, in Natchitoches Parish, where slave ownership was common among various members of the Metoyer clan. As early as 1810, a few members of the group had begun to purchase blacks, and, by 1830, 99 free people of color with the surname Metoyer owned 226 slaves, while other family members related by marriage owned an additional 61 bondmen and bondwomen. Augustin and his brother Louis Metoyer were the largest owners, each possessing 54 slaves. Indeed, by the 1830s, the great majority of the Metoyer clan had entered the slaveholding class. The average member of the colony actually owned more slaves than the average white in the parish (Mills 1977: 108–9, 218).

Although some of the slaves owned by colored Creoles were members of their own families who could not be legally manumitted, or wives and mistresses with whom the men cohabited,[5] most were acquired to labor in the fields or work in various other capacities. Artisans and small shopkeepers purchased slave apprentices and helpers; businessmen and women bought haulers, carters, and stock handlers; and plantation owners purchased house servants, cooks, mechanics, and field hands. Maximillian Collins and Zeno Chastang, both large landowners and children of white fathers, gradually acquired 45 blacks, including stockmen, herdsmen, and field workers, to work their farms. Though once a slave himself, Jean Baptiste Meullion of St. Landry Parish acquired slaves on a regular basis, traveling to the slave market in Natchez, Mississippi, or making arrangements with a slave-trading firm in New Orleans. He used his chattel to produce sugar and cotton on his 1,240-acre plantation, selling his sugar crop in 1834 for $1,418, and his cotton crop four years later for $19,349. Cotton planter Dominique Metoyer of Natchitoches Parish steadily increased the number of slaves he owned, working them on land he originally acquired in a grant from the Spanish government. He produced successive cotton crops with his 32 slaves on his 500-acre Red River plantation (Mills 1977: 57; Sterkx 1972: 204–7).[6]

In their treatment of their bondmen and bondwomen, colored Creoles differed little from their white neighbors. A few felt some compassion for those in bondage, especially slaves who might be related by blood or marriage, but most considered their blacks principally as chattel property. They bought, sold, mortgaged, willed, traded, and transferred their slaves, demanded long hours in the workshops and fields, and disciplined recalcitrant blacks. Nor did they seem especially concerned about slave families or unproductive or elderly blacks. Following the death of her husband in the late 1830s, Marie Marguerite Le Comte, a free woman of color in Natchitoches Parish, sold two children away from their mothers, disposed of an old woman for fifty dollars, and tried in vain to sell several other slaves described as "sickly" and "infirmed." On sugar estates, where harvesting and pressing of the cane demanded sixteen-hour workdays, mulatto owners pushed their slaves incessantly, and, when women were unable to work such long hours, they stocked their plantations with young men. Among the twenty-eight field hands on Louise Oliver's Plaquemines Parish sugar estate, the men outnumbered women three to one. "You might think, master, dat dey would be good to dar own nation; but dey is not," one anonymous slave explained to a white traveler in Louisiana during the mid-1850s. "[T]hey is very bad masters" (Olmsted 1953: 262).[7]

With land and slaves, Creoles of Color emerged during the nineteenth century as the wealthiest group of free blacks in the nation. By 1850, exactly one out of three rural free African-American landowners in Louisiana (181 of 543) owned at least $2,000 worth of real estate. These farmers and plantation owners, largely colored Creoles, controlled a total of $1.8 million worth of land, 24 percent of the property owned by blacks in the entire South. Typically, they cultivated a few hundred acres, owned several slaves, and tended small herds of livestock, but among them were quite wealthy free mulattoes. Louisa Ponis of St. John the Baptist Parish owned 1,300 acres valued at $35,000; Adolphe Reggio of Plaquemines Parish owned 700 acres valued at $40,000, with sugar-refining machinery worth $20,000; his neighbor Andrew Durnford, whose 2,660-acre St. Rosalie plantation, with large herds of livestock and 70 slaves, was worth $161,300. In Iberville Parish, the Ricard clan, including Madam Cyprien and her son Pierre Ricard, owned large plantations. The Ricard clan acquired not only land and slaves, but also various other types of property: livestock, buildings, machinery, buggies, guns, wagons, boats, fine clothing, jewelry, paintings, and silverware. One observer described them as "doubtless the richest black family in this or any other country" (Clarke 1859: 13; Whitten 1981: 85, 88).[8]

If they had an intense desire to accumulate property, they were equally devoted to assisting one another in financial matters. Whenever possible they attempted to keep fiscal affairs within their own families and clans by loaning one another money, cosigning notes, selling one another slaves, extending credit, and countersigning land deeds. In 1843, Mobile resident Martin Durand filed suit, claiming that he had legitimately purchased a valuable lot from "one Margaret Collins a Colored Woman" in 1825 but that now various members of the Chastang-Collins clan "have combined and confederated together to oppress your orator in the premises."[9] When the Dubucelets, Honorés, Deslondes, and Decuirs of West Baton Rouge and Pointe Coupée Parishes convened in 1829 to discuss various financial transactions following the death of a clan member, they were described in a local court record as "all free persons of colour, Relations & friends." These two court records typified the unity and solidarity among various clan members when it came to economic matters. Indeed, it was not uncommon for family members to provide gifts of land or slaves to young married couples, to make financial arrangements to assist relatives, and to distribute land or notes to other members of their families.[10]

The networks extended beyond economic affairs to marriage, education, religion, language, and social and cultural values. To a remarkable degree, colored Creoles married within their group. Occasionally the wishes of parents were ignored, and children ran away with slaves, free blacks, or whites, but most often they married their "own kind." In some locations, marriage contracts were signed; in others, there were less formal arrangements. In either case, parents were heavily involved with the choice of mates. In Mobile, young Creoles of Color invariably intermarried within one or another of a half-dozen families: in 1830, Joseph Lorent married Isabelle Chastang; in 1832, Bazille (also spelled Bazil) Dubroca married Louise Chastang; in 1841, Edward Chastang married Celeste Collins; in 1844, Zeno Chastang, Jr. married Patrone Andre; and, in 1854, Peter Chastang married Corielie Chastang (King and Barlow 1985: 1, 27, 28, 47).[11]

The situation was the same in Louisiana. Marital arrangements were made between the Donatto, Meullion, Simien, Guillory, and Lemmelle families in St. Landry Parish, the Reggio, Oliver, and Leonard families in Plaquemines, the Llorens and Metoyer families in Natchitoches, and the Decuir and Dubuclet families in Pointe Coupée. In the case of Antoine Decuir and Antoine Dubuclet, whose son and daughter were married in 1835, the two wealthy planters drew up a four-page document (in French) specifying the date of the wedding, the size of the dowry, and arragements for future property distribution.[12]

Colored Creoles placed a high value on education. Most were literate, and a significant proportion, at least until the 1830s and 1840s, spoke and wrote in French. Those who could afford to do so provided tutors for their children, or they sent their children away to private schools, to France, or to the North for an education. Plaquemines Parish sugar planter Andrew Durnford, the son of Englishman Thomas Durnford and a free woman of color, Rosaline Mercier, sent his son Thomas away to a boarding school, and when Thomas reached the age for higher training, Durnford sent him to Lafayette College in Easton, Pennsylvania (Whitten 1981: 7, 102, 103). In St. Mary Parish, Romaine Verdun, a planter and head of the Verdun clan, built a school and hired a full-time teacher for his children and those of his neighbors. Mulatto planters in St. Landry and several other parishes erected school buildings and employed teachers (Rawick 1972–, vol. 5, pt. 4: 4038; Stahl 1942: 361). "Out of nearly two hundred colored families who were free before the war," one observer in Pointe Coupée Parish noted in 1866, "only one family is unable to read and write while among the white people from twenty to twenty-five percent are in ignorance" (Willey 1866: 248–49).

Next to the family and education, the church was the most important cultural institution. Most Creoles of Color in the Gulf region were conscientious churchgoers, and the vast majority among them were practicing Catholics. In Pensacola, Mobile, and the Louisiana Parishes, they were baptized, married, and received their last rites in the Catholic Church. Marriage was especially important, since it linked the past with the present and the future socially, culturally, and economically. Couples obtained permission from parents, posted bans, confessed, took marital vows, and attended church wedding celebrations. Most often, colored Creoles attended church with whites, but occasionally they built and maintained their own churches. In Natchitoches Parish, the Metoyer family built the Church of St. Augustin. The free mulatto patriarch of the clan, Augustin Metoyer, explained that the church had been erected principally for various members of the Metoyer clan, but in his last will and testament in 1839 he said that "[white] outsiders professing our same holy, catholic, apostolic, and Roman religion will have the right to assist at the divine office in the said chapel" and enjoy "all the rights and privileges which I and my family are able to have there" (Hall 1988: 144–48; Mills 1977: 153).

Metoyer's reference to "outsiders" provides remarkable insight into the cultural and social values of colored Creoles during the antebellum era. Whenever possible, they sought to avoid contact with either whites or free blacks, socializing instead with other members of their clans. Of course, the stigma of race prevented social mingling with whites in most sections, but it was more than attitudes of whites that motivated Creoles of Color to look inward for spiritual and social renewal. Precariously balanced between whites, free blacks, and slaves, they felt survival depended on clan and family loyalty. Thus, they socialized almost exclusively with one another, hunting, fishing, riding, target shooting, dancing, dining, partying, and traveling together. Part of the social commingling was the result of their relatively high economic standing, and, in other sections of the Lower South where different traditions prevailed (such as in South

Carolina and Georgia), small groups of prosperous free people of color socialized, commingled, and even intermarried with one another. But the fierce determination to maintain clan exclusiveness was more pronounced and more widespread in the Gulf region than elsewhere.

Despite the desire of members of various clans to live in harmony, disputes did arise and sometimes spilled over into the public arena. Perhaps no case better illustrates this than the 1847 civil suit brought by Margaret Collins, described as a "creole mulatto," against her daughter Louise Laurendine. The mother explained that she had transferred ownership of her slave grandson Edward to her daughter, but only with the understanding that the boy would eventually be manumitted. When her daughter hired Edward out as a slave, Margaret brought suit, arguing that it was not her intention that he should be treated as a slave, despite his legal status. Among those who testified in her behalf were clan members Joseph and Edward Collins and Augustus and Jean Chastang; they affirmed that "the old lady" had always "treated the boy as her grandchild." Another witness, Catholic Bishop Michael Potier, provided a copy of Edward's 1828 baptismal record showing that he was the illegitimate son of Joseph Collins and his slave Emily. "An act of emancipation by the Master & Father," the Bishop said, "appears contemporaneous with the act of baptism."

This was not true, but the evidence revealed that the boy was indeed Margaret's grandchild and was entitled to his freedom. Louise Laurendine's response to the suit added two more dimensions to the conflict: the unique role of women in colored Creole society and the anomalous nature of free blacks owning slaves. Louise's husband, Benjamin Laurendine, a turner by trade, was an alcoholic and unable to support his wife and seven children. As a consequence, Madam Benjamin, as Louise was called, managed their estate, although the property was "subject by law to the control of the husband." To provide for her family, she turned Edward over to a hiring agent, who transported him to New Orleans "& hired him to a butcher for 3 years." Within a few weeks, however, Edward ran away and returned to Mobile. After being discovered, he was returned to the Crescent City, but ran away again. Then he "was taken up & put in the work house at New Orleans & before [the agent] could receive him, he had to pay about $86, for jail fees, & physicians fees." Despite these difficulties, Louise contacted a second agent, William C. Griggs, to hire the boy out, but Griggs quickly discovered that Edward was of "bad character & that he is of no value to Mad Benjamin"; indeed, during a two-year period she "did not receive one cent profit for the hire of the boy." Others said Edward was a "good for nothing, do nothing boy"; he was "lazy, & idle, indisposed to do any Kind of work."[13]

That a colored Creole woman would seek to profit from the hire of her own slave nephew in order to support her children reveals not only the ambiguous nature of slaveholding among Creoles of Color but also the special role of women. While Creoles of Color exerted every effort to maintain stable families—husband, wife, children—within the clan, there were numerous factors working against the "norm," including disease, alcoholism, premature death, and the peculiar demographic configuration of the free black population. Due to the selective manumission process in the Lower South, free black women often outnumbered free black men, creating a limited pool of suitable mates who were neither white nor slave. In 1830 in Escambia County, including a section of Walton County between the Yellow and Escambia Rivers, adult free women of color (over the age of twenty-four) outnumbered the men nearly two to one; in Mobile, and in various Louisiana parishes, although the margins differed, the ratios were often skewed in much the same manner. As a result, free women of color often became sole breadwinners— they lived alone and provided for their families. In the areas of substantial colored Creole concentrations outside of New Orleans in 1850 and 1860, between one-fourth and one-third of the African-American real estate owners were women (Schweninger 1990: appendix 5).[14]

Some of these free women of color continued to maintain relationships with white men. Although on the decline during the late antebellum period, interracial unions could be found in various sections of the Gulf region. In Plaquemines Parish, a few free mulatto women cohabited with white planters and farmers, including thirty-eight-year-old Antoinette Angelette, who lived with sixty-year-old sugar planter Sylvester Dobard, and Harriett Burlard, who lived with farmer Etienne Burlard. Among the Cane River Creoles of Color, emancipated slaves Rose Metoyer and Adelaide Mariotte were the plaçees of a succession of white "protectors." Similarly, in other sections, free mulatto woman maintained separate residences while white men provided them and their children with financial assistance. By the 1850s, however, such unions among colored Creoles were less common than in earlier years (Mills 1977: 158).[15]

In their relations with whites, colored Creoles sought to maintain cordial rather than intimate relations. They realized that however much they sought to lead separate lives, they were inextricably connected to whites in their communities. This was especially true in economic relations: those who maintained shops and stores or owned farms and plantations relied on white customers and merchants to sell their goods or staple crops. But they also came in contact with whites when appearing in court, traveling, seeking to free a family member, and attending church. During periods of rumored slave revolt or during a political crisis, even the most established and prosperous members of the group could feel threatened. In 1829, shortly after the appearance of David Walker's *Appeal* demanding that southern blacks rise up against their masters, free mulatto planter and slave owner Jean Meullion sought to protect members of his family who might be "reduced to slavery." While this did not happen, his fears were more than justified. M. S. Fayman, the granddaughter of a French-born planter and Haitian black, recalled: "I was taken up bodily by a white man"; after being kidnapped in Louisiana, she was sold to the famous Kentucky slave trader, Pierce Haynes. While most were able to avoid such violence, the incident pointed to the fragile and precarious nature of race relations (Rawick 1972–, vol. 16, pt. 3: 10–13).[16]

Nonetheless, during the late antebellum period, Creoles of Color outside of New Orleans in the Gulf region were remarkably successful in carving out a middle ground between slaves and whites. Part of their success was due to their drive and ambition in the economic realm. Included in their ranks were some of the richest free persons of color in the United States. But their success was also the result of their being able to maintain clan loyalty and cohesion, to isolate themselves from whites—but also maintain congenial relations with them—and to rely on the labor of bondmen and bondwomen. It is true that a few of them felt keenly the inhumanity of holding their brethren in bondage. But most of their despair seems to have had more to do with their being victimized by legislation designed to control all free blacks rather than by any compassion for their less fortunate brethren. Indeed, the emigration of "literate and respectable free colored people" from the Gulf region to the black republic of Haiti in 1859 and 1860 had to do not only with the oppression of blacks, but with the failure of whites to differentiate between Creoles of Color and other African Americans.

At the outbreak of the Civil War, most free Creoles of Color in the Lower South sympathized with the Confederate cause. As slave owners and property owners, they had a stake in maintaining the status quo. In 1861, a substantial majority of the able-bodied free men of color in Louisiana formed military or militia units on behalf of the Confederacy; later, a small but significant group of light-skinned mulattoes, including St. Landry Parish's Jean-Baptiste Pierre-Auguste, Charles Lutz, and Leufroy Pierre-Auguste, actually joined the Confederate army, seeing action at Shiloh, Fredericksburg, and Vicksburg. Still others supported the southern cause by donating slave laborers to work on fortifications, by purchasing Confederate bonds, or by providing food and supplies for the army (Bergeron 1986: 248; Berry 1967: 167; Schweninger 1989: 353–54).

The intrusion of Union gunboats in the lower Mississippi River Valley in the spring of 1862, the fall of Mobile and Vicksburg, and the Union cavalry raids during the last two years of the war brought destruction and devastation to many areas of the Lower South. Like their white counterparts, Creoles of Color suffered from confiscations, looting, burning, and pillaging. "When [the] war commence it purty hard on folks," a free person of color in St. Mary Parish recalled. First came Confederate soldiers, who took away their slaves; then came the Union cavalrymen, who confiscated the sugar and corn crops. In St. Landry Parish, the Meullion family, owners of thriving farms and plantations, lost most of their holdings during the war. Antoine Meullion gave up slaves, cattle, sheep, hogs, and five thousand fence rails when a band of Union soldiers under the command of Nathaniel Banks rode through his neighborhood. Other families that suffered substantial losses during the war included the Ricards of Iberville Parish, the Ponis families of St. John the Baptist, the Verduns of St. Mary, and the Porches of Pointe Coupée (Rawick 1972–, vol. 5, pt. 4: 185; Schweninger 1989: 354–55).[17]

For many Creoles of Color, wartime destruction was only a harbinger of things to come. As was the case for their white neighbors, the unsettled political situation, the lack of credit and currency, the difficulty securing farmhands, the refusal of former slaves to work under the same conditions as before the war, and flooding and crop failures in 1866 and 1867 forced many formerly prosperous free Creoles of Color to the brink of disaster. In 1871, following the death of her husband, Josephine Decuir was forced to auction off her plantation house, stables, cabins, machinery, sugarhouse, and 840 acres of land. She received only $25,752 for her land and other holdings, which before the war included 112 slaves, real estate, livestock, and machinery worth in excess of $150,000.

Decuir's case was not unusual. Within five years after the war, the prewar property holdings of colored Creoles in the Gulf outside of New Orleans had declined precipitously.[18] Having not only lost their slaves, they now witnessed the breakup of their farms and plantations and a sharp decline in the value of the lands they were able to maintain. Between 1860 and 1870, total black wealth—real and personal holdings—in Iberville Parish went from $665,100 to approximately $104,600; in Natchitoches, from $739,700 to $370,800; in Pointe Coupée, from $796,000 to $259,600; in St. Landry, from $609,900 to $236,200; and in St. Mary, from $228,700 to $83,100. In addition, these comparisons do not capture the losses incurred a few years later with the onset of a severe depression. In 1873, during the first year of the downturn, forty-four members of the Metoyer family clan were listed as having had their land sold at tax sales. Often these sales were conducted for nonpayment of assessments amounting to only a few dollars (Schweninger 1989: 364).

The precipitous economic decline was only part of the wrenching adjustments colored Creoles in the Gulf region would have to make during the postwar era. The emancipation of slaves, the newly won political rights of freedmen, the migration of tens of thousands of blacks seeking new locations, and racial violence and murder were only a few of the difficulties they faced. Now it became clear that their distinctive position in the region as a middle group had dissolved, and whites as well as other blacks looked upon them as indistinguishable from former slaves.

For some colored Creoles the new conditions meant that they should seek accommodation with formerly free blacks and emancipated slaves. How could any black support the old system of government, one queried, which had been designed to keep his brethren and kindred in eternal slavery.[19] "But now, we see that our future is indissolubly bound up with that of the negro race in this country," a free person of color who had previously held himself aloof from blacks and had taken great pride in his French ancestry explained to northern journalist Whitelaw Reid. "We have no rights which we can reckon safe while the same are denied to the fieldhands on the sugar plantations." An Alabama Creole of Color echoed the same sentiment: "We are all tarred with the same stick, knit together by bonds of common sympathy and suffering, and must rise or fall together" (Reid 1866: 244).

But faced with severe economic difficulties and a rapidly changing society around them, the great majority of colored Creoles outside of the Crescent City looked to the past rather than the future. Even those who saw that making compromises with other blacks was perhaps inevitable, given the new economic, political, and social milieu, did so as a political expedient or as a means of possibly assisting other colored Creoles rather than out of any deeply felt compassion for their "brethren and kindred." It is difficult to believe that the pro-emancipation Republicanism professed by Cornelius Donato and Dubreul Olivier of Pointe Coupée Parish, Antoine Meullion of St. Landry Parish, and other members of antebellum slaveholding class was altruistic. Rather, they hoped that such professions would help them receive compensation from the Southern Claims Commission for their losses during the war (Penn 1989: 405).

Indeed, the Civil War proved to be the watershed for the fortunes of Creoles of Color. Grouped together with former slaves and formerly free blacks, the once proud and prosperous families experienced increasing social degradation. Abandoned by their white "allies" and "friends," forced off the land or dividing it up into small plots, they were no longer a privileged group in a slave society. Even more than before they looked inward for social, intellectual, and cultural sustenance. In the Cane River colony, they formed *Societe des amis unis de L'Ile Brevelle* to provide a social and morale boost to members of the Metoyer and related clans.

As blacks in the Deep South became increasingly "Americanized," colored Creoles, one historian writes, "clung tenaciously" to their French heritage, "to the Creole culture that was for all practical purposes the last remaining tie between their postwar society and the life they had once known" (Mills 1977: 248). Indeed, within a generation after the war, few among them had more than dim memories of those early years of prosperity. However much they sought to re-create their past glories and fortunes, their unique position in a society based on human bondage was gone forever.

Notes

1. Only two years after the transfer of Florida from Spain to the United States, free people of color in St. Augustine, including a number of Creoles of Color, petitioned the Legislative Council to extend to them the same citizenship rights as whites enjoyed. Petition of the Free Colored People of St. Augustine [to the Territorial Legislative Council], 13 May 1823, Record Group 910, Series B76, Territorial Legislative Council, box 1, folder 6, Florida State Archives, Tallahassee, Fla.

2. Records of the County Court (hereafter abbreviated as RCC), Mobile Co., Ala., *Will Book I 1813–1837* (July 26,1820), 94 [John Chavanna]; ibid., (May 9, 1825), 109–10 [Daniel Juzan]; ibid., (Apr. 27, 1821), 115–16 [Hilaire Dubroca], in Clinton P. King and Meriem A Barlow, *Transcripts of Will Book I 1818–1837,* typescript in possession of the authors, 44, 50, 51, 54.

3. Records of the Parish Court (hereafter abbreviated as RPC), Plaquemines Parish, La., Inventories, vols. 1846–1858 (May 16, 1857), 404–9; ibid., Pointe Coupée Parish, La., Successions, no. 176, Apr. 5, 1839; ibid., St. Landry Parish La., Successions, no. 1544, Feb. 1, 1851; Deed of Emancipation for Jean Meullion, Feb. 12, 1775, in Meullion Papers, Louisiana State Univ.; RPC, Natchitoches Parish, La., Successions, no. 375, July 26, 1839.

4. RCC, Mobile Co., Ala., *Will Book II 1837–1850* (Jan. 18, 1813), 112–14 [copy of previously recorded will], in Clinton P. King and Meriem A. Barlow, *Transcripts of Will Book II 1837–1850 Mobile County Alabama* (Mobile: typescript, 1988), 98–99, at the Univ. of South Alabama Archives (hereafter abbreviated as USAA), Mobile, Alabama.

5. See, e.g., Petition of Bazil Chastang to the Senate and House of Representatives of Alabama, ca. 1826, in Records of the Alabama Secretary of State, Legislative Bills and Resolutions, HR no. 8, Alabama Department of Archives and History, Montgomery, Alabama (hereafter abbreviated as ADAH). An act to emancipate the "coloured woman slave named Nancy and her four children" passed the house and senate, and was signed by the governor on Jan. 11, 1827. Records of the Alabama Secretary of State, Administrative Division, Enrolled Acts, 1826–1827, 131, ADAH.

6. United States Manuscript Slave Census (hereafter referred to as USNMSSC), Mobile Co., Ala., 1860, 11, 14; United States Manuscript Population Census (hereafter referred to as USMSPC), Mobile Co., Ala., 1860, 27, 137; Receipt, William Shipp to Jean Meullion, Feb. 5, 1811, Meullion Papers, Louisiana State Univ.,

Baton Rouge, La.; RPPC, Natchitoches Parish, La., Successions, no 375, July 26, 1839.
7. RPC, Natchitoches Parish, La., Successions, #375, July 26, 1839; RPC, Plaquemines Parish La., Inventories, vols. 1846–58 (May 6, 1857), 404–9; RPC, St. Landry Parish, La., Successions, no. 2, 256, Sept. 9, 1859; RPC, Pointe Coupée Parish, La., Successions, no. 176, Apr. 5, 1839, and no. 355, Jan. 31, 1844.
8. Computed from USMSPC, 1850; USMSPC, St. John the Baptist Parish, La., 1850, 661; USMSPC, Plaquemines Parish, La., 1850, 278, 485, 549; USMSPC, Iberville Parish, La., 1850, 329; United States Manuscript Agriculture Census, Iberville Parish, La., 1850, 81.
9. RCC, Mobile Co., Ala., *Martin Durand* vs. *Polite Collins, et al.,* May 23, 1843, Case #1,030, USAA, Mobile, Alabama.
10. RPC, West Baton Rouge Parish, La., Successions, no. 176, July 18, 1829.
11. For a rare Creole of Color divorce case, see RCC, Mobile Co., Ala., *Chastang* vs. *Chastang,* Aug. 14, 1863, Case no. 2, 534, USAA.
12. "A Contract of Marriage Between JOSEPH METOYER and MARIE LODOISKA LLORENS," Jan. 18, 1840, Cane River Collection, Historic New Orleans Collection; USMSPC, St. Landry Parish, La., 1860 (in 1860 census takers in St. Landry Parish often included the maiden names of women in each household who were probable spouses); RPC, Plaquemines Parish, La., Successions, no. 167, May 12, 1840; RPC, Pointe Coupée Parish, La., Marriage Contract, Feb. 26, 1835.
13. RCC, Mobile Co., Ala., Chancery Cases Not Divorces, *Collins* vs. *Laurendine,* Dec. 20, 1847, Case no. 1,373, USFA.
14. *Fifth Census; or, Enumeration of the Inhabitants of the United States, as Corrected at the Department of State. 1830* (Washington: Duff Green, 1832), 98–101, 104–7, 156–59; *Statistical View of the United States . . . Being a Compendium of the Seventh Census* (Washington: Beverley Tucker, 1854), 397.
15. USMSPC, Plaquemines Parish, La., 1850, 272, 276, 279.
16. RPC, St. Landry Parish, La., Conveyances, book H (Mar. 22, 1830), 32–33; Creoles of Color were vulnerable because as slaves they often brought high prices. "The gang of slaves," one observer wrote from New Orleans in 1833, "[is] the most valuable for their number in the state (being all Mechanics and Creoles of the Country)." John Chinson to Ralph Gurley, Dec. 16, 1833, Records of the American Colonization Society, reel 19, Library of Congress.
17. Petition for Relief of Antoine Meullion, Dec. 1889, no. 8,090, in Meullion Family Papers, Louisiana State Univ.; J. Ward Gurley Jr. to Charles Benjamin, May 18, 1875, Records of the Claims Commission, Records of the Treasury Department, Record Group 56, reel 6, National Archives.
18. RPC, Pointe Coupée Parish, La., Successions, no. 203, July 11, 1865; United States Manuscript Argicultural Census, Pointe Coupée Parish, La., 1850, 579; USMSPC, Pointe Coupée Parish, La., 1870, 324.
19. *The (Mobile) Nationalist,* July 11, 1867.

References

Amos, Harriet E. 1985. *Cotton City: Urban Development in Antebellum Mobile.* Tuscaloosa: Univ. of Alabama Press.
Bergeron, Arthur W., Jr. 1986. "Free Men of Color in Grey." *Civil War History* 32 (3): 247–55.

Berlin, Ira. 1974. *Slaves Without Masters: The Free Negro in the Antebellum South.* New York: Pantheon Books.

————. 1976. "The Structure of the Free Negro Caste in the Antebellum United States." *Journal of Social History* 9 (3): 297–318.

Berry, Mary. 1967. "Negro Troops in Blue and Gray: The Louisiana Native Guards, 1861–1863." *Louisiana History* 8 (2): 165–90.

Blassingame, John. *Black New Orleans, 1860–1880.* 1973. Chicago: Univ. of Chicago Press.

Clarke, James F. 1859. *Present Condition of Free Colored People of the United States.* New York: American Anti-Slavery Society.

Foner, Laura. 1970. "The Free People of Color in Louisiana and St. Domingue: A Comparative Portrait of Two Three-Caste Slave Societies." *Journal of Social History* 3(4): 406–40.

Hall, Gwendolyn Midlo. 1992. "The Formation of Afro-Creole Culture." In *Creole New Orleans: Race and Americanization,* Arnold R. Hirsh and Joseph Logsdon, eds. 58–87. Baton Rouge: Louisiana State Univ. Press.

Hall, Robert L. 1988. "Black and White Christians in Florida, 1822–1861." In *Masters and Slaves in the House of the Lord: Race and Religion in the American South, 1740–1870.* John B. Boles, ed. Lexington: Univ. Press of Kentucky.

Hirsch, Arnold R., and Joseph Logsdon, eds. 1992. *Creole New Orleans: Race and Americanization.* Baton Rouge: Louisiana State Univ. Press.

Holmes, Jack D. L. 1975. "The Role of Blacks in Spanish Alabama: The Mobile District 1780–1813." *Alabama Historical Quarterly* 37(1): 5–18.

King, Clinton P., and Meriem A. Barlow, comps. and eds. 1985. *Marriages of Mobile County, Alabama 1813–1855.* Baltimore: Genealogical Publishing Co.

Logsdon, Joseph, and Caryn Cossé Bell. 1992. "The Americanization of Black New Orleans, 1850–1900." In Arnold R. Hirsh and Joseph Logsdon, eds. 201–61. *Creole New Orleans: Race and Americanization.* Baton Rouge: Louisiana State Univ. Press.

Mills, Gary. 1977. *The Forgotten People: Cane River's Creoles of Color.* Baton Rouge: Louisiana State Univ. Press.

Nordmann, Christopher. 1990. "Free Negroes in Mobile County, Alabama." Ph.D. diss., Univ. of Alabama.

Olmsted, Frederick Law. 1953. *The Cotton Kingdom: A Traveller's Observations on Cotton and Slavery in the American Slave States.* Edited by Arthur M. Schlesinger. New York: Alfred Knopf.

Penn, James. 1989. "The Geographical Variation of Unionism in Louisiana: A Study of the Southern Claims Data." *Louisiana History* 30 (4): 399–418.

Rankin, David. 1974. "The Origins of Black Leadership in New Orleans During Reconstruction." *Journal of Southern History* 40 (3): 417–40.

————. 1977–78. "The Impact of the Civil War on the Free Colored Community of New Orleans." *Perspectives in American History* 11: 379–418.

Rawick, George, ed. 1972–. *The American Slave: A Composite Autobiography* 19 vols. Westport, Conn.: Greenwood Publishing Co.

Reid, Whitelaw. 1866. *After the War: A Tour of the Southern States, 1865–1866.* Reprint edited by C. Vann Woodward, New York: Harper and Row, 1965.

Schweninger, Loren. 1989. "Antebellum Free Persons of Color in Postbellum Louisiana." *Louisiana History* 30 (4): 345–64.

————.1989. *Black Property Owners in the South, 1790–1915.* Urbana: Univ. of Illinois Press.

Stahl, Annie. 1942. "The Free Negro in Ante-bellum Louisiana." *Louisiana Historical Quarterly* 25 (4): 300–96.

Stampp, Kenneth. 1956. *The Peculiar Institution: Slavery in the Ante-Bellum South.* New York: Vintage Books.

Sterkx, Herbert. 1972. *The Free Negro in Ante-Bellum Louisiana.* Rutherford, N.J.: Fairleigh Dickinson Univ. Press.

Sutton, Leora. "Creoles in Pensacola." Unpublished paper, used by permission of the author.

Thomas, David. 1911. "The Free Negro in Florida before 1865." *South Atlantic Quarterly* 10: 335–45.

Whitten, David. 1981. *Andrew Durnford: A Black Sugar Planter in Antebellum Louisiana.* Natchitoches, La.: Northwestern State Univ. Press.

Willey, Nathan. 1866. "Education of the Colored Population of Louisiana." *Harper's New Monthly Magazine* 33: 244–50.

Woodson, Carter G. 1924. *Free Negro Owners of Slaves in the United States in 1830.* Reprint, New York: Negro Univ. Press, 1968.

FOUR

Carl A. Brasseaux

Creoles of Color in Louisiana's Bayou Country, 1766–1877

Creoles of Color are among the "first families" of southwestern Louisiana, and, in the more than two centuries since their establishment in the Bayou Country, they have forged one of America's most distinctive rural societies. Yet, this remarkable group has aroused but little interest among African-American scholars, whose attention has been firmly riveted upon New Orleans's more "exotic" urban Creole population. Annie Lee West Stahl afforded but passing mention of the Attakapas and Opelousas Creole of Color communities in her 1942 article on the free black community in antebellum Louisiana. A generation later, H. E. Sterkx provided greater, but still marginal, coverage of the early development of the Bayou Country's Creole of Color communities. Only Joseph H. Jones's 1950 master's thesis focuses exclusively upon the region's long-overlooked community, but this study's highly circumscribed geographical and chronological foci significantly lessen the work's significance and utility. As a consequence, the remarkable story of the Bayou Country's Creoles has remained largely untold.

Most Creole of Color families trace their ancestry to African slaves imported from present-day Mali, Senegal, and, to a lesser extent, from other west African states (Brasseaux 1986: 52–60; Hall 1992) who later were manumitted for various reasons. Some slaves earned their release through military service, particularly during the Natchez War (1729–31), or for outstanding public service (Brasseaux 1980: 139–58; Everett 1966: 28; Sterkx 1972: 20, 26–28). Other bondsmen were emancipated as a reward for long and faithful service (Sterkx 1972: 18–19), while still other slaves who could prove any degree of Indian ancestry were freed by Louisiana's Spanish colonial government (1769–1803) in compliance with a ban on Indian slavery in the Spanish empire (Hanger 1990: 237–64). Finally, some manumitted slaves were the mistresses or natural children of white farmers (Sterkx 1972: 59–67). As the eighteenth century progressed, however, manumissions for heroic or faithful service and emancipation of slaves able to prove Indian ancestry grew increasingly rare, while the release of mistresses and their mulatto children became more and more commonplace, resulting in the dramatic growth of Louisiana's free black population in the late eighteenth and early nineteenth centuries. The 1763 census of lower Louisiana, for example, lists only 82 free persons of color, all of whom resided in the New Orleans area; the free black community, however, grew rapidly in subsequent years, rising to 1,701 in 1788, 3,350 in 1806, 16,710 in 1830, 17,462 in 1850, and 18,467 in 1860. Rapid population growth was matched by a corresponding rise in economic status (Ficklen 1910: 117; Mills 1977; Roussève 1937: 49; Schweninger 1989: 345–64; Voorhies 1973: 5–103; Woodson 1927: 244).

The development of the free black communities in Attakapas (in present-day Lafayette, St. Martin, Iberia, Vermilion, and St. Mary Parishes) and Opelousas (in modern-day St. Landry, Evangeline, Acadia, Calcasieu, Cameron, Jefferson Davis, Allen, and Beauregard Parishes) offers a microcosmic view of these statewide economic and demographic trends (Brasseaux, et al. 1977). Small numbers of slaves accompanied the few French settlers—mostly retired military officers and enlisted men—who established themselves in the frontier districts of Attakapas and Opelousas in the early 1760s (Conrad 1990; Voorhies 1973). These black and white pioneers were joined in subsequent years by numerous retired French enlisted men, Acadian exiles, African slaves, and *gens de couleur libre*—free blacks whose descendants now constitute a majority of the Creoles of Color in the prairie parishes (Brasseaux 1979: 112–17; Brasseaux 1987).

The first free black mentioned in the records of the prairie posts was one Louis, identified in contemporary census reports as a "free mulatto"— probably originally from the New Orleans area—who, in 1766, resided with his wife, Josine, and daughter, Nanette, in the Opelousas district. (The term "mulatto" is used here and elsewhere in the same sense in which it was commonly utilized in the nineteenth century as a generic designation for all persons of mixed racial, i.e., Caucasian and Negroid, background.) The 1774 census of Opelousas, which identifies "Louis" as "Louis Ricar[d]" (Bergeron 1979: 44), indicates that the free man of color had become quite prosperous during the intervening eight years. According to the census, he owned two slaves, fifty cattle, six horses or mules, and ten hogs—at a time when only 22.79 percent of all Opelousas district households possessed slaves, and only 18.38 of all freeholders possessed as many as fifty cows (Archivo General de Indias, Seville, Spain, Papeles Procedentes de Cuba [hereafter abbreviated as AGI-PC], legajos 189A: 106–10).

Other free blacks who subsequently made their homes along the southwestern Louisiana frontier, settling in the Attakapas District, also fared well economically, thanks largely to the beneficence of their liberators. Sometime before 1774, André Masse, the largest slaveholder among the Attakapas/Opelousas pioneers, emancipated six Negro families and endowed each with significant numbers of livestock. Three slave families freed around 1774 by Attakapas Commandant Gabriel Fuselier de la Claire also received generous quantities of cows, horses, and pigs. To put their collective economic standing into broader perspective, median livestock holdings for the black ranchers were 9.7 cows, 3.7 horses (or mules), and 5.0 hogs—figures exceeding comparable holdings for 20 percent of all local white households (Voorhies 1973: 282; AGI-PC, 189A: 106–10).

Though small, the new free black populations of Attakapas and Opelousas compared favorably—in terms of size and economic status—with the more established, but equally tiny, free black communities in the New Orleans area. And, in the late eighteenth and early nineteenth centuries, the Attakapas and Opelousas free black populations grew quickly, both in terms of demographic and economic importance: By 1810, there were 269 *gens de couleur libre* in Attakapas and 380 in Opelousas (1810 census).

This rapid growth—which paralleled the explosive growth of Louisiana's other free black communities—resulted in large part from the gender imbalance existing in the white community. There were 1,400 white males in the Attakapas in 1810, but only 1,064 white females. White males twenty-six years of age or older outnumbered comparably aged white females by a margin of 727 to 583. A similar imbalance existed in the Opelousas district, where, in 1810, white males outnumbered white females by a substantial margin—1,746 to 1,293. As a consequence, white men quite predictably exploited sexually their female slaves. Some of the resulting liaisons endured for a number of years, eventually evolving into extralegal marriages. Many such common-law wives were manumitted by their owners, particularly if they had borne children, because, under Louisiana law of the early nineteenth century, natural children derived their legal status (i.e., slave or free) from that of their mothers.

Along the southwestern Louisiana frontier, emancipated concubines usually remained a part of planters' households long after their manumission. It is thus no coincidence that the demographic profiles of early free black households in both the Opelousas and Attakapas regions generate a composite portrait of a "typical" free black household containing small numbers of white men, larger numbers of free blacks (usually the planter's black consort and several mulatto children), and still larger numbers of black slaves.

The 1810 census of the Territory of Orleans affords abundant additional evidence of the interracial character of the early free black households in the Attakapas and Opelousas districts. According to the census of the Attakapas district, whites were the heads of forty of the sixty-seven households (59.70 percent) containing free persons of color. Twenty-four of the forty white-dominated households (60 percent) contained no white women.

This trend toward white-male-dominated, mixed-race households was far more pronounced in the Attakapas area than it was in the Opelousas area, where, in 1810, fifty-two of the eighty-two enumerated free black households (63.41 percent) were dominated by free persons of color. By 1820, the percentage of free black–dominated households had grown to 71.43 percent. The greater independence of the Opelousas free black community stemmed in part from the greater availability of cheap land, which made economic autonomy more easily attainable, and in part from a small-scale migration of economically independent free black families from the Mississippi River parishes.

The 1820 census of the Attakapas and Opelousas regions demonstrates this point quite clearly. The domination of free black households by white males was highest in St. Mary Parish, where topography militated against land usage outside the narrow natural levees bordering the local bayous and rivers. Available arable land in the parish was thus claimed and exploited far more quickly than in neighboring parishes to the north, where prairie lands supplemented the natural levees. It is thus hardly surprising that, in 1820, twenty-two of the thirty-four St. Mary Parish households containing free blacks (64.7 percent) were dominated by whites, usually white men. In neighboring St. Martin Parish, on the other hand, where the availability of prairie land helped reduce land prices, only twenty-four of forty-four households with free blacks (54.54 percent) were headed by whites. Finally, in St. Landry Parish, which possessed vast expanses of unclaimed prairie land, whites headed only 28.57 percent (sixteen of fifty-six) of all free black households.

The number of households dominated by free black women was inversely proportional to the number of households headed by white men. As suggested above, the smallest number of female-dominated free person of color households was located in the lower Teche Valley, with the highest concentration of female-dominated households in St. Landry Parish.

The establishment of female-dominated Creole of Color households in the early antebellum period resulted from the dissolution of the common-law marriages between whites, usually white Creoles, and free black women. Many such living arrangements endured for the life of the white householder, but many other liaisons ended when the host planter took a white spouse. In either instance, the former concubine and her children were usually well provided for, and the mistress's patrimony furnished the economic basis for the family's elevated status in the region's three-tiered social system. For example, on January 21, 1804—approximately four years after his marriage to a white woman—Jacques Fontenette donated Louise, a free black woman, and her nine mulatto children a parcel of land with five arpents frontage by forty arpents depth at "Isle á Labbé." Fontenette also donated slaves to Louise and her family (Hébert, 1: 214; 2: 322; St. Martin Parish Original Acts, Clerk of Court's Office, St. Martin Parish Courthouse, St. Martinville, La. [hereafter abbreviated as SMOA]; Everett 1966: 46–47).

Matriarchal free black households grew increasingly less common as the antebellum period progressed. Although interracial alliances remained a fixture in the region's cultural landscape, despite the prohibition against interracial unions in the 1825 civil code (Sterkx 1972: 243), they constituted, by 1850, less than 10 percent of all free persons of color households in the old Opelousas district (now subdivided into St. Landry and Calcasieu Parishes). Vermilion Parish, in which free blacks were practically nonexistent, was a notable exception. Indeed, the 1850 census lists only two free black residents in Vermilion Parish. Interracial unions constituted less than 15 percent of all free black households in the old Attakapas district (then consisting of St. Martin, St. Mary, Lafayette, and Vermilion Parishes).

These interracial unions, which in the late eighteenth and early nineteenth centuries had normally been created by white Creole men and Creole of Color women, were, in mid-nineteenth century, more commonly established by French immigrant, Anglo-American, or Acadian/Cajun men and Creole of Color women. Liaisons between white women and Creole of Color men were far less common; indeed, the 1850 census notes only a handful of such instances, primarily because of local biases against such unions. Yet, they were nevertheless noteworthy, primarily for the violent reaction that they elicited from the white community.

Second- and third-generation Creole of Color households, on the other hand, were consistently patriarchal in organization throughout the prairie districts, as free black men married within their caste and established stable nuclear families. The resulting network of blood relationships within the still emerging Creole of Color caste helped bring to the community a common identity and shared values that overshadowed the subregional economic differences between individual group members (Baker and Kreamer 1982: 78–79). Undergirding this emerging group identity was its marginal status in antebellum Louisiana society, a social condition established and maintained by laws and the prevailing racial biases of the day.

Beginning with the promulgation of the *code noir* (Black Code) in 1724, Louisiana's legal system fostered the creation and maintenance of a three-tier social system, with a white elite and a black servile population at the polar extremes, and, between them, a free black class that enjoyed the legal rights and privileges, but not social status, of whites (Allain 1980: 127–37). The colonial records of the Attakapas and Opelousas posts, for example, list a surprising number of conveyances between whites and free persons of color—both men and women; the records also list conveyances among free persons of color; business contracts between whites and free blacks, as well as exclusively among free men of color; marriage contracts among free blacks; suits against free blacks by whites; suits involving only *gens de couleur libre*; and suits against whites by free blacks (St. Landry Parish Original Acts on deposit at the Louisiana State Archives and Records Service, Baton Rouge, Louisiana [hereafter abbreviated as SLOA]; SMOA).

Though free blacks could successfully sue whites in court, they could not—as a result of legal prohibitions and social conventions—share a meal or a church pew with whites, even with whites of inferior economic status. By the end of the Spanish period (1803), free blacks in New Orleans were not even permitted to copy the clothing and jewelry of their white neighbors (Everett 1966: 34; Gayarré 1879, 3: 179; Burson 1940: 104). Further, under the terms of the 1724 code, emancipated blacks were required to show respect to Caucasians, particularly their former owners (Sterkx, 1972: 39), and, in the early nineteenth century, white Louisianians institutionalized this time-honored practice.

Historian H. E. Sterkx, in his landmark work on antebellum Louisiana's free people of color, insisted that free blacks maintained a social status only marginally above the slave level, despite their extraordinary legal and economic privileges. State legislation adopted in 1806 obliged free blacks to exhibit "special respect" to whites. According to a law of that year, they were not allowed to insult or strike whites under penalties of fine or imprisonment. Free Negroes were not only obligated by this law to speak and answer whites with respect, but they also were required never "to conceive themselves equal" in any way with persons of the Caucasian race (Sterkx 1972: 240–41).

The institutionalized social isolation of free blacks from the white elite was supplemented by sporadically enforced legal attempts to isolate the *gens de couleur libre* from the servile population. Fearing collusion between the free black population and slaves in the event of servile insurrection, whites periodically established—but only haphazardly enforced—legal impediments against social and economic intercourse between members of Louisiana's two lower social orders (Brasseaux 1990: 12).

Such artificial barriers between free blacks and slaves, however, were largely unnecessary. Though contacts necessarily persisted between the two groups, most (but by no means all) early free blacks in the prairie districts appear, from all accounts, to have distanced themselves as much as possible and as quickly as possible from the horrors of slavery, which they themselves had experienced. The course of the group's early development seems to have been charted by matriarchs of the first free black families, who, after separation from their white paramours through either death or abandonment, set about the task of making themselves and their children economically independent. This task was, in some cases, greatly facilitated by bequests from their now departed white benefactors. Others succeeded by dint of their unflagging industry, tenacity, and formidable business acumen (Baker and Kreamer 1982: 75–76).

Among the most notable early Creole of Color matriarchs were Marie Simien and Marie-Jeanne Lemelle of the Opelousas district. Simien, who settled with her four sons in the Opelousas district around 1796, invested her substantial financial resources—evidently derived from her former white paramour—in real estate, developing, by 1818, a vast personal empire. According to the 1818 tax rolls of St. Landry Parish, Marie Simien owned four parcels of land totaling 7,766 acres. Much of this land—6,350 acres—consisted of undeveloped prairies and pine forests west of present-day Eunice—lands then considered nearly worthless. Most of the remaining acreage (1,416 acres), however, was prime farmland in the Bellevue area south of present-day Opelousas that she cultivated with nine slaves. The uncultivated portion of the estate was used to graze over 300 head of cattle. Having carved a niche for herself, Simien established an 800-acre plantation for her son George near present-day Eunice (Baker and Kreamer 1982: 75–76).

Marie-Jeanne Lemelle, who was manumitted at New Orleans on December 5, 1772 (Hanger 1990: 258; New Orleans Notarial Archives, Juan Bautiste Garic Papers, 3: 366), followed the precedent established by Marie Simien. Lemelle, mistress of François Lemelle, *fils,* son of a prominent St. Charles Parish planter, migrated from the New Orleans area to the Opelousas district in the 1780s—approximately ten years after François had established himself in the same area. Taking the name of her prominent lover (like most of her local free counterparts), Marie-Jeanne settled at Isle à L'Anglois, east of the present town of Opelousas and, with her five sons, set about the task of improving her property, consisting of more than 800 acres, much of which she had acquired from her former lover for an unspecified, but small, quantity of cattle (SLOA). This task was made considerably easier by the presence of fifteen slaves, also apparently provided by François Lemelle. Once improvements were in place, part of Marie-Jeanne Lemelle's plantation was parceled out to her sons "to give them status within the community" (Baker and Kreamer 1982: 75–76 [quotation]; Conrad 1974: 2, 3, 9, 12, 16, 17, 68, 344; Hanger 1990: 249, 250, 258).

By mid-nineteenth century, the Simiens, Lemelles, Donatos, and other economically successful families had come to share, to a considerable degree, the culture of the white Creole elite that the most prominent Creoles of Color emulated so obsessively (MacDonald, et al. 1979: 172; Brasseaux 1990: 12). This drive toward cultural amalgamation into the local mainstream culture began in the earliest days of the Creole of Color prairie communities' development, as most first-generation free blacks voluntarily abandoned their African names, taking for themselves and their children French given names and applying to their children the surnames of their French and/or white Creole paramours. Abandoning their traditional animistic beliefs and west African languages, Creoles of Color also became almost universally Roman Catholic and French speaking, in emulation of white Creoles. Most slaves in the region, on the other hand, were Protestant and English speaking, particularly during the antebellum period, and these religious and linguistic differences helped to underscore the widening cultural gap between the caste system's second and third tiers. Like white Creoles, Creoles of Color became preoccupied with their social status, and, because of Louisiana's forced inheritance laws and the resulting difficulty in transmitting wealth from one generation to the next, status was quite difficult to maintain. In a closed society, such as the antebellum Creole of Color community, the economic significance of marriage was thus magnified, and marital alliances between free blacks were carefully arranged to preserve their rank within the caste (Hébert, vols. 1–6). Many of these marriages involved first or second cousins, requiring religious dispensations for consanguinity.

Such social dynamics had the effect of preserving the ethno-racial integrity of the Creole of Color group. By the time of the Civil War, the free black population of the Attakapas and Opelousas areas was almost universally "mulatto." Only in St. Landry Parish, where mulattos composed nearly 84 percent of the free black total, did mulattos constitute less than 90 percent of local free blacks.

The racial composition and homogeneity of the free black community helped set it apart from the enslaved population, which had remained 70 to 80 percent black. And, with the group's increasingly white cultural orientation, skin color became a matter of growing importance to the Creole of Color community (Sterkx 1972).

While embracing many facets of white Creole culture, numerous first-generation free blacks also adopted the economic capitalism of their white neighbors. Most at least attempted to acquire land, and many eventually purchased slaves. In addition, like members of the white elite, they educated their children either by means of tutors or private schools. Historian H. E. Sterkx notes that many free black planters sent their children to the Grimble Bell School at Washington, Louisiana. The students, who paid fifteen dollars a month for board and tuition, were instructed in "reading, writing, arithmetic, history, geography, bookkeeping, English, French and Latin" (Sterkx 1972: 269–70).

By the late antebellum period, such cultural mimicking had become so successful and so pervasive among economically successful free blacks that white Creoles—and particularly white Creole planters—who came into contact with *hommes de couleur libre* felt an immediate sense of cultural kinship with them. As H. E. Sterkx has noted, "[S]ocial relationships between well-to-do [free black] planters and White planters were usually cordial. When coming into contact with each other for business or other purposes both parties exhibited the amenities characteristic of the 19th century" (Sterkx 1972: 282–83).

But the impression made by free black planters upon their white counterparts went far deeper than the customary exchange of civilities would suggest. An immediate sense of camaraderie developed that tended to dissolve the artificial legal barriers to free association between the white and free black communities as reflected in state statutes. Creole historian Charles Etienne Arthur Gayarré recorded two notable white and Creole of Color encounters in his memoirs. In the first, a white planter riding on a steamboat struck up a conversation with a cultured mulatto sugar grower. "When dinnertime arrived, a solitary table was set aside for the latter. Moved by the colored man's quiet acceptance, the White man went to him with a friend: 'We desire you to dine with us.' The free colored man expressed his appreciation for their hospitality, but declined as his presence at their table, even though acceptable to them, might displease the other passengers" (Gayarré Papers).

In the second encounter, an unidentified white traveler who called upon a free black acquaintance, refused to eat unless his host joined him in the repast; as suggested by the first episode, a social encounter not only unacceptable to, but unthinkable for, most antebellum white Louisianians (Sterkx 1972: 282–83).

Such limited social equality as respect and good will of white planters afforded was confined largely to those second- and third-generation free blacks who reaped the benefits of their ancestors' investments in land, livestock, and slaves. Perhaps the most notable of these cultured scions of Creole of Color pioneers was Martin Donato Bello (often rendered as Martin Donato), the son of Donato Bello, an Italian-born Opelousas militia officer, and Marie Jeanne Talliaferro, a free mulatto woman. In 1803, Donato and his bride, Marianne Duchesne, established a community of gains and assets valued in excess of $20,000. Their assets included not only 2,142 arpents of land, but also a cotton gin and a small number of slaves. Over the next fifteen years, Donato, who managed the estate, expanded the family holdings to 5,096 acres and 49 slaves. At the time of his death in 1848, Donato's slaveholdings had grown to 88, making him perhaps the largest black slave owner in the antebellum South. In addition, the Creole of Color farmer and rancher accumulated so much cash that, in the 1830s and 1840s, he often served as a private banker to local white planters (Baker and Kreamer 1982: 78–79).

Creoles of Color of the prairies borrowed not only the agricultural capitalism and lifestyles of their role models, but their biases as well. By mid-nineteenth century, successful Creoles of Color—like their white counterparts—had come to consider themselves a social elite. As H. E. Sterkx has noted, "[C]olored aristocrats dressed, thought, and in many ways acted as haughty as their White counterparts towards the 'lowly' . . ." (Sterkx 1972: 382–84). Though these attitudes were shared by most members of the antebellum Creole of Color communities in the Attakapas and Opelousas districts, they cannot be said to characterize all of them. As with all of the major ethnic and racial groups in early Louisiana, Creoles of Color were not a monolithic group. In fact, the free population schedules of the 1850 census indicate that local free black society was highly stratified both economically and socially. According to the census, four free black families in south-central and southwest Louisiana owned at least $10,000 in real estate—an important criterion used by many modern historians to identify members of the planter class. Having the necessary economic resources and business expertise, successful free blacks participated fully in the prosperity enjoyed by the Attakapas and Opelousas regions in the 1850s. By 1860, there were 17 free black planters in St. Landry Parish alone (1850 census; Sterkx 1972: 207).

However, most free black landowners, like their white counterparts, possessed between $50.00 and $5,000 in real property. Many free blacks who owned little or no real estate were urbanites, living in the numerous small towns then developing in the region. In 1850, for example, 80 of the 159 free blacks residing in Lafayette Parish lived in Vermilionville, the parish seat. Indeed, these free persons of color then constituted the largest single element of the town's population (Brasseaux 1990: 12). Nearly 46 percent of the free black population in St. Martin Parish lived in the towns of St. Martinville and New Iberia, while 57 of the 414 free persons of color in St. Mary Parish resided in Franklin. Unlike their rural counterparts, who usually derived their livelihood from farming or ranching, both as freeholders and increasingly as day laborers, free black urbanites were usually involved in the building trades. The building trades would attract increasing numbers of *gens de couleur libre* throughout the prosperous 1850s. In addition, most local hotels—and many local houses of prostitution (Brasseaux 1990: 12; Barde 1861: 335)—would come to be owned and operated by free blacks in the last decade of the antebellum period. Like their rural counterparts, the urban Creoles of Color sought to improve their status economically, and many of them would eventually become small slaveholders. During the early antebellum period, many of these slave purchases, though less than half of all slave acquisitions, appear to have been made for the purpose of acquiring and then manumitting relatives. The practice of purchasing relatives, moreover, appears to have become less commonplace over the passage of time (Brasseaux 1977: 105–6; Brasseaux 1986: 52–60).

Despite the disparity of wealth among individuals within the free black community, the perception among whites was that the freedmen were generally wealthy and thus a threat to white superiority. As regional tensions increased as a result of the slavery controversy in the 1850s, free blacks increasingly became a target for whites frustrated with the South's limited ability to defend the "peculiar institution" through normal political channels. St. Landry's free black community, the largest in the prairie region, bore the brunt of assault.

Crystallizing in the late 1850s, white hostility to local free blacks took the form of legal and extralegal efforts to eradicate the free black population—by intimidation if possible, through violence if necessary. Responding to the escalating threat, many free blacks fled the prairies for Latin America. As early as 1832, members of St. Landry Parish's Donato family began to forge cultural and economic ties with the Vera Cruz region of Mexico. The long-term importance of these contacts, however, would not be fully realized by the free blacks of the prairies until the late 1850s (Sterkx 1972).

The initial attempt to eradicate the free Negroes from south Louisiana had consisted of the peaceful efforts of the Louisiana Colonization Society to "repatriate" free persons of color to their African "fatherland." In the eyes of the Pelican State's proponents of colonization, repatriation was the best means of "getting rid" of the potential fifth columnists in the struggle to preserve slavery "without resorting to doubtful [legislative] acts of expulsion" (Sterkx 1972: 292). At the height of its repatriation activities in the late antebellum period, however, few free blacks—now firmly established second- and third-generation Louisianians for the most part—expressed any interest in leaving their native state, despite the rising racial tensions in the prairie parishes during the 1840s and 1850s.

Only 309 of the approximately 20,000 free blacks in Louisiana were transplanted to Liberia between 1831 and 1860 (Sterkx 1972: 153–58, 295–96; Brasseaux 1990: 12–14).

The recalcitrance of the state's free black population to move to Africa caused Louisiana's colonization advocates to laud instead Mexico's virtues as a potential colonization site. Partisans of Mexican colonization by Louisiana free blacks even solicited financial assistance from the federal government, but no funds materialized. Mexican colonization nevertheless became a reality, as many Louisiana free blacks—most of them former Attakapas and Opelousas residents—made their way to the Vera Cruz area. The vanguard of this colony consisted of an undetermined number of St. Landry Parish expatriates, led by members of the Donato family, who reportedly carried with them "a considerable fortune and technical equipment which promised to make the experiment a success." Settling along the Popolopan River, these "colonists" proved so successful at growing Indian corn that they soon began to invite relatives to join them in a country that, they claimed, harbored less racial animosity than their native state. Few Louisiana relatives, however, heeded this call to migrate until 1859, when numerous armed bands of vigilantes began their reign of terror in southwest Louisiana (Barde 1861: 337; Sterkx 1972: 296–97).

Acadiana's *comités de vigilance* were created in response to the local judicial system's failure to apprehend and/or convict numerous petty criminals credited with a crime wave sweeping the prairie country in the late 1850s. Local white property owners organized themselves into paramilitary groups of night riders who tried alleged criminals in absentia and, after apprehending their unsuspecting victims at their homes during nocturnal raids, executed sentence—usually a flogging followed by a warning to leave the country under penalty of death. Striking often and without warning, the vigilantes quickly drove much of the local criminal element into exile in Texas or to the western Louisiana prairies. Instead of disbanding, the vigilantes then turned their attention to local residents deemed undesirable either because of their unpopular political views or their flagrant disregard for existing social conventions. European immigrants suspected of socialistic political tendencies, poor whites with slave or free black concubines, free blacks with slave lovers, and poor persons of all walks of life and all racial backgrounds who openly defied the social controls maintained by the planter caste were victimized by the vigilantes (Barde 1861; Sterkx 1972: 285–315).

Free blacks were not spared the vigilante onslaught, and, as in white society, the lower economic orders of the free black community appear to have been the primary targets for vigilante terrorism. One of the raids most celebrated by the vigilantes was against the Coco settlement at Anse-la-Butte, in St. Martin Parish. Coco, a free black, had, for nearly fifty years, openly maintained a polygamous, extramarital relationship with two white sisters, by whom he had sired nineteen children. In the 1850s, Coco and his sole surviving wife appear to have enjoyed a peaceful existence—until the organization of the vigilante "Committee of Pont de la Butte." Coco's children had settled alongside their parents, establishing a veritable village called "Cocoville." The sons lived off the land as hunters and trappers, but the daughters, according to vigilante sources, supported themselves by means of prostitution. It was through prostitution that members of the Coco family reportedly became associated with various white "undesirables" who were among the first victims of the second phase of vigilante repression. Sometime in late February or early March 1859, a large party of vigilantes rode to the "Cocoville" settlement in Prairie Maronne and presented the community's "Black Mormon" patriarch with a "decree of exile" (Barde 1861; Sterkx 1972: 285–315).

Acknowledging the futility of resistance, the Coco family slowly migrated to the Marksville area over the course of the next month, with many junior members of the family finding new homes along the way. Coco, accompanied by five or six clan members, occupied a leaky, abandoned hut, only to be displaced once again by local white vigilantes. Subsequently chased yet again from Rapides Parish, Coco and his much-maligned family eventually found a haven in New Orleans (Sterkx 1972: 302, 304–5, 310; Barde 1861: ch. 5).

Many other free blacks of the Attakapas and Opelousas districts were also forced to abandon their homes, but, unlike Coco's family, they often tasted the lash before enduring exile. Every attempt at resistance was crushed, and, despite the vigilantes' public disavowal of violent intentions against "respectable" free people of color, many innocent free blacks were sufficiently intimidated to join the exodus. Like Coco's family, most of the refugees seem to have made their way to the Crescent City. Among the first emigrants to reach the city were one hundred exiles from St. Landry Parish, where inflammatory editorials by the *Opelousas Patriot*—a local pro-vigilante, anti–free black newspaper—had spurred local vigilantes into a frenzy of anti–free black activity. In fact, by 1860 the Grimble Bell School at Washington, Louisiana, had been closed by vigilantes, forcing many of its former students to seek an education in New Orleans's private institutions (Sterkx 1972: 302–10; Barde 1861: ch. 5).

Capitalizing upon the situation, the Haitian consul at New Orleans, P. E. Desdunes, a free man of color, began to recruit free black refugees from Attakapas and Opelousas for resettlement in Haiti. Desdunes offered free transportation to the black republic as an inducement for Haitian settlement, and he offered assurances of social equality and political rights and opportunities unavailable to them in Louisiana. Swayed by Desdunes's promises, 150 free blacks—most of them evidently from St. Landry Parish—boarded ships for Haiti in May 1859, while an additional 195 free people of color from St. Landry and East Baton Rouge Parishes sailed for the island the following month. Emigration to Haiti continued, though on a smaller scale, into early 1860 (Sterkx 1972: 302–3; *Opelousas Courier,* June 14, 1859; *New Orleans Daily Picayune,* Jan. 15, 1860; Barde 1861).

Few participants in this exodus found Haiti to their liking, and most returned to New Orleans by summer's end of 1859. Those who remained in Haiti, however, appear to have prospered. "Ch." Boisdoré (apparently Charles Boisdoré from St. Martin Parish), for example, reportedly became chief armorer for the Haitian government's Port-au-Prince arsenal by 1861 (Sterkx 1972: 302–5; Barde 1861).

Disillusioned by the Haitian experiment but unable to return their home parishes because of the continued vigilante activity, many expatriates chose to join the free black colony near Vera Cruz. Some of the colonists there became merchants, engaging in trade with New Orleans (Sterkx 1972: 302–5; Barde 1861).

As storm clouds gathered over the increasingly volatile slavery issue—and by extension the issue of race relations—free blacks in southwestern Louisiana found themselves increasingly targets of white violence. In the twilight of the antebellum period, most of this violence was confined geographically to the upper Teche region and socially to the lower strata of the free black community. Free black planters on the lower Teche, in an apparent effort to remain in the good graces of the local white population, reportedly contributed to the formation of Confederate military units. No such effort at good faith seems to have been made by the free black planters of St. Martin, Lafayette, and St. Landry Parishes, and free blacks generally appear to have maintained a low profile throughout the prairie country when war finally came in 1861 (Baker and Kreamer 1982: 82–90).

The exodus of Confederate volunteers to Virginia in 1861 and the conscription of many Attakapas and Opelousas poor whites into the Rebel army the following year greatly diminished the threat of violence to southwest Louisiana's free black population. New threats, however, appeared in the form of two devastating 1863 Union invasions of the Teche Valley and the simultaneous formation of Jayhawker bands—paramilitary groups of conscription evaders who lived off the land. The resulting problems were compounded in 1864 by the Confederate state government's attempt to conscript Attakapas and Opelousas free blacks for duty as

forced laborers in north Louisiana. Following the onset of free black conscription, free men of color in St. Landry Parish were admitted into the
largest and most active Jayhawker group in southwestern Louisiana—
the Bois Mallet band, commanded by Ozémé Carrière. Before the Civil
War, Carrière, a white Creole, had entered into an extramarital liaison
with the sister of Martin Guillory, a prominent local free man of color
who, in 1864, became Carrière's chief lieutenant. Following Carrière's
assassination by Confederate forces in 1865, Guillory accepted a Union
commission as captain and organized his Jayhawkers into the Mallet Free
Scouts (Brasseaux 1992: ch. 4).

The destructive, usually violent Jayhawker raids in the last two years
of the Civil War generated a tremendous grass-roots backlash in southwestern Louisiana, and, shortly after the cessation of hostilities, Martin
Guillory was assassinated by a group of white and black men at his home
near Opelousas.

Guillory's assassination signaled the beginning of a new and violent
chapter in the history of southwestern Louisiana—one that would see an
escalation of vigilante activities in the rural areas for the duration of the
postbellum era and throughout the 1880s. But, at the end of the Civil
War, most free blacks in the Attakapas and Opelousas areas were less
concerned with the threat of violence than with their changing economic
and social status. Like their white neighbors, free black property holders
endured devastating effects of long-term foraging by the Confederate and
Union armies; the widespread destruction and/or theft of private property by unruly soldiers and camp followers; the expropriation of property, produce, and livestock by the Confederate and Federal governments;
the initial depreciation and ultimate repudiation of Confederate currency;
and the emancipation of slaves. Free black men and women of substance
before the war found themselves impoverished at the war's conclusion.

Exhibiting their characteristic industriousness, most members of the
former free black community attempted to regain their antebellum prominence, but the challenges were formidable. Destruction of draft animals
and farm implements during the war and the resulting suspension or dis-
ruption of farming operations made it difficult, if not impossible, to resume cultivation of neglected, badly overgrown fields. Yet, mortgage
records indicate that, like their white counterparts, formerly prosperous
farmers within the old free black community encountered surprisingly
little difficulty in procuring the credit necessary to resume farming on at
least a modest scale. But, like their white counterparts, many of these
renewed farming endeavors were doomed to failure—largely as a result
of factors beyond the farmers' control. During the war years, the number of horses and mules declined by 48 and 43 percent respectively. The

resulting shortages in the early postbellum period caused prices for draft animals to rise to nearly $250 per head. Few farmers, even those who received credit, could afford such exorbitant prices, and most efforts at revival were thus immediately shackled. These problems were compounded by perennial labor shortages, insect infestations, unusual weather patterns, and repeated flooding. Repeated crop shortages, the deleterious local effects of two national recessions, and the high cost of credit (10 to 15 percent) gradually reduced many once prosperous former free black freeholders to tenantry between 1866 and 1873 (Brasseaux 1992: 76–79).

The 1870 decennial census bears grim testimony to the community's economic collapse. An examination of ten large antebellum free black landholdings in St. Landry Parish indicates that the median decline in the value of their estates during the war and early postwar years was a staggering 88 percent (see table 4.1).

Not all of the region's former free people of color were wartime and early postbellum economic casualties. As indicated earlier, some *gens de couleur libre* had managed to secret cotton and other agricultural commodities behind Jayhawker lines; these goods brought exorbitant prices on the New Orleans market at the war's conclusion. Some of the more enterprising members of St. Landry Parish's emerging Creole of Color community used these funds to speculate in undervalued farmlands placed on the local real estate market as a result of the area's early postbellum economic turmoil. An analysis of the real estate transactions of nine St. Landry Creole of Color families for the period from 1865 to 1881 indi-

Table 4.1
Economic Decline among Former Free Men of Color, St. Landry Parish, 1860–1870

	1860	1870	% Change
Auguste Donato, *père*	68,000	6,000	91
Antoine D. Meuillon	56,100	9,460	83
Evariste Guillory	26,520	2,500	91
Donate Guillory	23,790	1,800	92
Casimire Guillory	21,296	1,700	92
Zenon Rideau	16,660	3,000	82
François Simien	15,550	2,150	86
Antoine St. André	13,000	1,100	92
Joseph Lachapelle	11,500	1,800	84

SOURCE: 1860 and 1870 census reports, St. Landry Parish.

cates that the former *gens de couleur libre* were *purchasers* of land in 128 of the 159 transactions (80.5 percent) involving them. The median purchase price for lands acquired through these conveyances was $789.76, a princely sum during this period of protracted economic upheaval, when prime farmlands were available locally for only $10 to $15 per acre. The postbellum land acquisitions become still more impressive when one considers that many early postwar vendors demanded gold as payment (St. Landry Parish Conveyances, 1865–1881, Clerk of Court's Office, St. Landry Parish Courthouse, Opelousas, La. [hereafter referred to as SLC]).

The remarkable land acquisitions by some speculators in periods of economic stress during the postwar era masked the underlying financial problems within the Creole of Color community. Over the sixteen years following the conclusion of the Civil War, progressively fewer Creoles engaged in land acquisition as continually increasing numbers of speculators fell prey to the consequences of financial overextension. By 1876, many of these speculators were penniless, besieged by creditors, and faced with the prospect of bankruptcy (St. Landry Parish Civil Suits, 1866–1876, Clerk of Court's Office, St. Landry Parish Courthouse, Opelousas, La. [hereafter referred to as SLPCS]).

By 1910, most Creoles of Color had been reduced to tenantry. The federal decennial census of St. Landry Parish for that year indicates that fully 68 percent of the Creoles in Wards 1, 2, and 3—in which the most thriving antebellum communities were located—were tenant farmers. Among the Creoles of Color in the once flourishing Ward 1 area of neighboring St. Martin Parish, 54 percent were tenants.

Compounding the devastating economic impact of the war and its immediate aftermath was the sudden dissolution of the legal and social systems underpinning the privileged social position of Creoles of Color in Louisiana's three-tier caste system. With the emancipation of Negro slaves, the legal distinctions that had helped to set the *gens de couleur libre* apart as a people no longer existed. To the contrary, local black codes, such as the one adopted—but only briefly enforced—in Opelousas in July 1865, treated blacks as though they were a monolithic group and endowed them all with the highly circumscribed rights of freedmen.

Most of the former members of the free black caste rebelled against their loss of status and against the resulting inevitability of social amalgamation with the freedmen, from whom they had tried so long to distance themselves. To distinguish themselves from the Negro freedmen, former free blacks locally began to identify themselves as Creoles of Color, their former label—*gens de couleur libre*—being no longer a valid designation for their ethnic identity and special social status. Enclaves of Creoles of Color in the prairie parishes—at Leonville, Washington, Frilot Cove, and Bois Mallet in St. Landry Parish; at Grand Marais in

Iberia Parish; in and around Vermilionville in Lafayette Parish; at Grand Pointe and around St. Martinville in St. Martin Parish; near Verdunville and along Bayou Salé in St. Mary Parish—used every means possible to preserve the social distance between themselves and their black neighbors. Social contacts were discouraged with the freedmen and their descendants, while being simultaneously encouraged with other Creole of Color communities, particularly with other prairie enclaves but also with Creole of Color communities in other parts of the state. According to historian Claude Oubre, "[M]arriages arranged by the families perpetuated the contact between the various communities. As in earlier times these marriages held the land holdings intact while also preserving the racial composition of the community" (Baker and Kreamer 1982: 87).

Some Creoles of Color also sought political involvement as a means of regaining their prewar social status. The Donatos and other prominent former free men of color formed the backbone of the Republican Party in the prairie parishes. These Creole of Color politicians, who were allied politically with Gov. Henry Clay Warmoth, found it expedient to portray themselves as champions of the freedmen's causes as a means of furthering their own political interests. Former free black planter Gustave Donato of St. Landry Parish, for example, was a delegate to the 1868 state constitutional convention. Other Creoles of Color held less conspicuous positions either in local government (usually the police jury and local federal patronage positions) or on party committees in the Opelousas and Attakapas areas. Creoles of Color in Opelousas, however, appear to have curtailed their political activities significantly after the bloody Opelousas riot of 1868, which claimed between twenty-five and fifty "black and tan" victims. Free blacks remained active in other areas of the prairie country until the end of Reconstruction. For example, Victor Rochon represented St. Martin Parish in the state legislature between 1872 and April 10, 1875. He was joined in the general assembly by L. A. Martinet, also of St. Martin Parish, who was elected in 1874 and served until April 10, 1875. They were joined in the lower chamber by Arthur Antoine of St. Mary Parish. In the upper chamber, Alexandra François represented St. Martin Parish in 1868 and 1869, while Emile Detiege served the same geographic constituency from January 1874 through 1876 (MacDonald, et al. 1979: 97; Vincent 1976: 147, 148, 161, 192, 234, 235, 237).

Creole of Color participation in politics was sharply curtailed in the prairie parishes after the restoration of state control to white "Redeemers" in 1877 and completely extinguished by the white supremacist state constitution of 1898. With the erosion of political power came a corresponding erosion of civil rights. At the dawn of the twentieth century, Creoles of Color in the prairie parishes found themselves with little more than their lands, their pride, and their ethnic identity. Yet these were enough to sustain them and to propel them into leadership positions in the Civil Rights movement, which would eventually restore the community to its traditional position of prominence in local society.

References

Allain, Mathé. 1980. "Slave Policies in French Louisiana." *Louisiana History* 31: 127–37.

Archivo General de Indias, Seville, Spain, Papeles Procedentes de Cuba (abbreviated as AGI-PC), legajos 188A, 189A.

Baker, Vaughan B., and Jean T. Kreamer, eds. 1982. *Louisiana Tapestry: The Ethnic Weave of St. Landry Parish.* Lafayette, La.: Center for Louisiana Studies.

Barde, Alexandre. 1861. *Histoire des Comités de vigilance des Attakapas.* Lucy, La.: Le Meschacébé.

Bergeron, Arthur W., Jr. 1979. *Calendar of Documents of the Opelousas Post, 1764–1789.* Baton Rouge: Le Comité des Amis des Archives.

Brasseaux, Carl A. 1977. "Prosperity and the Free Population of Lafayette Parish, 1850–1860." *Attakapas Gazette* 12:105–10.

———. 1979. "Opelousas and the Alabama Immigrants." *Attakapas Gazette* 14 : 112–17.

———. 1980. "The Administration of Slave Regulations in French Louisiana, 1724–1766." *Louisiana History* 21: 139–58.

———. 1986. "Louisiana's Senegambian Legacy." *Senegal: Peintures Narratives/Narrative Paintings.* Lafayette, La.: Univ. Art Museum.

———. 1987. *The Founding of New Acadia: Beginnings of Acadian Life in Louisiana.* Baton Rouge: Louisiana State Univ. Press.

———. 1990. *Lafayette: Where Yesterday Meets Tomorrow. An Illustrated History.* Chatsworth, Calif.: Windsor Publications.

———. 1992. *Acadian to Cajun: Transformation of a People, 1803–1877.* Jackson: Univ. Press of Mississippi.

———, et al. 1977. *The Courthouses of Louisiana.* Lafayette, La.: Center for Louisiana Studies.

Burson, Caroline M. 1940. *The Stewardship of Don Esteban Miró, 1782–1792: A Study of Louisiana Based Largely on Documents in New Orleans.* New Orleans: American Printing Company.

Conrad, Glenn R. 1974. *St. Charles: Abstracts of the Civil Records of St. Charles Parish, 1700–1803.* Lafayette, La.: Center for Louisiana Studies.

———. 1990. *Land Records of the Attakapas District,* vol. 1: *Attakapas Domesday Book.* Lafayette, La.: Center for Louisiana Studies.

Everett, Donald E. 1966. "Free Persons of Color in Colonial Louisiana." *Louisiana History* 7: 21–50.

Ficklen, John Rose. 1910. *History of Reconstruction in Louisiana.* Baltimore: Johns Hopkins Univ. Press.

Gayarré, Charles Etienne Arthur. 1883. *History of Louisiana.* 4 vols. New Orleans: A. Hawkins.

———. "The Quadroons of Louisiana." Gayarré Papers, Department of Archives, Louisiana State Univ., Baton Rouge.

Hall, Gwendolyn Midlo. *Africans in Colonial Louisiana: The Development of Afro-Creole Culture in the Eighteenth Century.* Baton Rouge: Louisiana State Univ. Press, 1992.

Hanger, Kimberly. 1990. "Avenues to Freedom Open to New Orleans' Black Population, 1769–1779." *Louisiana History* 31: 237–64.

Hébert, Donald J., comp. 1974–90. *Southwest Louisiana Records*. 33 vols. Cecilia/Eunice, La.: Hébert Publications.

Jones, Joseph H. 1950. "The People of Frilot Cove: A Study of a Racial Hybrid Community in Rural South Central Louisiana." M.A. thesis, Louisiana State Univ.

MacDonald, Robert R., et al., eds. 1979. *Louisiana's Black Heritage*. New Orleans: Louisiana State Museum.

Mills, Gary B. 1977. *The Forgotten People: Cane River's Creoles of Color*. Baton Rouge: Louisiana State Univ. Press.

New Orleans Daily Picayune, 1859–60.

New Orleans Notarial Archives, Juan Bautista Garic Papers, vol. 3: 366, microfilm copy in the Colonial Records Collection, Center for Louisiana Studies, University of Southwestern Louisiana, Lafayette, Louisiana.

Opelousas Courier, 1859–60.

Rousseve, Charles Barthélémy. 1937. *The Negro in Louisiana: Aspects of His History and His Literature*. New Orleans: Xavier University Press.

Schweninger, Loren. 1989. "Antebellum Free Persons of Color in Postbellum Louisiana." *Louisiana History* 30: 345–64.

St. Landry Parish Civil Suits, 1866–1876, Clerk of Court's Office, St. Landry Parish Courthoue, Opelousas, La. Abbreviated as SLPCS.

St. Landry Parish Conveyances, 1865–1881, Clerk of Court's Office, St. Landry Parish Courthouse, Opelousas, La. Abbreviated as SLC. See particularly Conveyance Book U-1.

St. Landry Parish Original Acts on deposit at the Louisiana State Archives and Records Service, Baton Rouge, Louisiana. Abbreviated as SLOA. See particularly marriage contract between George Bolard, F.M.C., and Marie Jeanne, F.W.C., June 15, 1779, document 57; and slave sale from Luc Collins to George Bolard, free mulatto, July 4, 1780, document 95; manumission of a slave by Marie Louise, F.W.C., Mar. 30, 1781, document 146.

St. Martin Parish Original Acts, Clerk of Court's Office, St. Martin Parish Courthouse, St. Martinville, La. Abbreviated as SMOA. See particularly Donation by Jacques Fontenette, Jan. 21, 1804.

Stahl, Annie. 1942. "The Free Negro in Ante-bellum Louisiana." *Louisiana Historical Quarterly* XXV: 301–96.

Sterkx, H. E. 1972. *The Free Negro in Ante-Bellum Louisiana*. Rutherford, N.J.: Farleigh Dickinson Univ. Press.

United States Census Reports, Louisiana schedules, 1810–70.

Vincent, Charles. 1976. *Black Legislators in Louisiana During Reconstruction*. Baton Rouge: Louisiana State Univ. Press.

Voorhies, Jacqueline K. 1973. *Some Late Eighteenth-Century Louisianians*. Lafayette, La.: Center for Louisiana Studies.

Woodson, Carter G. 1927. *The Negro in Our History*. Washington, D. C.: Associated Publishers, Inc.

FIVE

Nicholas R. Spitzer

Mardi Gras in L'Anse de 'Prien Noir: A Creole Community Performance in Rural French Louisiana

The public celebration of Mardi Gras in the central Gulf Coast region of Louisiana, Mississippi, and Alabama prominently recalls the area's historical and cultural differences from the rest of the South. Mardi Gras ("Fat Tuesday") or Carnival ("fleshly excess") is celebrated with costumed float parades, neighborhood marches, informal parties, and formal balls in New Orleans, Lafayette, Biloxi, and Mobile, among other Gulf Coast cities. In rural French Louisiana, the Cajun and Creole courir de Mardi Gras, or Mardi Gras run, is carried out on horseback and flatbed trucks by revelers in small communities on the bayou- and marsh-laced prairies extending from Lafayette and St. Landry Parishes in the east westward to the Texas border.[1]

Mardi Gras is historically associated with French and Spanish populations along the Gulf Coast, although African-American-Caribbean people have long created their own distinct versions of Carnival. Mardi Gras takes place in February or March just prior to Ash Wednesday, forty days before Easter. The Mediterranean-Latin roots of Mardi Gras are to be found in the pre-Roman rites of spring and later Roman festival/ritual occasions such as Bacchanalia, Lupercalia, and Saturnalia (Leach 1972: 192–93). Over time, such occasions were incorporated into the Catholic liturgical calendar. The festive eating, dancing, and drinking associated with Mardi Gras is followed by the relative austerity and penitence of the Lenten period.

The idea for the *courir de Mardi Gras* in southwest Louisiana arrived with the Old World French early in the eighteenth century and was reinforced by the Acadians in the years after their arrival in 1765. Cajun Folklorist Barry Ancelet suggests that this rural French style of Carnival has sources in *La fête de la quémande* of medieval France, which was celebrated by a procession of revelers who traveled through the countryside offering some sort of performance in exchange for gifts (1982: 1). In southwest Louisiana, a band of masked (usually) male revelers goes from house to house, in a manner which might further be compared to

Christmas mumming in Europe, the West Indies, and parts of French-speaking Missouri or Nova Scotia. The African-French Creole version of Mardi Gras is held in about a half dozen small settlements across southwestern French Louisiana.

The Creoles—many of whom are ancestrally linked to Cajuns as well as to Continental French, Spanish, and Native Americans—share much culturally with Cajuns, including the French language, Catholicism, foodways, aspects of music style, and, most important for this essay, the celebration of Mardi Gras. However, social relations between Cajuns and Creoles have historically been ambivalent and sometimes hostile. Given this ambivalence, the Mardi Gras run is used by rural Creoles to address cultural and social similarities and differences with Cajuns—and African Americans—as well as to comment on many aspects interior to Creole family and community life, such as age, gender, kinship, and community relations.

The African-French Creoles of these small southwest Louisiana communities have adapted this European-derived form of festivalizing into one that is aesthetically pleasing and socially useful to them. Creole Mardi Gras participants use this traditional public performance occasion to intensify and transform everyday life domains of home, family, work, and worship and to provide aesthetic shape and commentary on Creole values, behavior, and social relations. Of special interest in this regard is the distinction made in the rural Creole community between the values of "respect" and "reputation" in the personal comportment of men and women.[2] Respect or respectability refers to the ideal normative behavior at the family, neighborhood and community level. Respect is associated with home life, land ownership, family bonds, hard work, devout Catholicism, and self-improvement. Respect has a special connection to women and domesticity associated with the house and yard area. Mature men, especially farmers and tradesmen, are also affiliated with respectability through their work and perceived sense of responsibility to the community. Involvement with cooperative labor parties, called *coup de main,* and in Catholic benevolent societies that provide medical and burial insurance are among many ways men show their respectability.

In the post-colonial context of much of Louisiana Creole culture, respect has also often associated with things French and Spanish, with ancestry connected to the antebellum free people of color, and phenotypically with more European features in skin color, hair, etc.—all of these traits, tendencies, and nuances are increasingly well documented in the scholarly literature. This orientation is not to suggest that people of strongly African descent are not respected, respectable, or proud of their ancestral or cultural orientation, but to observe the evaluative criteria for certain behaviors and historical associations that often obtain within Creole communities.

In contrast and conflict—but also essentially interlocked—with the value of respect is the domain associated with "reputation." This non-normative value, and the aesthetics and behaviors associated with it, is generally linked to a world of men acting individualistically in pursuit of pleasure with women, in drinking, and in boasting about their exploits. Reputation-oriented behavior is group-centered to the extent that men may gather in bars, camps, or clubs to act *cannais* ("tricky"), recount their previous triumphs, and plan new exploits. While "respectable" people may characterize a "man of reputation" as *couyon* ("stupid"), *une fou* ("a fool"), and lazy, this does not mean that such individuals do not participate in Creole community life or are all jobless. However, many of their jobs, such as itinerant or seasonal agricultural labor, construction, oil field work, and truck driving, have lower status than work associated with landed agriculturists, artisan-craftsmen, businessmen, educators, and other community leaders.

As a parallel to the association of "respect" with French/Spanish ancestry and culture, "reputation" is often linked by Creoles with African and African-American ancestry and cultural style—especially to those people who dwell in the "quarters" (black district) of a town and urban Creoles or African Americans in general. Again, the associations of reputation do not prohibit culturally or ancestrally African-Caribbean or African-American people from emphasizing their respectability through all manner of behavior. Nor are people descended within a French-oriented Creole community exclusively respectable if their behavior draws criticism from other members. Likewise, people of Cajun ethnicity may be characterized as not respectable if their behavior is considered too rough, rowdy, drunken, or otherwise lacking *politesse* ("politeness")—as many Creoles assert. Further, while respect and reputation are useful ideal descriptions for domains of meaning and action, they are in no sense immutable categories. Daily life is invariably complex, and there are many avenues in which people of respect can engage in activities like hunting, dancing at zydeco clubs, giving a boastful account of one's love life and so on, all of which assert their personal reputations. Just as surely, those who inhabit the clubs and bars, or who otherwise occupy a more marginal social and economic status, can claim respectability, such as when they assist at a *coup de main,* show courtesy to elders, or marry into a respectable family—often with a partner considered "bright," or of more European appearance.

Creole Mardi Gras illuminates these complex, contrasting value domains for participants and observers alike. Mardi Gras annually engages the full range of the community: men and women, those of more African-American or French orientation, young and old, urban and rural, high and low social and economic status, families and individuals, married and unmarried, those maintaining respectability or seeking a reputation. Mardi Gras displays personal, social, and cultural identity. It brings the many contours, contrasts, and complementarities of Creole life and its constant transformation into high relief. It is the traditional means of expression about the nature of Creole experience in rural French Louisiana used by Creoles themselves. It is one of the best lenses available into the complexities of Creole consciousness and identity.[3]

Mardi Gras in L'Anse de 'Prien Noir

L'Anse de 'Prien Noir (Black Cyprien's Cove) is a small Creole farming settlement located in a partially cleared *pinière* ("pine grove") near the boundary of St. Landry and Evangeline Parishes.[4] The community, according to oral history, was founded in the 1830s by Cyprien Ceazer, a French-speaking (and probably Spanish-speaking) free man of color whose parentage, like that of many who today call themselves Creole, was Spanish, French, Native American, and African. The L'Anse de 'Prien Noir settlement (referred to by locals and hereafter as "'Prien Noir") was part of a general early- to mid-nineteenth-century westward movement of landless free persons onto the prairies from the plantation regions to the east along Bayou Teche. Members of the Ceazer family today believe that Cyprien was born in St. Martinville, the post of the Attakapas district. Cyprien Ceazer is buried in the community cemetery his family provided when the community was settled.

There are still Ceazers in the community, and another branch of the family lives twelve miles to the west in the small settlement of Soileau. In addition to Ceazers, the most common family names include Ardoin, Fontenot, Guillory, Victorian, and Thomas. Members of the 'Prien Noir and Soileau communities share the view that their land was at one time more extensive than in the present day. While many still own their modest farmsteads (two to eight acres), others are sharecroppers on land owned by local Cajun farmers and outside agribusinesses. In Soileau, in particular, the Creole holdings tend to be larger and less broken up from earlier days. One member of the Ceazer family owns forty acres and suggests that his kin controls as much as four hundred acres, which he says is less than they formerly held.

The resident population of 'Prien Noir during the period of field study (1975–1983) was roughly eighty people composed of portions of six Creole extended families of approximately sixty persons total and three Cajun families of twenty persons total. Two of the Cajun families operate grocery stores, and one is a farmer. 'Prien Noir is part of the larger unincorporated settlement of Duralde, which has approximately four hundred residents including the eighty mentioned. Duralde, which has several stores and a church, but no school, post office, or town center, is about 60 percent Cajun and 40 percent Creole overall. The Creoles tend to live in a series of small settlements like 'Prien Noir.

The Duralde area is bounded to the northeast by the Cajun prairie farm town of Mamou (with approximately five thousand residents). To the west is Soileau (with three hundred residents), which, like Duralde, is unincorporated. To the southwest is Basile (with twenty-five hundred residents). To the southeast is the small city of Eunice (with nine thousand residents). Eunice's larger size is based in part on rail distribution of rice and soybean crops, as well as on the oil industry. Unlike the rest of the towns and settlements noted above, Eunice is located in St. Landry Parish. Residents of 'Prien Noir view Mamou as the nearest town for shopping and other business and for health and educational services, but many receive their mail from the Eunice post office and are listed in the Eunice phone book.

The Mardi Gras run in 'Prien Noir has gone on as long as anybody can remember. Unlike the well-known nearby Cajun Mardi Gras in Mamou, which was revived by local civic leaders in the 1950s (Oster and Reed 1960: 1–17), the 'Prien Noir Creole Mardi Gras is continuous from earlier times. In the words of Marceline Ardoin, a respected matriarch in the Creole community, the Mardi Gras in 'Prien Noir has been run "since people was people I guess. For years they say. They never stopped running it. It used to be bigger. They had horses, but they could walk. All the houses was close. They used to be over one hundred men about a mile long. I was so scared. They was all well-dressed and they knowed how to sing Mardi Gras. They had their long *capuchon*. It would come sharp with bells on it. They'd ring 'dingy, dingy, dingy,' oh it was nice." Her husband, the respected musician Alphonse "Bois Sec" Ardoin, added: "Mardi Gras has never changed that I know. Mardi Gras is the same all the time. I don't believe it can change."

Mardi Gras in L'Anse de 'Prien Noir during my field visits consisted of a band averaging thirty men who mask and dress mostly as clowns and gather at 7:30 A.M. Tuesday morning at the club/dance hall. The group is led by an uncostumed captain, assisted by truck driver(s) and two musicians. The musicians play a special role in service to the band of clowns and the community: they do not mask and they comport themselves with an air of special dignity. Although the rest of the year some may be known for their late hours and carousing, on Mardi Gras they play it "straight."

The clowns, often collectively called the "Mardi Gras," or *paillasse* (literally "straw men"), led by the captain, spend much of the day riding from house to house, singing as they go, and dancing together as they beg for *charité*. The clowns include those who are teenagers—just en-

Fig. 5.1. The lead musician, Alphonse "Bois Sec" Ardoin," and the clowns of the Creole Mardi Gras in L'Anse de 'Prien Noir leave the Ardoin family dance hall at 8:00 A.M. to begin the *courir*. Evangeline Parish, Louisiana, 1979. Photograph by Nicholas R. Spitzer.

tering the world of men—and the older men who will watch the young men's moves and act as their mentors and critics. In this community, which has lost many of its men due to lack of jobs and urban residency, there has been a tendency for the clowns to be primarily younger men and teenage boys. The captain and musicians, as well as a few of the lead clowns, are elders. Thus among an average of thirty Mardi Gras participants, approximately fifteen are between ages fourteen and eighteen, ten are between ages nineteen and forty, and five are between ages forty and seventy. No one over age seventy, in my experience, has run Mardi Gras in this community; however, one captain in the nearby Creole community of Soileau was still running at seventy-nine. The most significant fact is that the young adult and especially middle-aged men are represented so slightly. In part this is due to the fact that Mardi Gras has elements of a *rite de passage* event for the young. Thus while all the young should pass through Mardi Gras, many older men do not continue to run. As one elder clown, referring to the main attraction of the *courir* and house visit, the chicken chase, says: "Them young boys has got to prove they can do it, that they can catch that chicken and kill it."

The Mardi Gras spend much of the day begging for *charité* at twenty to forty households and stores in and beyond the L'Anse de 'Prien Noir and Duralde area as a whole. A Mardi Gras visit begins with the captain entering the yard to speak with the woman or man of the house and respectfully asking permission for the band to perform in exchange for *charité*. The answer from the householder is nearly always "yes," especially at Creole homes and at the homes of Cajuns in the *voisinage* ("neighborhood"). The captain uses a white flag to wave the band forward and into the driveway in front of the house and yard. As they arrive they begin singing a call-and-response chant called the Mardi Gras Song (for a sample transcription, see the text near the end of the *On est bon des politessiens:* Playing the Roles of Captain and Clowns subhead below). Although the clowns occasionally present themselves as thieves and outlaws, as is common in Cajun Mardi Gras, the Creole approach, dominantly that of a beggar-clown, is less forceful and more polite. This is reinforced through palms-open supplication by the singers and self-effacing comments found in the song text, such as "It's not often we do this. We are polite people from far away."

The positioning of the performers is consistent at all visits. The householder stays back or behind the yard fence if there is one. The captain and musicians are nearby on the other side, but separate from the Mardi Gras, who are en masse unto themselves. After singing, the clowns dance together—something not done by men at any other time of the year.[5] This dance and the chant of request is observed by the householder and spectators. Upon its completion, the Mardi Gras is either tossed a chicken (or a duck or turkey) or allowed to chase a designated bird or birds in the yard. Sometimes a frozen chicken is humorously thrown into the air, or offerings of rice, sausage, money, candies, spices, and cooking grease are made, but it is the chicken chase that is usually the center of attention. The chase is carried out by the young men, who may scramble over fences into the yards, past junked cars, under bird roosts, and into muddy rice fields in their competition for the catch. When caught, the bird is killed, usually with exaggerated wringing of the neck, and handed over to an uncostumed "chicken man," who bags the *charité* and keeps a tally.

Thanks are offered to the householder in song, and an invitation to eat the evening's gumbo and attend the dance is made. The captain then commands the Mardi Gras to get moving, back on the truck, and on the road. Earlier, the Mardi Gras had urged the captain to get moving and bring the band to the house. Throughout the day the captain and clowns are at odds in this manner. He may tell them to dance better or to be quiet and orderly. He may also prohibit their going to a store or entering a yard or garden area, prevent the consumption of alcohol except when he allows it, or order them not to urinate in public. In short, he protects the householders and the ideal community values by respecting their property and not having them "dirty" themselves in contact with the clowns. The clowns in turn drink, play pranks, try to scare the women and children, and demand that they move on for more chicken conquests.

During the latter part of the 'Prien Noir run, the chicken man heads back to the club with the *charité* already gathered to give to women who have assembled to begin to clean and cook the day's spoils. Late in the day, the clowns return triumphantly to their club. Some take over the seasoning and light tasks at this point, consistent with the fact that men do nearly all the festive cooking in the Creole community. The entire band, and many of the people invited from house visits—mostly Creoles, men, and women, young and old, and a few Cajuns—then arrive to join in a communal gumbo supper.

At about 8:00 P.M., over twelve hours after the start of the run, a zydeco dance commences with the clowns marching into the dance hall lead by the captain, the musicians, and lead clowns. They circle the hall, dance two dances with one another, and unmask. At this point the rest of the visitors join the dancing in the usual male-female couples. The dance, typically the noisiest and most exuberant of the year, concludes at midnight and the beginning of the Lenten season. The following day is a work day for most men, but a few join a congregation dominated by women and children on Ash Wednesday, a Holy Day of Obligation among Catholics.

Carnival Knowledge: Aesthetics of Mardi Gras in 'Prien Noir

Mardi Gras in 'Prien Noir is a special type of community-wide performance comparable historically to calendrical ritual and festival occasions worldwide. Given the communal nature of the activity and the fact that it provides an aesthetic commentary on the social and ethnic dimensions of everyday life in the community, the term "cultural performance" is usefully applied to Mardi Gras (Singer 1959: xii). The late anthropologist Victor Turner describes such cultural performances, including Carnival, as "commentaries and critiques on, or celebrations of, different dimensions of human relatedness" (1984: 19). Turner also uses the term "multi-vocal" to refer to the many varied symbolic meanings in Mardi Gras. He further notes that "[i]ts referents are not all of the same logical order but are drawn from many domains of social experience and ethical evaluation" (1969: 52).

Mardi Gras, through such aesthetic devices as dislocation, juxtaposition, reversal, intensification, and obscuring, is a special day of "social drama" that expresses the meaning of everyday reality in the rural Creole community. Creole Mardi Gras in Louisiana is not, as the French anthropologist Duvignaud suggests for festivals in general, "a powerful denial of the established order" (1976: 19). It is better understood as a powerful restatement of the established order *and chaos* of everyday life. The values and behaviors associated with chaos and licentiousness, which I have glossed as "reputation," are not the community ideal—but they are tolerated as a fact of life. Places such as camps, bars, and nightclubs do exist where these disruptive energies are played out, and, to some degree, they are contained, if not legitimized.[6] As to the ultimate issue of respectability and order at the Mardi Gras in 'Prien Noir, the word of the captain is final. If a clown should go beyond the bounds of decorum (by becoming too sassy, violent, or drunk), and the captain is viewed as a fair man, no one would complain if the too licentious clown were ejected from the *courir*. Thus, despite the chaotic aspects of Creole Mardi Gras and the symbolic tension involved in bringing together the elements of order and disorder in the community, order prevails.

Respectable values are attacked at Mardi Gras by the method of dislocation and displacement of reputation-oriented activity as the rowdy life of the men's club in intensified forms finds its way into the respectable house/yard area. The respectable routine of daily work at homes, farms, and stores is thus displaced by festive play. Brazilian anthropologist Roberto Da Matta, who has looked at the renowned Carnival in his country, describes this dislocating mode of symbolizing found in such festival settings as the movement of meaning carried by roles or objects and other means between domains: "The heart of the symbolizing process is thus the passage of an object or its appearance in a different domain . . . to symbolize—is fundamentally to dislocate an object from its place, a process that brings a clear consciousness of the nature of the object, of the properties of its original domain, and of its adaptation to a new locale. Thus dislocations bring on a consciousness of all the reifications of the social world" (1984: 213–14).

In rural Creole Mardi Gras, community members symbolically move their songs, dances, talk, play, and other behaviors into locations that provide the kind of consciousness and commentary described by Da Matta. As in Brazilian Carnival, the actions and appearances of the clowns at Creole Mardi Gras invoke an array of symbolic devices, such as exaggeration (intensification, reinforcement), inversion (or reversal), and neutralization (or diminishing) of meaning from life in the rest of the year (Da Matta 1984: 215). These are ways in which the personalities, politics, and values, as well as age, gender, class, and ethnic relations of everyday life, are placed into the festival frame and examined. The symbolic and aesthetic means of Mardi Gras in 'Prien Noir include: 1) use of time and space (calendrical event, processing along a travel route, visiting the house and yard); 2) special roles (captain, clowns musicians, householders, spectators, women as cooks and costume makers); 3) performances (music, dances, songs, boastful talk, commands, and polite requests); and 4) tangible materials (masks, costumes, flags, and chickens and other foods gathered and cooked). All these aesthetic contours and acts of Mardi Gras operate in a complex, interpenetrating manner—what Da Matta calls the "multiple planes" of Carnival. To understand the many meanings of Mardi Gras in 'Prien Noir, one must also know something of the everyday life circumstances as we have briefly sketched them. To understand life and local Creole culture, one must also look closely at the symbolic means and meanings in Mardi Gras. Between these vantage points a perspective on Creole aesthetics, identities, values, and behavior emerges.

Creole Mardi Gras in Time and Space

Time and space of the Mardi Gras celebration mark it as separate from everyday life. Mardi Gras occurs once a year on the day prior to the beginning of Lent. It is in the same place each year in the liturgical calendar, but it fluctuates on the secular calendar over several weeks from early February to early March. Mardi Gras in the Latin-Catholic world is part of the historical juxtaposition of Carnival excess to Lenten abstinence. Le Roy Ladurie notes the extreme significance of this temporary context in the sixteenth-century French Carnival in Romans: "As concerns the place of Carnival-Lent in the Christian time cycle. . . I gave the definition I find best suited to the primordial concept of Carnival and the essence of Lent: burying one's pagan ways, having one last pagan fling before embarking on the penitential rigors of the catechumen's Lententide, which would result in spiritual and baptismal rebirth at Easter. In short, the rites of Carnival were a logical prelude to their opposite: Lenten fasting and preaching" (1979: 307–8).

People in 'Prien Noir do not have a developed rationale for why Mardi Gras occurs prior to Lent. No one in the community suggests that the festival and the following ritual Holy Day of Ash Wednesday and the relatively austere Lenten period are strongly linked or that Carnival is somehow a "pagan fling" prior to a time of abstinence. For example, one man when questioned about how Mardi Gras is related to the teachings of the Church stated: "I don't know what Mardi Gras is for. The priest never said. Lent is to give something up. You go for the ashes and maybe the Church has a dance before Mardi Gras, but as far as being a Church day, it's not." Many Creoles, especially women, make Lenten sacrifices (i.e., giving up certain foods, attending dances, and other pleasurable behaviors). Ash Wednesday Mass is usually well attended by women. Though many persons have to work on this day, employers in the region are often Catholic as well and thus allow individuals time off for Mass. However, the importance of sacred activities temporally proximate to Mardi Gras is increasingly what individuals choose to make of it.

Thus I vividly recall seeing the respected lead musician of the Mardi Gras kneeling to pray at his home, his accordion at his side, prior to joining the men at the club for departure. It was a final sacred act prior to entering the time of license. Further, he was careful to be sure to end the Mardi Gras dance that evening precisely at midnight and the official beginning of Lent. A respectable man such as this chose to personally frame the day with a prayer for safety in what he was about to do and concern for the formal rules of the Catholic Church. He was also in church with his wife the next day.

In contrast, the lead clown, a man of vast reputation, was also in the Ash Wednesday service, as were a few members of his retinue. After receiving communion and the blessing of ashes on his forehead, signifying penitence and humility, he walked, with head bowed and eyes narrowed, right by where I was seated in a pew. As he passed, he looked sideways at me and winked. Where the respectable man allowed his sense of the religious life to penetrate and even inform his running of Mardi Gras, the man of reputation was willing to comically acknowledge that things had not changed so much from Mardi Gras day, even though we were now in church on Ash Wednesday.

Although the older, more home-oriented men—along with older women in the community—strongly endorse the sacredness of the time that follows Mardi Gras, for most the contrast based on time seems less essential than the more general juxtaposition of the festival to everyday life. The significance of the timing of Mardi Gras can, however, be understood more broadly as a manner in which people situate themselves within the year. A special day of disorder allows people to evaluate the more ordered daily and annual routine on both the sacred and secular calendars. Edmund Leach views this temporal aspect of Carnival generally as an ordering function. The festival becomes a measuring device against the passage of time in everyday life (1971: 135). Beyond the deep cultural and historical roots of Mardi Gras, Creoles today were born into this ritual/festival cycle. As a part of it (as the above examples of the lead musician and clown show), they use the boundaries of festival time in manners they find appropriate. Community members primarily reference Mardi Gras time in evaluation of people for the rest of the year. For example, the timeliness of the lead clown's behavior at Mardi Gras and its inappropriateness the rest of year is the subject of much comment. A person who rather appreciates the lead clown's antics year-round and especially likes to see him enjoying himself at Mardi Gras says: "Mardi

Gras is his day." On the other hand, a person critical of his ways in general says: "For him, every day is Mardi Gras." The lead clown then is elevated on Mardi Gras by his propensity for carousing and reputation-oriented behavior, but the rest of the year he is criticized by those who live according to the values and behaviors of everyday respectability.

The temporal appropriateness of begging and acting the clown on Mardi Gras is recognized in repeated lines of the chant used by the lead clown and others as they approach a house in search of *charité*. They say *"Une poule par an c'est pas souvent"* ("A chicken a year is not much") and *"On n'a pas souvent beaucoup fait ça"* ("We don't do this very often"). Both phrases are used as excuses for why the clowns dare to intrude into the yard, behave as they do, and beg for *charité*. Both clearly indicate that Mardi Gras is an infrequent (annual) time when everyday rules are suspended.[7]

Closely allied to the marking of Mardi Gras as a special time in the liturgical cycle for behavior inappropriate at other times of the year, is the intersection of time and space during the day itself. The Mardi Gras band begins at the club and ends at the club. Thus the informal "play world" of the club becomes for the day the official beginning and ending point of Carnival time. Comments by the clowns are heard throughout the day about the club as a home base to which those who give *charité* will be invited. The club as starting point is occasionally referred to in speech and song as *le moyeu* ("hub") around which the variegated circling path of the Mardi Gras is oriented: *tout le tour du moyeu* ("all around the hub"). When, late in the day, debates occur as to how far the band has gone and the possibility of returning with the *charité* already collected, the comments of the men who wish to go back are couched in terms of being far from the club and that "It's time to go back home!" On Mardi Gras, the club assumes the role of a communal household for the men as the central point on the map of the community.

In sketching the route of a Mardi Gras with its interior stops and also the exterior points beyond which the band will not travel, one sees a rough delineation of L'Anse de 'Prien Noir, as well as the broader Duralde and subregional Creole communities. As the band moves to the edge of the acceptable terrain for the 'Prien Noir Mardi Gras run, the homes are those of people they know less well and are not considered close enough physically or in terms of friendship or kinship to visit. Indeed, individual clowns who know family or friends on the outer bounds of the community territory may ask to make such visits, and these personal exceptions are often a source of debate revolving around the authority of the claim, the time of day, and whether other clowns also know of or are related to the household in question.

The excitement generated simply by being out on the road, en route in the midst of Mardi Gras, is obvious. A good deal of time is spent on the truck, drinking, jiving, and playing music. There is also extensive commentary on the houses and fields of community members passed en route regarding who has plowed, built a shed, fixed a fence, wrecked their car, and so on. Unlike a day in which work must be attended to on time, Mardi Gras sets only rough bounds of leaving (7:30 A.M.) and returning to the club (3:30 P.M.). The route is a secret held by the captain, and, while he controls the clowns in this aspect of disorder, as a whole the effect is to be headed in an unscheduled fashion to no set destination other than a sequence of homes. While their "work" of singing, dancing, and chasing chickens is cut out for them, the getting there is relatively free time within the already celebratory frame. Much pleasure is taken by the men as they simply ride the truck, drinking, singing, talking, and blocking traffic, all the while observing the landscape in a rolling party. As Da Matta notes regarding movement in space for Brazilian Carnivalgoers and paraders: "[I]t is the travel that becomes important. In this context leaving and arrival are less important than the movement itself. . . . Daily travel is functional, rational and operational, since it has a specific aim: work, shopping, business, or study. But in ritual travel, or rather the conscious travel of ritual, the aim and the travel itself become more or less the same" (1984: 216–17).

Mardi Gras travel and the activity en route are further examples of the special time and space created. The Mardi Gras brings the party to the people—disrupting quiet rural spaces and the households they visit. To travel in broad daylight in such a manner would be impossible the rest of the year with a large group. It might be considered a form of vigilante action by the average bystander. If undertaken by a smaller group of men who were drinking at night, it would be considered "cruising": men out looking for a party, women, or the "action." Men who go from club to club such as this at night and on weekends the rest of the year are sometimes stigmatized as "road runners."

If the special communal travel of Mardi Gras over the dusty back roads and "blacktop" highways of the community tends to bond the clowns as a unit, it also serves to distinguish them from other groups on a *courir*. The Cajun Mardi Gras from nearby towns and country settlements as well as another Creole Mardi Gras are occasionally encountered by the men of 'Prien Noir. The marginal intersection of the respective groups' routes reminds the Creoles of 'Prien Noir that their community has social as well as territorial bounds. Creoles are not welcome to run with the Cajun Mardi Gras (some Creoles in nearby Cajun towns come out to the country to run with Creole bands). There is also some apprehension in meeting up with the Cajun bands, which are likely to be rowdy and larger than the Creole groups. The 'Prien Noir Mardi Gras's movement about the countryside reminds the participants of social segregation from Cajuns based on race, as well as the different kinship and friendship networks that make up the rival neighboring Creole community's Mardi Gras. However, it is also a time of integration since Cajun and Creole bands both visit white and black households. The act of moving about the whole community and subregion to visit homes of people of another ethnic category, with whom the Creoles share many aspects of French culture, suggests a special level of familiarity and integration in the Mardi Gras period.[8]

Some aspects of time/space sequencing are related to the roles of Mardi Gras participants. Perhaps the most obvious is that the captain always leads the group. In the past this was done on horseback, and now it is usually done in the cab of a small truck, which may also hold the musicians. This truck is followed by the truck(s) of clowns. When the band stops along the roadside in front of a house, the captain walks first to the gate of a yard and then, if the householder has not come out in response to the approaching music and noise of the clowns, proceeds to the door to ask permission for the Mardi Gras to visit. If permission is granted the clowns take care not to leave the truck area until the white flag of the captain beckons them forward. As the captain walks back toward them, the clowns are also cautioned by him not to get between him and the house. Most often the captain will position himself at the edge of the yard, but outside the compound. The musicians position themselves near this location as well. The clowns stay to themselves, singing and dancing together as they sing and request *charité*. The householders remain on their porch, in their yard, or very close to the fence line when outside the yard. In visits where the householder hands the chicken to the captain, he in turn will taunt the clowns with his control of the space and the chicken on behalf of the householder: holding the bird by the feet, pretending to throw it, waving the clowns back with his white flag, saying, *"Fais pas ça!"* or *"Pas trop vite!"* ("Don't do it!" "Not so fast!").

When the chicken chase begins, the prohibited space boundaries necessarily dissolve. If the bird runs into the yard, gardens, trash pile, pig sty, fields, or across the street, the younger clowns head off in pursuit. At once they are free to break the boundaries of the respectable domain of the house/yard/farmstead complex, and, at the same time, they are doing it in a way that renders them foolish, since they have to follow the arbitrariness of a bird's flight over these various bounded areas—a foolishness accentuated by alcohol. In this critical moment of the visit, the boundaries of the yard domain—so highly marked by the householder with the respectable captain and musician close to either side of the boundary holding the clowns at bay—are suddenly crossed.

After the bird is caught or other *charité* is received, the clowns re-treat through the front of the yard singing their "thank yous" in a return to decorum. The net effect again is an oscillation: this time between or-der and chaos in the use of space. There are occasionally those house-holders who, to the disappointment of the clowns, will avoid this bound-ary breaking by providing *charité* other than a live chicken. Some will more pointedly tell the captain that the clowns are not to enter a garden area. This request is sometimes enforced by a dog in the compound, but usually the clowns obey the captain if such a request is made.

Space ordering of the band when on the road also has significance. Behind the leading captain, the elder clowns always ride in the front of an open truck. This is thought to have the least dust and the smoothest ride. The younger men and boys are found at the back of the truck, with the exception that the eldest among them controls the back entry gate under the orders of the older clowns and the captain. The spacing on the road and in the trucks expresses the hierarchy among clowns and the cap-tain, with the highest in the lead, the older clowns with most established reputations in singing and clowning at the front of the clown truck, fol-lowed progressively by lesser (younger) clowns. The latter are in turn followed by the more senior of the younger clowns, who have both the hardship and prestige of riding at the back and controlling safety on, and access to, the truck. Behind the last truck of clowns, there is the chicken man, who acts as something of a deputy captain in bringing up the rear. He is followed by spectators watching the Mardi Gras. This procession of trucks and cars may reach as many as twelve by the middle of the day. The spectators are often those who could not serve as clowns, such as non-Creole blacks, Creole women, Anglos, or Cajuns. They become a movable audience that stands in a neutral position to one side of the enactment at the boundary of the yard at each house visit.

On est bon des politessiens:
Playing the Roles of Captain and Clowns

Enacting the roles of captain and clowns in these festival times and spaces is at the symbolic core of Mardi Gras. Performances associated variously with these roles include: captain—requesting a visit, com-mands, speeches, and occasionally prayers; clowns—costuming, mask-ing, jiving, begging, singing, dancing, and chasing chickens. The cap-tain has the most important single role in the rural Creole Mardi Gras. He is distinct in authority, appearance, and behavior from the clowns, and he enforces the larger framework of rules against which they chafe.

Fig. 5.2. Mardi Gras *capitaine* Paul Thomas awaits the arrival of his bands of clowns in L'Anse de 'Prien Noir. Evangeline Parish, Louisiana, 1981. Photograph by Nicholas R. Spitzer.

He has ultimate authority for the choice of the houses visited and the route of the *courir,* the safety of the clowns and the spectators, and the lives and property of those visited. He may have to negotiate the trouble-free passing of another Mardi Gras band—including one of the more rowdy groups from a neighboring Cajun community—without losing face.

The captain embodies respectability and order in the Creole community. Paul Thomas, the captain of the 'Prien Noir Mardi Gras, makes the following assessment of the social and physical requirements to fulfill this role:

> Not everybody can become a captain. You need to be authoritarian and slightly mean, to have a good voice to command and give orders. You also have to appear big, strong, and powerful. In order to be respected, a captain must be around fifty years of age. Too young a man cannot be elected. A captain has to be well known in his town where he is. A fifty-year-old man will understand well the rules of the *courir.* There will not be abuses and complaints. He is in first position in the group. He is leading the *courir* with his flag held straight and high.

Although clowns may disagree with and chide the captain on Mardi Gras day, they acknowledge his ultimate authority. Alphonse Ardoin, well respected in the community, once served as captain, but did not wish to do so again because he believed he did not have the force of authority over the clowns. Ardoin, who regularly performs as a musician on the run, comments on the role of the captain and his respect for Paul Thomas: "He's a good man. A man you can depend on. You can be sure on that man. What he going to say is there. He waves his flag and it's this, it's that. You got to be serious. I've been captain, but I'm not fit for that me. I'm too chicken.[9] You got to be serious. You got to be a man. You going to say something, everyone got to take you at what you said. Just like me, they going to laugh at me."

The captain is a respectable supervisory figure in the play world of the festival—on a par in the everyday life of the rural Creole community perhaps with zydeco club owners. He lets people carouse, but must always be ready to enforce the rules should things get beyond the bounds of what is acceptable. The captain constantly badgers the clowns with orders: "Come on!"; "Let's go!"; "Make the show good!"; "I don't want no more drinking for a while!"; "Don't nobody go in this yard 'til I say so!"; "This lady is particular about her garden, so stay away!"; and so forth. At the same time the captain must "take a lot of things," referring to how the clowns will harass him to get their way. Both zydeco club owners and Mardi Gras captains are referred to by names of authority, such as "sheriff," "boss" and *"chef,"* which are most commonly reserved for whites in the region.

The clowns and other community members agree that a strong captain, like a strong club owner, is needed—one who will not "take too much shit or give too much shit." Alphonse Ardoin's son Morris Ardoin has also served as captain. He comments: "If you don't lay down your rules, you in trouble. 'Cause you got to have rules. Most of 'em know better, but they start drinking and say 'It's Mardi Gras today, I'm free.' Now Mardi Gras *is* a fun day. You're free . . . as long as you want to do right. You can do most all what you want to that day. As long as on the right side. Now if you start disturbing things, you're out." The very clowns who push the bounds of appropriate resistance to the captain are at the same time quite vocal about the importance of a proper individual in the role. Several commented:

> You need an older man that got the respect, that don't have to take that much. You got an older man and no one's going to try and hurt him 'cause you got to respect them. Now someone like Paul Thomas is a good captain, everybody respect him, black and white. They going to see Paul Thomas and say, "Yeah, that's the Mardi Gras, tell them to come."

> You need *un homme* straight, yeah. If a car comes, you need a man who can stop it (i.e., to prevent colliding with clowns on foot on the road).

Now you take C——, he was not a good captain. He drank too much.
Couldn't get you there on time, said bad things to women. He tried to use
a whip.

M—— was not a good captain. He going disturb you "do this, do that,
don't drink, stop, go," aaaaaah . . . that's not good!

Alcius "Bee-fie" Fontenot, the lead clown of the 'Prien Noir Mardi
Gras, who has the fluctuating task of both supporting and resisting the
captain, adds the most serious commentary about the captain's role and
the rules involved: "Mardi Gras is a free day, the Mardi Gras is free.
You obey only the captain. You got to listen to the captain. He's on top.
He keeps what you get (*charité* collected). You'll get it back at the
gumbo. The captain doesn't want us to drink a lot, maybe a young man
can't control himself, the captain sees that." When I asked two individuals familiar with the current lead clown and the demanding role of captain, if the lead clown could ever be considered for the captain's position. The responses were amused and incredulous:

Alcius could never do it, never, oh noooooo. Uh-uh. I'm not a man for
that, but I believe I could do better than Alcius [the lead clown]. I at least
understand how you got to be. But Alcius, he likes to play with all them
kids. You need to be a serious man to be captain.

Alcius goes around all the time saying, "Take it easy." If he went to
somebody's door to ask them to receive the Mardi Gras, he would probably just say, "Take it easy," instead of all the polite things you need to
say. He would mess up.

The notion above, that the lead clown "likes to play with all them
kids" points to the fact that the majority of the clowns are young and
that the older clowns, though figures who sit in judgment on the youthful performers, are themselves often thought of as men who never really
grow up and like to continue to drink, play, and be "road runners." The
captain, in contrast, is a source of ultra-adult style. He is supposed to be
physically strong, older, respected, stern, and polite all at once. Yet, one
of these characteristics alone may not be enough to gain respect. For example, one former captain, criticized as being "drunk" and "too rough,"
was a seventy-nine-year-old who was viewed as abusive of his power,
but not really able to enforce it physically in case of real trouble. Further, he violated the rules by not being "polite." The clowns actually refer to themselves in the song/chant as *politessiens,* an archaic usage referring to "polite ones." It is, however, the captain who is formally
charged with maintaining their "politeness" as they come to beg *charité.*

The captain shows concern that they "work" for the *charité* about to be given and he urges the clowns to perform well. Paul Thomas expects his clowns to obey:

> The rules is I want for him to do something for me in front of the people. It's for him to do it. . . . I don't want you to go by yourself and do something bad. The people is going to say, "Well the captain Paul is coming and he's got good clowns, make a good show, he's nice." But if something don't look too good and people say, "Well he pass here and didn't make too good a show, was acting bad," it's bad on me. They got to follow me like I tell them to do, or someone may say "Paul, how come the clowns made a good show there, but they come here and doesn't want to do good?"

The captain must use his words and behavior to show that he respects the householders and community, can "give a good show," can be tough with the clowns without causing a revolt, and protect the houses and yards of those he visits. His abilities are backed up with the threat of physical action. In that sense, he also is a man who relies upon his reputation for toughness.

The clowns' relationship to the captain is built on a series of symbolic contrasts: he dresses plainly, while they are gaudily dressed; he is a recognizable individual, respected as a leader, while they act collectively in masked anonymity as carousing followers; he makes polite requests and gives commands, while they harass one another and the captain; he works soberly to put on a good show and collects the group's rewards, while they sing, dance, drink, beg for their *charité*, and chase chickens. If the captain represents utmost Creole male respectability, the clowns are an intense caricature of men as makers of mischief. In contrast to everyday life, these two poles of behavior are brought into close proximity in intense stylized forms at Mardi Gras.

The elder lead clown, Alcius "Bee-fie" Fontenot, is a quintessential *homme de plaisir* in everyday life. The father of seventeen, always on the dance hall circuit, he greets all comers with lines like, "Chere, you going to make it, tu vas faire z-haricots?" ("You going to make/harvest beans?" I.e., "Are you getting it together?"). In answer to his own question, he often quickly adds: "We got to make it." In 'Prien Noir there is general acknowledgment that Fontenot is the best of the senior clowns, based on his singing ability, his reliable wit as a joker in the community, and his desire to see that younger men will learn from him.

Fontenot comments on his own ability as follows: "A head Mardi Gras (clown) must have good *politessiens* (polite people to follow him) and be polite. My old uncle started me when I was young, about eighteen. He was good. He taught me just like you go to school. We went for duck, the rice,

chicken, the grease, the *gratons* (cracklings), just like now. If you like Mardi
Gras and you been doing it since you was young, you keep doing it."

As lead clown, Fontenot presents himself as part of the tradition—
having learned from an elder—and as appropriately polite. This man, who
is charged with leading the clowning in the most raucous event in the
Creole community, in inversionary manner reflects with pride on his ex-
cellence at being "bad." Likewise, in his movement from everyday life—
where he is a sometimes disdained carouser—to Mardi Gras, he is provided with a realm in which he is accorded special respect—albeit not of
the same order as that given to the captain.

The lead clown's respect is founded on a turnabout of the everyday
context for his mode as a man of reputation, while the captain's respect
rests on a heightening of his everyday image to keeper of order on the
year's most chaotic day. Together, the lead clown and captain are paired
as the top men of the Mardi Gras. Though the lead clown may chide the
captain, he also basically supports the captain's call for order. While trying to show his raucous individuality, the lead clown equally emphasizes
the collective polite comportment of his fellow men of Mardi Gras. He
particularly scrutinizes the younger clowns, who, he cautions, "[m]ust
learn to do Mardi Gras right before I'm gone."

The Mardi Gras also instructs the young on how to behave and not
to transgress too far in their wayward youthful activities. When a boy
first runs Mardi Gras, it means that he is no longer dictated to by the rule
of his mother to stay home. He is able to go out and be seen publicly
with the band of adult male clowns. On several occasions, I have seen
young boys under age fourteen attempt to get a costume the night before
Mardi Gras, and talk "as if" they will run, only to be held in when mother
finds out the plan. Once a boy does get to join the band, he is usually
with a half dozen others who are new as well. The older young men in
their twenties try to intimidate new clowns, telling them they "better not
fuck up and ruin the Mardi Gras." Likewise, the oldest clowns watch the
attitudes and behavior of both the older young men and the newest
clowns. Some of the young clowns do come in with a rebellious attitude
about what they are going to do on Mardi Gras, as suggested in the comments of one youth who asserted, *"Mardi Gras c'est libre* (it's free) boy,
you sign your name and nobody can fuck with you." The older clowns
spend a fair amount of time before and during Mardi Gras complaining
about such overzealous attitudes and what may be overuse of alcohol
and other stimulants on the *courir*. At the same time, they encourage competition among the boys to catch the most chickens, sing well, and be
good clowns. The oldest men do not chase chickens except for a bird
that flies very near them. When they fortuitously catch such a chicken, a
great show is made with bragging like *"Ça c'est la mode pour 'trappé*

une poule!" ("That's the way to catch a chicken!") Most of the time the older men watch the young clowns in the act. One elder notes: "Them old men they can't run that much, they like to watch the kids run for it. The kids have to show they can do it. If you catch it you got to kill it. A boy has to show they can do it. Each year they do it better. If they put that in their head, they can stand up and see what the old know to do. I was listening to them, they can sing that chorus, *Mon cher camarade,* but not the words."

The younger boys are generally stigmatized as lowly ones who must learn the true way to run Mardi Gras. They get the least favorable position on the truck. The older young men sit or stand at the very back of the truck to act as gatekeepers and safety monitors. They help unload and load the human cargo at each stop—especially when the elders who need assistance are getting off the truck. They are being watched by the oldest clowns to see how well they behave in this intermediate role, but they too are competing with one another to intimidate the younger ones with stories of how they might be thrown off the truck, encounter a mean woman at a particular house, be bitten by a dog, or meet a very drunk and rough Cajun Mardi Gras band on the route.

These older young men also try to show that they can sing and play music. There is usually an up-and-coming singer who leads a chant with as many words as he knows or can make up as the truck rattles down the country roads. Likewise, one or two of these men will compete to see who can best play accordion, thus suggesting that one day they will play the role of the designated musician for Mardi Gras. It is also this group of older young men that urges the Mardi Gras to cover as much ground as possible. Late in the day when the oldest men are tiring and others are getting too drunk to carry on, some of these older young men—and some of the new clowns—may chide those who tire. Often the conflict about how far to go comes at a crossroads where the captain solicits opinions on how much longer the Mardi Gras wishes to run and how much more *charité* is needed to make a "good" gumbo for the supper and dance that evening. A sign of toughness is to be one of the last people to be urging that the Mardi Gras go to another neighbor or another community. At some point the captain takes a consensus reading and makes his evaluation of whether or not the band has gathered enough *charité,* visited all necessary households (i.e., those of close friends, kinfolk, and important people in the community), and how tired the group (especially the older men within it) has become. Finally, it is he who decides that the group will head back to the club for its gumbo supper.

The sense that the Mardi Gras is structured as a series of tests for the young as they mature (emphasizing chasing chickens, toughness for the run, proper singing, and politeness) is a condensed commentary on everyday life, in which men are expected to gain knowledge and hence respectability as they age. Both the young and the lifelong men of reputation of 'Prien Noir are described as "working" on this day of festival play. In everyday life, one criticism made of such men is that they are lazy and do just enough to get by. Young boys are also the focus of concern in everyday life with regard to how well they do their chores and adjust to the realm of work outside of the home. On Mardi Gras, these two groups of males (younger teenagers and older men) are put together as "workers" under the "boss," or captain, who must see to it that they do well. Within the structure of the clown group, the older men expect the boys to do the hardest "work," that of chasing chickens. Ironically, of course, all the "work" is in fact a form of sanctioned play, occurring roughly during the normal hours of everyday work. Compounding the sense of reversal, the work involves begging for food—and the primary food given is the chickens that women usually tend. The men beg for and chase the food source associated with women's work in the yard in order to satisfy their hunger and prove their worthiness as men and clowns.

There is a major difference in the mode of work as well. Creoles and Cajuns alike participate in a form of cooperative labor called *coup de main* in which individuals act collectively to aid one another at harvest time, on a job requiring a group, or when a person is sick and cannot fend for himself. The Mardi Gras clowns operate as a humorous *coup de main* of carousers who will collectively beg the food for the evening meal to which all who contribute will be invited. Thus Mardi Gras draws upon this aspect of everyday community life; however, the food so gained is received not from work but by begging, dancing, and singing. Rather than fully cooperative labor, the mode of gathering is an occasion of individual and intergenerational competition. Such competition runs counter to the "help your neighbor" aspect of a conventional *coup de main*.

Being able to sing the Creole version of the Mardi Gras Song is also bound up with the issues of workmanlike, competent, polite, and adult running of the Mardi Gras. The Mardi Gras song in 'Prien Noir has many variations depending on the situation the clowns wish to comment upon. I recorded this version, followed by an English translation, with all the basic elements in 1977.[10]

> Lead clown: Oh Mardi Gras allons-nous en.
>
> Chorus: Ouais mon/bon cher camarade.
> [not printed hereafter, but repeated after each line]
> Lead clown: On est bon des politessiens qui reviennent beaucoup de
>   loin.
> Mardi Gras est misérab'.

Une poule par an c'est pas souvent.
Not' gombo est réellement faible.
Nous t'invite à manger un bon gombo.
Mardi Gras t'a 'mandé po' nous recevoir.

[dance] "Johnny Peut pas Danser"

Mardi Gras t'a 'mandé pour nous recevoir.
Mardi Gras t'a 'mandé pour nous recevoir.

Une poule par an c'est pas souvent.
Not' gombo est réellement faible.
Not' gombo est réellement fable.
Mardi Gras allons-nous en.

[dance] "Johnny Peut pas Danser"

Mardi Gras est beaucoup satisfaits.
On vous invite pour grand bal à soir chez Monsieur Alphonse Ardoin.

Mardi Gras allons-nous en.
Capitaine voyage ton flag.
Mardi Gras allons-nous en.
On n'a pas souvent beaucoup fait ça.

[dance] "Valse du Grand-Bois"

Mardi Gras allons-nous en.
Allons-nous en de l'aut' paroisse.
Allons-nous en de l'aut' voisin.

Lead clown: Oh Mardi Gras let's go away.

Chorus: Yes my/good dear friend
[not printed hereafter, but repeated after each line]

Lead clown: We are polite people who return from far away.
The Mardi Gras is poor.
One chicken a year is not much.
Our gumbo is really weak.
We invite you to eat a good gumbo.
The Mardi Gras has asked you to receive us.
[dance] "Johnny Can't Dance"

[Next two lines same as above]

One chicken a year is not much.
Our gumbo is really weak.
Our gumbo is really weak.

Mardi Gras let's go away.

[dance] "Johnny Can't Dance"

The Mardi Gras are very satisfied.
We invite you for a big dance tonight at Mr. Alphonse Ardoin's place.
Mardi Gras let's go away.
Captain wave your flag.
Mardi Gras let's go away.
We do not often do that.

[dance] "Big Woods Waltz"

Mardi Gras let's go away.
Let's go away to another parish.
Let's go away to another neighbor.

A special significance of the Mardi Gras Song as performed in 'Prien Noir is how it differs in performance style and practice from that heard in many nearby Cajun Mardi Gras. The responding chorus, *"Ouais, mon/ bon cher camarade"* ("Yes, my/good dear friend"), marks the Creole Mardi Gras Song as different from most Cajun versions. The Cajun song is a continuous text for an individual singer or group of singers, or an instrumental based on the melody sung to this text. The Creole Mardi Gras Song is a chanted call-and-response song with leader(s) and chorus. It is difficult from an ethnomusicological perspective to fully suggest the origins of the 'Prien Noir Creole song style in relation to its survival in the African-French community. It appears to have sources in both medieval French religious chants—and the minor modal scale used in the chant suggests this—and an African-Caribbean leader and responding chorus style. This call-and-response style, with partially improvised text, especially marks the Creole Mardi Gras Song in 'Prien Noir as different from the Cajun Mardi Gras Song, which emphasizes the repetition of a more standardized text to a more elaborated melody by a voice or unison of voices (human or instrumental).

For 'Prien Noir Creoles the song is a means by which the beggar clowns elliptically suggest that they need help from individual households for a community gumbo that is "weak." The same claim is still made at the end of the day when much *charité* has been gathered. It is rhetorically directed at getting *charité* rather than depicting the actual condition of the gumbo. Thus the request in song is essentially a stylized one relating to the day's mission as a whole, rather than a particular paucity. It is asking community support for a community dish. The statement of weakness of the gumbo is tied to an initial invitation "to eat a good gumbo" with the idea that a contribution will make it such. Finally, the last line of the first part reiterates what the entire chant has been about, namely, being received into the yard and treating these clown-beggar-strangers as guests deserving of a gift of *charité*. The song concludes with thanks, *"Mardi Gras est beaucoup satisfaits"* ("The Mardi Gras are very satisfied"). Sometimes the comment *"Madame et Monsieur, merci bien"* ("Madam and Sir, thank you very much") is inserted. An invitation is made for the communal gumbo supper and dance sponsored by the Mardi Gras with a reminder of the location, *"On vous invite pour grand bal à soir chez Monsieur Alphonse Ardoin."* In addition to rewarding the householder with an exchange (an invitation to eat and dance for the *charité* given), it serves to remind all present under whose auspices the run is being carried out—in this case the musician whose family operates the club.

The chorus for the entire chant, *"Ouais mon/bon cher camarade"* ("Yes my/good dear friend"), is found as a single line in some Cajun versions of the song (Oster 1959: 9–10). "My" and "good" are interchangeably used perhaps because they sound similar and do not significantly change the meaning of the entire line. The chorus reinforces the communal nature of the activity as a group responds to a lead singer. The words also state collective assent and affirmation of support.

Although the chant is performed a cappella, it is punctuated by acoustic instrumental versions of the same variety of Creole waltzes and two-steps that would be found at a dance hall or club. These tunes are played so that the clowns, some in female costume, can dance as couples—another inversion of everyday life behavior. This humorous gender-bending behavior at each house symbolically raises the contrasts between the values, styles, work, and roles associated with the sexes.

Une poule par an c'est pas souvent:
Women, Children, Chickens, and Men in Masks

At most households visited in the immediate Creole community, the Mardi Gras runners must deal with a woman.[11] The reason is that the men, unless they are old, are either in the Mardi Gras band or off on their regular job for the day. The presence of the woman as the leader of the house deciding who will get what represents a reversal of the public ideal that the respected male is the final authority on the wealth of the house. In fact, women often privately control the household economic distribution. One woman states flatly, "I decide what to throw for Mardi Gras. They are my chickens, and I'm here. So who's going to decide but me?" The focus that Mardi Gras brings to this situation is an intensification of the reality that women are major contributors to the household economy and have an important, if not publicly acclaimed, say in the everyday use of such family resources. The Mardi Gras in 'Prien Noir also has a long history of being exclusively a men's activity, bent on scaring women and children at the house visit. One woman recalls her childhood view of the Mardi Gras. "You could see them with them high hats from far and they wouldn't run unless they would all be well dressed. Pretty suit, nice costume. I was scared because they was so ugly. They would run after the children outside. They would run you boy, I would stay locked in the room, they'd look in the window and I'd go under the bed." Women are often still frightened by the Mardi Gras. One married woman in her twenties, whose father has been the captain on several occasions, comments: "I've always been scared of the Mardi Gras. I was home alone this year, so I just told daddy to let them pass. I guess ever since I was small, I was afraid of the clowns. You don't know who they are or what they'll do."

Children may scatter or run to the arms of their mothers when the Mardi Gras come. Some who do not get away will cry should the clowns chase them, pick them up, or try to dance with them. Most householders—men, women, and children—stay behind their fences. If a woman is at home with family, she may stay on the (screened) porch area and allow the captain to carry out her directions and act as a temporary male head of the household. Other women show their respectability through personal fortitude in the face of the Mardi Gras. One young woman said jauntily: "I'm not scared of the Mardi Gras, me. I know it's some men. I been raised with Mardi Gras."

Although Creole women have historically not run in the Mardi Gras bands, many are quite frank about demanding respect from the revelers, particularly their own husbands, children, and other kinfolk. Eva Fontenot, the wife of the lead clown and a mother of seventeen children, says:

> There are some days when he don't respect what I do for him. I tried to change him. I couldn't change him, so let him go. I have enough of that Mardi Gras with six of mine (husband and sons) running already. What it is, I'm nervous. Too much drinking and noise get on my nerves. Mardi Gras is a men's run. I guess I'm old-fashioned, but I think women should stick with women, men with men, and childrens with children. I don't think it's right for men and women from everywhere to go together.[12]

Mrs. Fontenot's comments reflect the quintessential standoff between reputation and respectability as played out both in everyday life and symbolically at Mardi Gras. Women are usually the ones at home to receive the Mardi Gras band. As such they remain defenders of their house/yard and respectability-related values in regard to its annual performance. They often control giving of *charité,* and some of them are relied upon to later clean and cook the chickens they largely have provided for the communal gumbo supper.

Chickens are generally a food resource produced in the yard under the supervision of women. In slang, women are often referred to as *une poulette* or *une poule* (a chick, a chicken). In English, men sometimes also refer to wives as "the old hen." Thus, an everyday association between women and their chickens and women as chickens is often drawn. Chickens are also the primary form of *charité* in a Mardi Gras. Without the chicken, there would be no chase in the yard; there would be no meat in the evening gumbo, except for sausage. Chicken is a common, "mainstay" meat in the Creole diet. It does not have the prestige of the hog butchered at Easter or other ceremonial occasions. It is not accorded the status of beef or lamb, which are also butchered for social events and stored frozen for other times. When families want to reward a son, they give him his own cow, sheep, or pig to care for. No one would give chickens as a reward, although women do trade and sell chicks as well as eggs.

At Mardi Gras, the chicken takes on a special status. It is the best *charité* and it is the central food. At Mardi Gras the chicken becomes a hunted animal, coveted by clowning men and taken from its everyday domestic yard domain controlled by women. The transformation of the yard bird into hunted prey is a comic transformation of the everyday. The degree to which it stands for women, their work, and their respectability is also an intensification of how chickens are usually viewed. At Mardi Gras, chickens are beheaded—usually by twirling them by the neck—and afterwards treated with a degree of violence that suggests this is more than the usual killing of a yard chicken. For example, the dead birds, which still move spasmodically, are sometimes passed and kicked like footballs. Sometimes their blood is painted on the face of a clown and the feathers are pulled to use as costume decoration. It is the younger boys, some of whom are squeamish, that are commanded to do these acts.

Carnival is historically laden with food symbolism, especially where the day was oriented toward a final consumption of flesh for the more austere time of Lent (Le Roy Ladurie 1979: 316–17). The men of the 'Prien Noir band confirm their belief that Mardi Gras, at least in part, is about food: "Mardi Gras is to get hungry so that when you go out, you looking for food. When you get back, if it's a good Mardi Gras, then you get your gumbo." The captain, in describing the food activity, adds: "At night, with all the food gathered, the women are cooking outside a gigantic gumbo and everybody stuffs his face. We should not forget that it is Mardi *Gras*. This last word means 'fat.'" While it is women who generally raise the chickens, women who mainly hand them out at Creole Mardi Gras, and women who do most of the cooking, it is men who return with the *charité* and do most of the eating. The wives and daughters of the captain and the elder clowns usually gather earlier in the day to do the food preparation. On the day in which men "work" at play, women do a form of collective toil—plucking, cleaning, and cooking the birds—that they, and others of their gender and the community, gave as *charité*.[13] During this afternoon women's work session, disgruntlement at the Mardi Gras division of labor is often heard. One older woman comments, "This is the way it always is; we always have the hard work us, but not the credit."

Women also handle most of the serving chores at the supper. They wash dishes and utensils for reuse. The cooking, in large iron pots over wood fires, and eating, at makeshift tables of scrap wood, is all done outside, like outdoor festive cooking and eating events run by men at other times. As is often true with everyday rural household meals, women eat after the men. While men's work for the day is transformed to play and begging, women's work becomes intensified in contrast to the play of the Mardi Gras band to include a festive form of cooking usually done by men as well as all the preparation and cleanup work. Yet, the entire community contributes to and consumes the kind of meal (chicken gumbo) which is normally prepared and consumed at home on an everyday basis.

In addition to their major involvement with the *charité* and preparing the food at Mardi Gras, women also work to contribute to at least one other primary material aspect of Mardi Gras symbolism: the costume. Masks are increasingly store bought, but women continue to assemble and sew costumes. Eva Fontenot, the wife of the lead clown, says: "Making a costume is easier than other clothes. You use something that is green, red, odd colors. This year I used orange and black." Ironically, it is also women (and children) who are scared by the Mardi Gras in their costumes of "odd colors." One woman who is scared recalls, "They say don't wear red on Mardi Gras (if you are a woman) or the clowns will get you." Another woman adds, "Red and green are 'show off' colors, and that's what the Mardi Gras does." In daily life, men who consider themselves "hot" or "bad" in reputation often do wear red. Red is also a primary color in Mardi Gras costumes. Red and other colors considered gaudy are thus emphasized in a manner that foregrounds the reputation style of the Mardi Gras. However, as with cooking, women provide the support services for this costumed enactment.

The whole matter of masking and costumes in Carnival and other festival settings has received much attention in the ethnographic literature. The mask at Mardi Gras clearly marks that this is a different time and place than everyday life (Ogibenin 1975: 1–2). A mask isolates the wearer from everyday life, but affirms the wearer's bond to the immediate group of fellow maskers. Within the Mardi Gras, the lack of a mask clearly marks the respectable captain, musicians, and householders in a different grouping, that of respectability, from the clowns who are intensified versions of everyday reputation-seekers. The mask is both a face and an "anti-face" (Ogibenin 1975: 7). It confers anonymity on the clowns at the same time as it inspires fear in some of those visited—even those who know who is who. The mask may embolden the clowns to special feelings and acts of bravado. One clown comments on how a mask makes him feel: "Mardi Gras is *libre*. Nobody can tell you shit for Mardi Gras, white, black, nothing. . . . That's a free day you got. After a while you got that thing on your face and you change into Mardi Gras. They don't know who you are. You can be a Ku Kluck, and you can be a robber, and you can kill somebody and they don't know who you are."

Barry Ancelet suggests that Mardi Gras was traditionally a day to "settle scores" (1982: 1) for men who could not be recognized. This seems more true historically and particularly in the Cajun community celebration than in the Creole Mardi Gras. Though many young Creoles suggest that the mask frees them to do as they please, as with other aspects that near the bounds of propriety in the Mardi Gras, masked license is moderated by the elders. The lead clown Alcius Fontenot says: "You wear a mask so no one knows who you are. You got to wear one. All the Mardi Gras wears one. When you arrive, they can't know you. You don't even want your family to know. They got to treat you as Mardi Gras. You can act nice, but they have to take you seriously as Mardi Gras. But if you go to a store you got to raise that 'cause some store owners get worried."

The clowns of 'Prien Noir insist that the mask be worn at all times in the presence of non-Mardi Gras. En route, they pull them off to drink, smoke, and talk. The older clowns call out to lower the masks when a house is approached. The masks come off for the gumbo supper, but they are put on again for the evening entrance to the dance hall when the men dance together for the final time. The captain explains that the mask makes the dancing of men with men acceptable throughout the day. "When they dance they are masked and it's OK. But we usually don't want that. For women it's OK [to dance together] like that. Women are women, but men do that only on Mardi Gras." Men are affirming their membership in the male festival group where the rule is to break the everyday rule. In a normal dance hall setting, men would not dance with men, but would instead be competing with one another to dance with women.

Masks and costumes in general show a variety of functions and messages. One that is especially significant in the 'Prien Noir Mardi Gras has to do with the external bounds of the community. The Mardi Gras band, in its road travels, behavior, and costuming, becomes marginal to respectable family groups of the community, represented by the householders. Materially this is done by using masks and costumes to be something from outside the community. The traditional pointed *capuchon,* with its medieval origins, is still common in the Creole Mardi Gras, as are harlequin-like (diamond) color sequences. Window screen masks with painted faces have largely been replaced by store-bought, mass-produced masks of specific pop culture characters. Mr. Spock, American presidents, R2-D2, and Spiderman are common, along with devils, women, clowns, and Arabs (very popular in oil-producing south Louisiana since the embargo of the mid-1970s).

There are still some homemade masks that one sees regularly. For example, there are painted female faces (not always fully a mask, but with the same transforming effect) with false breasts and clothing to match. Beyond parodying women, some of the costumes specifically parody whites. In addition to white clown faces, one usually sees at least one Ku Klux Klan outfit with a pointed hood referring to the fearful image of masked white vigilantes—a historical reality in Cajun Louisiana recalled as a present-day problem in the strong support received by former Klansman turned gubernatorial candidate David Duke in many Cajun communities.[14] All these "faces" and guises take the clowns outside the bounds of everyday reality and even beyond the complex color and caste lines characteristic of French Louisiana.

Creole Mardi Gras and Ethnic Boundaries

Mardi Gras involves both Cajun and Creole communities in the southwest Louisiana prairie area. Cajuns, as the dominant social and cultural group in the region, consider the Mardi Gras to be a Cajun cultural activity. Many Cajuns are not aware of the smaller Creole country bands. Some Cajuns tend to view them as a less impressive version of their own run. Creole runners, on the other hand, are very aware of the Cajun bands, partly because the Cajun bands are dominant in the local and national news media prior to Mardi Gras, and they attract increasingly large numbers of tourists. The Cajun Mardi Gras also have a different rhetorical posture toward the community as a whole than the Creole bands. Creoles often experience this posture of the Cajun Mardi Gras when they meet on the road. Whereas Creoles place great emphasis on a good "show" and "politeness," Cajuns tolerate more drunkenness and the potential for individual acts of aggression toward one another (Reed 1975) and occasionally toward tourists and some community figures. Ancelet has characterized the image of the Cajun Mardi Gras in part as "vandalizing" (1989: 4). To this I would add "macho," "frontier," and "cowboy" as words to describe the overall tone of the Cajun runs. Creoles are quite aware of the rougher Cajun style of Mardi Gras. Most do not approve of it and, in some cases, are intimidated by it. The Cajun Mardi Gras style seems to be an intensification of the way things are in everyday life: Cajun males dominate the social, economic, and cultural discourse of the region.

The Creole captain, who in his public-spirited mode generally emphasizes the communality and togetherness of all people in the region as a whole, adds: "In spite of all that togetherness, one thing has to be mentioned. The black men, the Creoles, never mix with the Cajun at Mardi Gras." Historically darker black Creole Mardi Gras also did not mix with lighter *mulâtre* bands either. However, at some point in the 1960s, 'Prien Noir locals say, "*Mulâtres* began to run with blacks, but none tried to run with white. Oh Lord, they'd kill if they did that!" Creoles also use Mardi Gras to differentiate themselves from the black Americans, saying, "They don't know how to do this." There is often amusement in the band when a young Creole man brings home a black friend from college or an urban job site. Everyone watches the visitor for sure signs that he knows nothing about the tradition. Jokes are often played on such black outsiders as a way to encourage them to join the fun and remind them of their status.

More pertinent to the primary ethnic boundary in the countryside, Creoles generally regard the Cajun Mardi Gras as unruly, drunken, and somewhat dangerous. Commenting on a nearby Cajun Mardi Gras group, a Creole clown says:

> It's dangerous to go there 'cause them white guys, them son-of-a-guns get drunk and they want to do this and that, and that's bad. . . . Now they got some good men that's going to handle them if they get too drunk, they going to put them in jail, but they can't fine them 'cause it's Mardi Gras. The captains there really have to watch those men. Here we agree more on how Mardi Gras should be. We don't use a tape of the music, our men know how to sing and run Mardi Gras. . . . A bunch that's small like us, it's pure, we got the real music and dancing here.

Creoles are sometimes stigmatized by Cajuns as "ignorant" and not "real Frenchmen," as well as socially lower. These views particularly infuriate the descendants of the traditionally higher-caste, landowning Creoles of Color. The Creoles at the 'Prien Noir Mardi Gras use the event to assert respectability for their community and for the ethnic group as a whole. This sense of respectable behavior on the part of Creoles comes into high relief particularly when Creoles visit Cajun householders and store owners. In these locations they are determined to do well and prove that they know the tradition. They are also careful to contain the more rowdy elements of their own bunch. They especially delight in positive comments by Cajuns they visit, and they repeat these praises. "People at the [Cajun-operated] country store told me that we had a good Mardi Gras and that we deserved good *charité*. They told me that the L'Anse Maigre Mardi Gras [Cajun] was drunk, didn't dance or anything. They said, 'You're not drunk, you're polite.'"

There are historical reports of violence between whites and blacks at Louisiana Mardi Gras (Tassin 1970: 76–77) and accounts of chicken stealing by Cajun whites from black Creole bands in earlier days (a reversal of the southern stereotype if there ever was one). One man recalls: "In the old times we battled with the L'Anse Maigre Mardi Gras [Cajun] when we met on the road. They tried to get our chickens. Things were worse back then. We couldn't go to their schools. They thought we knew nothing. We were undeveloped. It was closer to slavery then. Things are better now. When we meet now we listen to each other's music. The captain there is a man of good character." Many Creoles disagree that things are completely better now. For example, Alcius Fontenot, the lead clown, says: "Those guys from L'Anse Maigre was drunk [this year]. They say, 'Oh nigger, oh nigger, oh nigger.' They was really drunk, didn't mean nothing, but they did raise the word." In contrast, another person comments as follows about a different Cajun band: "We met the Oberlin Mardi Gras and shook hands with them . . . knew every one of them." It appears, then, that the social relationships between Cajun and Creoles at Mardi Gras are intensified versions of those in everyday life, both good and bad. There are those communities and individual relationships where people get along and there are those where suspicion and distrust are common. In 'Prien Noir, several whites follow the *courir* in cars over some of the route. Local Cajuns also come to the gumbo supper, and some even come to the dance (normally Cajuns do not go to a Creole dance). Sometimes the encounter with a Cajun Mardi Gras is tense; sometimes it is uneventful. The intensification of the festival occasion and the alcohol adds to the seriousness of any overt problem in everyday life.

If Creole Mardi Gras is a time of relative integration (e.g., visits to Cajun homes, Cajuns and other whites following the band, and attending the supper and dance), it is also a time of segregation with the history of the social barriers heightened in the minds of some (e.g., separate bands, chicken stealing, racial epithets, and tense encounters on the road). If there is a central message regarding ethnic boundaries at the 'Prien Noir Mardi Gras, it is the assertion by the group that Creoles as a whole are respectable people, knowledgeable about their traditions, and that they have the right to show off their respectability as well as their reputation in carrying out their Mardi Gras on this special day.

Mardi Gras as Heritage and the Future of Creole Culture

In recent years the Creole Mardi Gras in 'Prien Noir and other communities where I attended have shown elements of change. In the mid-1980s, women and young children began to run. Along with this new inclusiveness, a mood of reflection about Creole heritage was emerging. There was an increasing consciousness about wearing costumes that showed "African" influences or showed careful homemade work to emphasize "authenticity." Youths who had gone off to college brought back friends, black and white, to share in the Mardi Gras and "experience my culture," in the words of one young man. Other youths who had moved to town in search of work also came back with friends. Together an array of perspectives, from urban African America, from working class to upwardly mobile—all more conscious of varieties of cultural heritage—came to the Mardi Gras and Creole community life in general.

This transformation was and is part of broader social change as Creoles of all shades of ethnic, class, and regional affiliation entered a period of the greatest reflexivity in their over two-and-a-half-century history as a group in Louisiana and the Gulf South. Historically, such group consciousness has come about in periods when questions of Creole ethnic identity were raised along racial lines from the Civil War to the Civil Rights era. Creole self-scrutiny of ethnicity has been accelerated in the later twentieth century as people have left the land and the relative social isolation of rural communities to move to towns and cities in and beyond Louisiana, from Lake Charles and Houston to Los Angeles and Oakland. In urban settings, Creoles have encountered and been assimilated into black American society and culture at a much greater rate than possible in country settings. In urban settings Creoles are also more frequently evaluated by others as black Americans. The increased identity shift from African-French Creole to African American through urbanization has been augmented by the national media, which provides black entertainment genres and projects a social order in which to be black is to be an English-speaking African American. However, the acculturation and assimilation of Creoles has by no means been complete.

There remain many rural speakers of French Creole and Cajun French in the Creole population. French folk Catholicism persists among Creoles, and, most germane to our interests, Creole communities still run Mardi Gras and participate in zydeco dances—the latter genre, transformed as a regional/ethnic commercial music, has become the most prominent symbol of Creole culture. With Creoles now at both the most acculturated and most reflexive period in the history of the group, their surviving cultural traditions—particularly those symbolic forms that can address the nature of their ethnic identity and community life—have been thrown into high relief.[15]

At the local level the 'Prien Noir Mardi Gras has undergone transformations in recent years that reflect changes in both the Creole value system and larger social and cultural contexts. The presence of women, girls, and young children running Mardi Gras, though they usually have made up no more than 7 to 10 percent of the *courir,* has reduced some of the symbolic tension between domains of men and women and young and old as the event and ones like it in other Creole communities move more toward a local celebration of group heritage. The boys are no longer as strictly part of a socially delimited male *rite de passage.* Children are clearly not as scared by the older symbols and actions of the Mardi Gras or they would not feel comfortable running with them. However, changes in the content of Creole Mardi Gras have been rationalized in traditional terms by Captain Paul Thomas. "When all them girls and young ones started coming it must be that we got something good, if they wanted to come. Running after a chicken is a big thing now. Looks to me like the young ones is getting with that."

As a revered elder, he accepts the change and deems it good for the community. He also admonishes the clowns in his morning speech to "respect them girls" and thereby invokes the traditional ideal value adhering to women. The same captain also carefully watches the women runners and sees that they sit in the back of his smaller truck, a place once reserved for male elders, and considered the best ride on the run. An elder clown also accepts the girls' presence in terms of tradition, saying, "Well Mardi Gras is *libre* you know so you can put into Mardi Gras what you want, even girls I guess."

Young Creole men increasingly now use Mardi Gras to new ends that satisfy their more urban African-American aesthetics. For example, some of the men from the city, in a mocking of urban gangs and their own return to the country, painted "The Duralde Gang" (referring to the place name nearest 'Prien Noir on the map) on the back of their costumes. Another man from the country, who now lives in Lake Charles and is very interested in his "African roots," had his wife make a costume in the African nationalist colors of red, black, and green—which are not that different from traditional Mardi Gras colors anyway. He also added primary blue and yellow trim and commented that his costume "looks African, man, you know like all that African art with them intense colors." While these new costumes still conform generally to a rural Creole Mardi Gras aesthetic, they also indicate the African-American orientation of the urban men as well by commenting on urban social life and pride in perceived African ancestry and culture.

The young men returning from the city also have made some transformations in the song as well. Though some have tried to learn the French words and even play the accordion, many interject their own lyrics, in which the response to the leader's song may be parodied. Instead of *"Ouais mon cher camarade,"* the youthful chorus has been heard to chant "We don't mess around!" as they pursue the chickens. In so doing, they use urban black (non-French) "rap" style (with reputation-oriented content) in a rural Creole French festival setting, thus showing a dual affiliation and competence in two cultural realms of expression. The elders did not approve, but neither did they forbid the young men from singing in this manner. One of the urban clowns, descended from the first family to settle in 'Prien Noir, said, "I don't speak no French, this is my first year running from Lake Charles. We the punks from the city."

In contrast to the urban African-American influences in costume and song style, another new symbolic use of rural Creole Mardi Gras is found in the subgroup formed by some of the more educated young urban and suburban Creoles called "the Executives." The Executives wear a variety of masks, from a gorilla mask to a white clown mask, but all try to show in some way that they are businessmen. Some wear wide, out-of-fashion ties, others carry briefcases, still others have their costumes tailored to look like suits, although they are in the outrageous colors of Mardi Gras. They usually ride in their own separate "executive car" (a customized Volkswagen Super Beetle one year). In one instance an executive caught a chicken and stuffed it into his briefcase to return it to the captain. The festive conjoining of the rurally raised food source with the trappings of middle-class status is another example—in this case a new layer—of symbolizing by dislocating. The Mardi Gras setting gives these young men a chance to express humor about and frustration with middle-class professional life (from which they are still largely excluded) by uniting the supposed high-status accouterments of that life (clothes, briefcase, and car) with the costumes, chickens, and antics of Mardi Gras.

Beyond all the transformations of content, in the years since my primary field study the younger kinfolk who grew up in 'Prien Noir have moved the celebration to the back streets of urban Lake Charles. This has occurred as elders have retired or died and fewer young men live in the rural area to carry it on. The initial results in Lake Charles were not totally satisfying; as one participant recounted, "Man did you ever try to stop city traffic or dive on concrete to chase a chicken?" However, lately, with the leadership of Alphonse Ardoin's son Lawrence "Black" Ardoin, also a musician, this event has grown to embrace a larger dance and Creole cultural festival in the city.

Such developments are important in the regional dialogue in French Louisiana about cultural significance and conservation. Cajuns are the organizers and primary participants in the vast array of product and food festivals (rice, sugar, oyster, boudin, frog, *cochon de lait,* etc.) in the region (Spitzer 1985: 331), many of which started in the 1930s. When Creoles participate in Cajun-dominated festivals, it is historically in a secondary manner. Some communities celebrate Cajun heritage days with French food and music, and there is even a Cajun Hall of Fame. Creoles and their culture are rarely foregrounded or given credit in such settings—despite the profound Creole influences on cuisine and music in the area, including those influences considered to be Cajun that are actually Creole.

Creole control of their own community performance genres, like a small Mardi Gras, is especially important in light of the "Cajunization" of the public regional discourse of south Louisiana. Mardi Gras retains symbolic significance within the Creole community as well. Several rural Creole Mardi Gras runs and historically related trail rides continue to this day, and the Lake Charles festival evolution from the original 'Prien Noir run shows how a tradition may be transformed to reflect new conditions. The future of the African-French Creole culture of Louisiana depends in large part on Creoles who have not been displaced and separated from their cultural landscapes or traditions by social and economic conditions. Creoles who are aware of their traditional aesthetics and values will be best suited to control the evolution and representation of their cultural symbols for themselves and larger society. The increasing public presentation and self-consciousness involved in the new urban running of the 'Prien Noir Mardi Gras suggests that this traditional group performance genre—along with more widely traveled zydeco music—will continue to be an aesthetically accepted and enjoyed expression of Creole values and ethnicity at a community level appropriate to conditions of the late twentieth century.

Notes

1. For an overview of Mardi Gras celebrations on the Gulf Coast, see my entry "Mardi Gras" in *The Encyclopedia of Southern Culture* (1989: 1230–33).
2. Observations of a similar sort are reported from an array of Mediterranean and African-Caribbean societies. See especially the work of Peter Wilson (1969). For more in-depth examination of this topic in Creole Louisiana, see Spitzer (1986a: 225–99).
3. The most significant group expression of Creoles throughout the region is zydeco music and the dance events where it is performed. For an examination of rural zydeco and its relation to Mardi Gras see Spitzer (1986a: 300–410 and 522–51) and also my entry "Zydeco" in *The Encyclopedia of Southern Culture* (1989: 1037–38). See also the film *Zydeco: Creole Music and Culture in Rural Louisiana.* For an additional perspective, see the chapter by Barry Ancelet in this volume.
4. The fieldwork observations in this essay were made at several Mardi Gras cel-

ebrations between 1975 and 1983. Oral quotations in this chapter are based on interviews conducted during this fieldwork and in the two years thereafter. Given the constantly changing nature of Mardi Gras and the social and cultural flux in Creole communities, the descriptions here should be considered a part of the recent ethnohistory. A larger work in progress will update many of the observations herein and deal more broadly with Mardi Gras, zydeco, and Creole identity.

5. One exception to this is a pageant form of parody known as a "womanless wedding" held at a benefit zydeco dance. This occurred only once in my experience over a ten-year period.

6. Folklorists Roger Abrahams and Richard Bauman, in their comparison of the European-derived Nova Scotian Christmas festival and a creolized (with strong African influence) West Indian Carnival, similarly suggest that festivals are not an antithesis of everyday life behaviors, but the "antithesis of behavior called for by the *ideal* normative system" (1978: 195).

7. For an elaboration of the ways in which festival time and festivals in general operate in a variety of cultures, see Falassi (1987).

8. This oscillation between organizational principles and behavioral realms, what Beverley Stoeltje calls "repetition and simultaneity" as a form of festival communication (1983: 40), characterizes many of the symbolic means of the Mardi Gras celebration.

9. This usage reminds us that chickens, unlike captains and men in general, are associated with timidity and fear. This association of meaning with chickens will be elaborated upon later.

10. For recorded samples of the Cajun Mardi Gras song listen to Swallow LP 6019, *The Balfa Brothers Play More Traditional Cajun Music* (1976), and *Folksongs of the Louisiana Acadians,* Arhoolie 5009, edited by Harry Oster (1959). For an example of this Creole chant, listen to my LP *Zodico: Louisiana Créole Music* on Rounder Records LP 6009 (1978) or Lamberton and Spitzer's National Public Radio program, "Bon Cher Camarade: Cajun and Creole Music of Southwest Louisiana" (1980).

11. Out of twenty-five Creole house visits in one year, eighteen were tended to by women. The percentages reverse drastically when visiting Cajuns, where three out of fifteen visited had women acting as the household leader, and one of those refused their visit because no men were home.

12. She is alluding to the fact that women and children are now starting to run Mardi Gras, a change discussed below.

13. Claude Levi-Strauss suggests that animal species and their use often provide "conceptual support" for social differentiation (1963: 92–104). In this case the use of the chicken provides a symbolic means for social criticism based on such differentiation.

14. Although the Klansman is a solitary figure in my observations of Creole Mardi Gras in and beyond 'Prien Noir, many of the Cajun Mardi Gras runs feature one or more *negresse* figures. This is a large black-faced, ape-like female impersonator with exaggerated features. Her behavior, in addition to general mischief making, usually involves assaulting the clowns in a sexual manner. This race and gender stereotype figure widely used by Cajun Mardi Gras has no exact parallel among Creole Mardi Gras. As noted, Creoles do have white-faced clowns and there is sometimes a Ku Klux Klan costume, but the former is not a widespread, grotesque, or as central a figure—and of course Klansmen really do exist. Why the *negresse* figure is so popular with Cajuns merits further examination. For vi-

sual documentation of the Cajun Mardi Gras *negresse*, see Pat Mire's film *Dance for a Chicken* (1993).

15. For more commentary on the new Creole reflexivity, see the chapter by James Dormon in this volume. See also my earlier comments on the roles of zydeco and Mardi Gras in the public representation of Creole culture in and beyond French Louisiana (1986a: 522–51).

References

Abrahams, Roger D., and Richard Bauman. 1978. "Ranges of Festival Behavior." In Barbara A. Babcock, ed. 193–208. *The Reversible World: Symbolic Inversion in Art and Society*. Ithaca: Cornell Univ. Press.

Ancelet, Barry Jean. 1982. "Courir de Mardi Gras." *Louisiane* 54: 1–10.

———. 1989. *"Capitaine, voyage ton flag": The Traditional Cajun Country Mardi Gras.* Lafayette: The Center for Louisiana Studies, Univ. of Southwestern Louisiana.

Balfa Brothers. 1976. *The Balfa Brothers Play More Traditional Cajun Music.* Swallow LP 6019.

Da Matta, Roberto. 1984. "Carnival in Multiple Planes." In John J. MacAloon, ed. 208–40. *Rite, Drama, Festival, Spectacle: Rehearsals Toward a Theory of Cultural Performance.* Philadelphia: Institute for the Study of Human Issues.

Duvignaud, Jean. 1976. "Festivals: A Sociological Approach." *Cultures* 3 (1): 13–25.

Falassi, Alessandro, ed. 1987. *Time out of Time: Essays on the Festival.* Albuquerque: Univ. of New Mexico Press.

Lamberton, Deborah Jane, and Nicholas R. Spitzer. 1980. "Bon Cher Camarade: Cajun and Creole Music of Southwest Louisiana." 90-minute radio documentary. Washington, D.C.: National Public Radio.

Leach, E. R. 1961. *Rethinking Anthropology.* Reprint, London School of Economics Monographs in Social Anthropology No. 22. London: Athlone Press, 1971.

Leach, Maria, ed. 1949. *Standard Dictionary of Folklore Mythology and Legend.* Reprint, New York: Funk and Wagnalls, 1972.

Le Roy Ladurie, Emmanuel. 1979. *Carnival in Romans.* Trans. Mary Feeney. New York: George Braziller.

Levi-Strauss, Claude. 1963. *Totemism.* Translated by Rodney Needham. Boston: Beacon Press.

Mire, Pat. 1993. *Dance for a Chicken: The Cajun Mardi Gras.* Documentary film. Eunice, Louisiana: Attakapas Productions.

Ogibenin, B. L. 1975. "Mask in the Light of Semiotics—A Functional Approach." *Semiotica* 13: 1–9.

Oster, Harry, ed. 1959. *Folksongs of the Louisiana Acadians.* Arhoolie LP 5009. Recorded and edited with brochure notes by Harry Oster.

Oster, Harry, and Revon Reed. 1960. "Country Mardi Gras in Louisiana." *Louisiana Folklore Miscellany* 1 (1): 1–17.

Reed, Roy. 1975. "Mardi Gras Cajuns Revel on Horses." *New York Times,* Feb. 12, 1975.

Singer, Milton, ed. 1959. *Traditional India: Structure and Change.* Philadelphia: American Folklore Society.

Spitzer, Nicholas R., ed. 1978. *Zodico: Louisiana Créole Music.* Rounder LP 6009. Recorded and edited with booklet notes by Nicholas R. Spitzer.

———, ed. 1985. *Louisiana Folklife: A Guide to the State.* Baton Rouge: Louisiana Folklife Program.

————. 1986a. "Zydeco and Mardi Gras: Creole Identity and Performance Genres in Rural French Louisiana." Ph.D. diss., Univ. of Texas, Austin.

————. 1986b. *Zydeco: Creole Music and Culture in Rural Louisiana.* El Cerrito, Calif.: Flower Films.

————. 1989. "Mardi Gras." in Charles R. Wilson and William Ferris, eds. *Encyclopedia of Southern Culture.* 1230–33. Chapel Hill: Univ. of North Carolina Press.

Stoeltje, Beverley J. 1983. "Festival in America." In Richard M. Dorson, ed., *Handbook of American Folklore.* 338–246. Bloomington: Univ. of Indian Press.

Tassin, Anthony. 1970. "Mardi Gras in Edgard." *Louisiana Folklore Miscellany* 3 (1): 76–77.

Turner, Victor W. 1969. *The Ritual Process.* Chicago: Aldine Publishing Company.

————. 1984. "Liminality and the Performative Genres." In John J. MacAloon, ed. *Rite, Drama, Festival, Spectacle: Rehearsals Toward a Theory of Cultural Performance.* 19–41. Philadelphia: Institute for the Study of Human Issues, 1984.

Wilson, Peter J. 1969. "Reputation vs. Respectability: A Suggestion for Caribbean Ethnology." *Man* 4: 70–84.

SIX

Barry Jean Ancelet

Zydeco/Zarico:
The Term and the Tradition

Like the blues and jazz, rock and reggae, the music of the Louisiana black Creoles usually called zydeco is the result of a typically American experience that blended European (primarily French, but also Spanish, German, and English), Native American, and Afro-Caribbean musical traditions. Lawrence W. Levine describes a similar blending process in Afro-American music which produced "a hybrid with a strong African base" (Levine 1977: 24). The American colonial context was basic to the development of these hybrid music forms. Nothing quite like them developed in Europe where direct contact with African culture was rare and exotic. In Africa, the closest parallel is the high-life tradition, born of the influence of the colonial French on native African culture. In America, both European and African cultures were far from home, on new ground. Settlers and slaves learned some old ways from each other and made up lots of new ways for themselves as they carved out a new world on the frontier.

Among the most important influences in this new blend was percussion. This new music was hard-driving, polyrhythmic dance music. Early planters tried with more or less success to prohibit drumming on the plantation (Epstein 1977: 52). For one thing, planters supposedly feared that slaves would use a secret language of drums to communicate among themselves. For another, drumming was the heartbeat of African cultural expression. Eliminating the practice would help to assimilate any reluctant subjects. Yet, it is impossible to prevent people from drumming in real life. There are too many opportunities to improvise. A log, box, table, or chair can easily become a drum with the simple addition of two sticks. Even without any additional objects, the body can be used to produce rhythmic sounds: slapping hands on thighs, clapping hands, stomping feet, etc. Put several people doing complementary rhythms together with such improvised "drums" and the result is remarkably close to the polyrhythmic beat of an African musical event. This critical African tradition may also have been reinforced by an overlap with Native American drumming. In any case, it survived to provide a beat for zydeco and Cajun music, as well as for rock, rhythm and blues, jazz, soul, hip hop, and other black-influenced American music styles.

Zydeco, zarico, zodico, zordico, and even *zologo* represent a few of the spellings used by folklorists, ethnomusicologists, record producers, and filmmakers, as well as dance hall owners and fans, to transcribe the word performers use to describe Louisiana's black Creole French music. The word *creole,* which originally meant simply "native or homegrown, not imported," served, among other things, to distinguish *esclaves africains* (African slaves) from the more valuable *esclaves créoles* (Creole slaves). In south Louisiana, where the French language is an important cultural identity marker, French-speaking blacks often call themselves *Créoles noirs* (black Creoles) or *Créoles de couleur* (Creoles of Color) to distinguish themselves from French-speaking whites, who might be either *Créoles français* (French Creoles) or *Cadiens* (Cajuns), as well as from English-speaking blacks, who are called *nègres américains* (American Negroes). Historically, black Creoles spoke a French-influenced Creole dialect. Many who live in the old plantation belt along the Mississippi River and on the western edge of the Atchafalaya Basin still speak a version of that Creole dialect. Eventually, most of those living on the southwest prairies came to speak a French dialect resembling that of their Cajun neighbors. Today, many members of the older generations still speak French or Creole or both, as well as the English they learned in school, while members of the younger generations tend to speak little or no French or Creole.

Because its first language was French or Creole, the zydeco tradition was a mystery to most outsiders. Native Louisiana Creoles explain that the word comes from *les haricots* because of the expression, *"Les haricots sont pas salés"* ("The beans aren't salty"), a phrase often heard in traditional songs. The spelling *zydeco* was the first one to appear in print. It was first used by record producer Mack MacCormack to transcribe the sound he heard from musicians in the Houston area in the early 1960s, and the term is the most widespread. Most record companies favor it, including Chris Strachwitz's California-based Arhoolie Records, which released most of "Zydeco King" Clifton Chenier's major recordings. This spelling comes from an Anglo-American's attempt to render the flapped [r] in *les haricots.* The "z" sound would then come from the liaison with the "s" of "les" as in *les hommes* or *les hôtels.* Although contemporary French grammar frowns on this liaison because the "h" in *haricot* is now considered aspirate, Cajun and Creole French dialects preserve the former pronunciation of *les haricots* without the aspirate "h."

So, then, what's in a name? Sometimes that depends on how you spell it, and who's doing the spelling. Québecois filmmaker André Gladu drew criticism from Strachwitz for entitling his 1984 film on Louisiana black Creole music *Zarico.* Strachwitz maintained that the standard spelling of the term was *zydeco* and that derivations unnecessarily cloud the issue and dilute the potential for interest. Gladu claimed this was a colonialistic foul and countered with the explanation that *zydeco* is based on superimposed English phonetics, while *zarico* respects the tradition's own French language connection by using French phonetics to render the term. Ironically, this French connection is the result of an earlier colonial influence. Thus, the politics, not to mention the economics, of culture spilled over into the realm of linguistics. The debate over whether to spell the term according to precedent or to perceived cultural appropriateness continues. This question is complicated further by the recent discovery of apparent African influences that may need to be taken into account.

Folk spellings and folk etymologies often develop to explain or rationalize words and expressions whose origins or exact meaning have become unclear, especially among people who had no way of knowing what a word looked like until relatively recently, when they learned to read. The attempts of folks to make sense of a term which has strayed, for one reason or another, from its original usage often yield related, though indirectly connected, meanings, much like "for all intents and purposes" can become "for all intensive purposes" and "taking something for granted" can become "taking something for granite." Similarly, in south Louisiana, the name given to the nocturnal witch-rider, the widely perceived cause of what is medically described as sleep apnea, is *couche-mal,* literally "sleep poorly," an adaptation of *cauchemar,* French for "nightmare."

In the same way, words sometimes survived the efforts of antebellum planters to eliminate African languages among their slaves, but they shifted slightly in the process. In Louisiana French Creole animal tales, for example, the dupe of Lapin (rabbit) is named Bouki. The word *bouki* is Wolof for "hyena," traditionally the hare's dupe in West African animal tales. No traditional storytellers report knowing the original meaning of *bouki,* yet the term has survived and been extended to cover generally any foolish character or person. Another African survival, *gumbo,* is still used in its original sense to refer to okra, but also has come to mean the soupy dish it is used to make. Similarly, *congo* came to mean "dark" or "black" and, by extension, "water moccasin," a snake that is dark grayish brown or black in color, by association with the color of the slaves who came from that area of Africa. The popular Cajun song, "Allons danser, Colinda," in which a singer exhorts a young lady named Colinda to dance with him while her mother is not around, is a borrowing from Creole tradition (Bernard and Girouard 1992). The calinda or kalinda was an African dance slaves performed despite the interdictions of their masters (Epstein 1977: 30–33), and the expression *"Allons danser calinda"* probably meant "Let's dance the calinda."

The explanation that zydeco comes from the expression "Les haricots sont pas salés" has generally been "taken for granite" by musicians, record producers, and scholars. A collection of traditional Creole music recorded by French ethnomusicologist Jean-Pierre LaSelve (1980) on Rodrigue, a remote island in the Indian Ocean, includes an intriguing song entitled "Cari zarico," a group song accompanied by clapping hands, stamping feet, drums and a triangle, with the following verse:

Idée moi, idée toi, Azéline.	I'm thinking the same thing you're thinking, Azéline.
Cari zarico.	Hot bean soup.
Quand la lune fé séga mouliné.	When the moon dances the séga, we'll harvest.
Cari zarico.	Hot bean soup.
	(LaSelve 1980)

Despite the literal translation, it seems safe to assume that bean soup was not uppermost on the singer's mind; courtship was. Yet, the singers used the expression "cari zarico" as a repetitive, seemingly unrelated chorus throughout the song. When asked about this, LaSelve explained that singing about beans is part of a musical tradition called "séga zarico," which exists on Rodrigue and several other Creole-speaking islands in the Indian Ocean. The traditional dance associated with this music re-enacts the planting of beans: the woman walks backward, pretending to make a hole with her heel by stamping on the floor, and the man walks toward her, placing an imaginary seed in the hole and covering it with his foot. The obvious connection between beans and dance, harvest and fertility rituals among Indian Ocean Creoles suggests that a look beneath the surface of the Louisiana Creole zydeco tradition might prove interesting.

Louisiana Creole and Rodrigue Creole cultures share similar origins and development patterns. They were both colonized by French planters in the eighteenth century. The first slaves brought to the Indian Ocean islands were not from the nearby east African coast, but from the west coast, the same area exploited for the American slave trade. Both cultures speak closely related varieties of French-based Creole. Both share preoccupations derived from a common heritage, such as the setting sun and the rising moon, stemming from both harvest rituals and ordinances that forbade slaves to be away from the plantation after dark. From Rodrigue, we hear:

Soleil couché, maman, la lune levé,   The sun is setting, mother, the
   no allé.   moon is rising, we go.
O hé, la saison là.   O hey, the season (the time) has
                                      arrived.

La saison, la saison, la saison là,   The season, the season, the season
   no allé.   (the time) has arrived, we go.
O hé, la saison là.   O hey, the season (the time) has
                                      arrived.

                                             (LaSelve 1980)

and from Louisiana:

O soleil après coucher,   Oh the sun is setting,
O la lune après lever.   Oh the moon is rising.
Mmm, mon nègre est pas arrivé   Mmm, my man has not arrived.

Mmm, malheureux, nègre,   Mmm, unhappy one, man,
O c'est malheureux . . .   Oh it's sad . . .

O mais quinze jours passés,   Oh fifteen days ago,
O les promesses tu m'as fait,   Oh the promises you made to me,
O chèr ami, mon nègre.   Oh dear friend, my man.

O soleil apé coucher   Oh the sun is setting
To connais la promesse tu   You know the promise you
   me fais moi   made to me
Sur un jeudi soir qui passé.   On a Thursday night past.

O la lune après lever,   Oh the moon is rising,
O soleil après coucher,   Oh the sun is setting,
Mmm, là-bas chez Moreau.   Mmm, over at Moreau's place.
O cherche ton candi, nègre . . .   Oh seek your candy, man . . .

                (Lomax 1934)

    In Louisiana, instrumental dance bands play waltzes and two-steps. In Rodrigue, they play waltzes and ségas. In both cultures, the dance bands are built around an accordion, a fiddle, and a triangle. Since they share so many elements, it is at least plausible that their preoccupation with beans is more than coincidental. English blues scholar Samuel Charters alluded to a similar realization in his book *The Roots of the Blues: An African Search* when, faced with a ceremonial procession in Banjul that looked for all the world like those of the black Mardi Gras Indians of New Orleans, it occurred to him that "To Weh Bakaweh" (a traditional Mardi Gras chant) "must be African, a phrase from one of the languages along this coast, though I was never able to locate it" (Charters 1982: 69).

The languages of west African tribes affected by the slave trade may provide some clues as to the origins of zydeco, though they are admittedly still vague. In at least a dozen languages from this culture area of Africa, the phonemes [za], [ré], and [go] are frequently associated with dancing and/or playing music, most notably among the Yula, where "a zaré" means "I dance" (Sigismund 1963). With the cultural and circumstantial evidence enhancing the case, it is tempting to pursue the link between these tribal languages and the proverbial expression concerning unsalted beans. The recurring refrain supposedly about unsalted beans may be built upon older sounds, no longer understood, and now distorted into more familiar, intelligible words, changing the denotation while preserving the connotation.

Levine maintains that "in America as in Africa Negro music, both vocal and instrumental, was intimately tied to body movement" (1977: 16). In south Louisiana, zydeco refers to dance styles as well as to the music associated with them. The meaning of the term has expanded (or survived) to refer also to the music, the musicians, the dance, and the entire social event. Creoles go to a zydeco to dance the zydeco to zydeco music played by zydeco musicians. The term is used to exhort dancers, as in the opening dialogue between zydeco king Clifton Chenier and his brother Cleveland on their classic recording of the tradition's title song, "Zydeco est pas salé":

Clifton: Hé, toi! Tout quelque est correct?	Hey, you. Is everything all right?
Cleveland: C'est bon, *boy.*	It's good, boy.
Clifton: Tout quelque chose est magnifique, hein?	Everything's wonderful, eh?
Cleveland: O oui. Qui to veux dire avec ça?	Oh, yes. What do you mean by that?
Clifton: Allons les haricots/zydeco, nègre!	Let's ———, man!
Cleveland: Allons couri à la yé.	Let's run after them.
	(Arhoolie 1082)

If zydeco meant only beans, then Clifton's last sentence would not be grammatically sound: "Let's go the beans, man!" Yet, neither the late Clifton Chenier nor his Creole compatriots were in the habit of speaking nonsense in their own language. If, however, zydeco is taken to be verb, with "les" being a direct-object pronoun, instead of an article, Clifton makes much better sense: "Let's zydeco them, man!" or "Let's go zydeco, man!" One connotation seems to be associated generally with Creole music and dancing. There are many other examples of this usage, such as "Nous autres va zydeco," "Zydeco tout la nuit," or, in English, "Zydeco, baby!" "Zydeco down!" and "We're going to zydeco all night long." Community musicians are described as zydeco kings, queens, and princes. Community dance events, which provide the primary opportunity for courtship, are announced as zydecos. Dance events are also referred to as "la-las" or simply as French dances, to distinguish black Creole events from disco, soul, or rhythm and blues gatherings.

Clifton Chenier's classic song, recorded in the 1950s, is thought by some to have given a name to this musical style. It is based on "Hip et Taïau," a French Acadian folk song about two thieving dogs:

C'est Hip et Taïau, [cher],	It's Hip and Taïau, dear,
Qu'a volé mon traineau, [cher].	That stole my skid, dear.
Quand [ils ont] vu j'étais chaud, [cher],	When they saw that I was mad, dear,
Ils ont ramené mon traineau, [cher].	They returned my skid, dear.
	(cf. Whitfield 1939 [1969]: 106)

Clifton's version continues to tell basically the same story in fractured form, but adds seemingly unrelated bridges ostensibly about unsalted beans:

O Mama!	Oh Mama!
Quoi elle va faire avec le nègre?	What's she going to do with the man?
Les zydeco est pas salé.	The beans/zydeco aren't salted.
Les zydeco est pas salé.	The beans/zydeco aren't salted.
T'as volé mon traineau.	You stole my sled.
T'as volé mon traineau.	You stole my sled.
Regarde les Hip et Taïau . . .	Look at Hip and Taïau . . .
	(Arhoolie 1082)

The occurrence of the expression "Les zydeco sont pas salés" in the seemingly unrelated bridges of several Louisiana Creole songs from the 1934 collection of Alan Lomax, as well as in modern zydeco music, suggests origins even beyond the phrase's functional folk etymology. In one Lomax recording, Wilbur Charles, a Creole migrant farm worker, concludes an unusual song—again borrowed from French Acadian tradition—about Italians lying in ditches apparently ill from having eaten rotten bananas with the following verses:

Quoi il n-a? Quoi il n-a avec ma femme?	What's the matter? What's the matter with my wife?
Ma femme, elle est malade, couchée côté de les vieux Dégos.	My wife is sick, lying next to the old Italians.
Dégo.	Italian.
Les haricots sont pas salés.	The beans/zydeco aren't salted.
Quoi il n-a, mon cher ami? Quoi il n-a?	What's the matter, my dear friend? What's the matter?
Les haricots sont pas salés.	The beans/zydeco aren't salted.
O yaïe! O mon nègre! Les haricots sont pas salés.	Oh yaïe! Oh my man! The beans/zydeco aren't salted.
Pas mis de la viande, pas mis à rien, Juste des haricots dans la chaudière. Les haricots sont pas salés.	Didn't put meat, didn't put anything else, Only beans in the pot. The beans/zydeco aren't salted.

(Lomax 1934)

The beans are unsalty because the cook has no meat to add to the pot. Before the days of refrigeration, a common way of preserving meat was to salt it away. Adding this salt meat to sauces, soups, and beans provided seasoning as well as protein. "Les haricots sont pas salés," then, may refer to hard times and, by association, to the music that helped to endure them. One is also left to wonder what the singer's wife is doing lying in the ditch with the old Italians in the first place, sick or not. Thus "Les haricots/zydeco sont pas salés" seems also to appear in situations that feature frustrated courtship or unhappy relationships. In English-speaking African-American tradition, this music is called the blues, whether it is a "low-down" blues lament, which relieves by purging, or a jumping, juking blues, which relieves by distracting.

The laments and field hollers that were in English in the rest of the plantation South were in French in south Louisiana. Consequently, zydeco's bluesy side is sometimes based on melodies and rhythms that resemble those of the southern blues tradition. Other times, the confluence of European and Afro-Caribbean rhythms and sources produced haunting songs in 3/4 time that function equally well as blues laments and as waltzes. Creole fiddler Canray Fontenot explained that, as late as his own youth and young adulthood in the 1930s and 1940s, the blues were considered barroom music, and respectable families did not allow the blues to be played at their house dances (Fontenot 1977). Musicians circumvented this proscription by converting their blues tunes into acceptable dance forms, such as the waltz. Fontenot's recording of "Les barres de la prison" is an excellent example of this style (Arhoolie 1070).

An important step in the development of what is now called zydeco was juré tradition, recorded in Louisiana by Alan Lomax during 1934. The Louisiana Creole counterpart of French Acadian *danses rondes* and Anglo-American play-party songs, these unaccompanied group songs were performed for dancers during times when instrumental music was either proscribed (as during Lent or periods of mourning) or simply unavailable. They resemble the Rodriguais séga zydecos in style and beat as well as in their frequent, seemingly unrelated references to beans in the chorus or bridge. *Juré* is apparently derived from the French word for "sworn" or "testified," though Epstein notes that a similar word, Juddy, was reported by seventeenth-century trader Ben Jobson to be used to refer to "professional" musicians in Guinea and Benin (Epstein 1977: 4). In Louisiana, jurés are the Louisiana French parallel for shouts and spirituals resulting from the blending of Afro-Caribbean, French-Acadian, and southern Protestant traditions. Some texts were religious, as in the case of "Feel Like Dying in [Joining] His Army," a bilingual recording made by Lomax in 1934:

O Lord, Lord, Lord, my God.
Feel like dying in [joining] His army.

| O oui, mon cher ami, o quoi tu vas faire? | Oh yes, my dear friend, oh what will you do? |

Feel like dying in [joining] His army.

| O quoi tu vas faire, comment, hein, petit monde? | Oh what will you do, how, eh, dear one. |

Feel like dying in [joining] His army.

O oui, ma petite, si to pries pas . . .   Oh yes, my little one, if you don't
pray . . .

Feel like dying in [joining] His army.
O si to pries pas, tu vas brûler   Oh if you don't pray, you'll burn
dans l'enfer.   in hell.

Feel like dying in [joining] His army.

(Lomax 1934)

Others were secular, often adapting the story line of French Acadian folk songs to a highly syncopated Afro-Creole style. In a similar vein, Gilbert Chase reported that "[t]he English musician Henry Russell, who lived in the U.S. in the 1830s, was forcibly struck by the ease with which a slave congregation in Vicksburg, Mississippi, took a 'fine old Psalm tune' and by suddenly and spontaneously accelerating the tempo, transformed it 'into a kind of negro melody'" (1966: 235–36; quoted in Levine 1977: 26). This is the case with Clifton Chenier's signature song, "Les zydeco est pas salé," and with several of the Lomax recordings, such as "Je veux me marier, je peux pas trouver," based on the French Acadian song, "Je veux me marier, mais les poules pendent pas." Compare the two:

French Acadian:

Je veux me marier,	I want to marry,
Je veux me marier,	I want to marry,
Je veux me marier,	I want to marry,
Mais la belle veut pas.	But my sweetheart does not.
La belle veut,	My sweetheart accepts,
La belle veut,	My sweetheart accepts,
La belle veut,	My sweetheart accepts,
Mais les vieux veut pas.	But her parents do not.
Les vieux veut,	Her parents accept,
Les vieux veut,	Her parents accept,
Les vieux veut,	Her parents accept,
Mais j'ai pas d'argent.	But I have no money.
J'ai pas d'argent,	I have no money,
J'ai pas d'argent,	I have no money,
J'ai pas d'argent,	I have no money,
Et les poules pend pas.	And the chickens aren't laying.

(traditional; e.g., Gilmore 1970)

Juré:

Je veux me marier,	I want to marry,
Je peux pas trouver,	I can't find,
O, c'est malheureux.	Oh, it's sad.
Je veux me marier,	I want to marry,
Je peux pas trouver,	I can't find.
Mais comment donc je vas faire?	What am I going to do?
Je veux me marier,	I want to marry,
Je peux pas trouver,	I can't find,
Mais Mam et Pap veut pas.	And Mother and Father don't want.
Je veux me marier,	I want to marry,
Je peux pas trouver,	I can't find,
Mais o, c'est malheureux.	Well oh, it's sad.
Je veux me marier,	I want to marry,
J'ai pas d'argent,	I have no money,
J'ai pas de souliers,	I have no shoes,
Mais o, c'est malheureux	Well oh, it's sad.
Comment donc	What then
Tu veux moi, je fais,	Do you expect me to do,
Mais comme un pauvre misérable. . . .	Well, like a miserable wretch. . . .

(Lomax 1934)

The French Acadian version is lyrically and rhythmically structured in typically European-influenced fashion. The juré is lyrically reformulated and impressionistic, with a fragmented story line, uneven lines, and a completely retooled melody, all of which come from the African influences of its singers' past. The juré version preserves the basic theme of the young suitor whose courtship is frustrated because he has no money, but develops the story in a completely different way.

Juré singers provided dance music during times of Lent or official mourning periods when instrumental music was forbidden, or whenever musicians simply could not be found or afforded. The French Acadian counterpart to this tradition was called danses rondes, or round dancing. In Anglo-American tradition, this was sometimes called play-party singing. ("London Bridge" and "Ring around the Roses" are two well-known examples of play-party singing.) Lomax called juré style "the most African sound I found in America." The singers are accompanied only by improvised percussion (stamping feet, clapping hands, spoons rubbed on corrugated washboards, etc.) and a vocal counterpoint.

Sexuality is a common feature in African tradition and survives in

Afro-American cultural expression. "Jazz" and "rock," which describe other related African-American musical styles, originally were euphemisms for making love in the black oral tradition. The connection between music and dance and sexuality and courtship may give additional clues to the origins and meaning of zydeco. In "J'ai fait tout le tour du pays," based on the French Acadian "J'ai fait tout le tour du grand bois," the story line concerns another frustrated young lover who cannot visit his sweetheart again because he is poor (his clothes are tattered, his horse is sickly . . .), but the bridge is a complaint ostensibly about unsalted beans. If one considers that zydeco has possible roots in courtship and fertility ritual music and dancing, however, a possible relationship appears between the bridge and the verses that describe frustration in courtship.

J'ai fait tout le tour du pays	I went all round the land
Avec ma jogue au plombeau	With my bottle on the pommel
Et j'ai demandé à ton père pour dix-huit piastres, chérie.	And I asked your father for for eighteen dollars, dear.
Il m'a donné que cinq piastres.	He gave me only five dollars.
O Mam, mais donnez-moi les haricots.	Oh Mama, give me the beans.
Mais o chérie, les haricots sont pas salés.	Well, o dear, the beans ain't salted.
O Mam, mais donnez-moi les haricots.	Oh Mama, give me the beans.
Mais o yé yaïe, les haricots sont salés.	Well, o yé yaïe, the beans ain't pas salted.
Toi, comment tu veux je te vas voir	You, how do you expect me to visit you.
Mais quand mon chapeau rouge est fini.	When, my red hat is worn.
Toi, comment tu veux je te vas voir.	You, how do you expect me to visit you.
Mais quand mon suit est tout déchiré?	When my suit is all torn.
O Mam, mais donnez-moi les haricots.	O Mama, give me the beans.
Mais o yé yaïe, les haricots sont salés. . .	Well, o yé yaïe, the beans ain't pas salty. . .
	(Lomax 1934)

Again, compare the French Acadian source with its even lines and lyrical narrative style to the juré version:

J'ai fait [tout le] tour du grand bois	I went all around the land
Avec ma [jogue] au pombeau,	With my bottle on the pommel,
Mon [pe]tit [cheval] blanc tout blessé	My little white horse lame
Et mes culottes rapiécetées.	And my clothes in tatters.
Comment tu [veux] que [je vas te] voir?	How do you expect me to visit you?
Tu [restes l'autre] bord du grand bois.	You live on the other side of the woods.
Comment tu [veux je te] marie?	How do you expect me to marry you?
J'ai [rien qu']une paire de souliers.	I have only one pair of shoes.

(Whitfield 1939 [1969]: 96–97)

Juré and zydeco may be even more directly linked to courtship and its results. The Rodrigue Island dance tradition described earlier is obviously associated with courtship rituals. In antebellum Louisiana, part of the planters' systematic efforts to eradicate their slaves' African heritage included outlawing slave dances like the calinda. The pretext that they were lewd and lascivious was not entirely unfounded, however, especially from a European point of view. Descriptions of these dances suggest that they may have been associated with African courtship and fertility rituals (Levine 1977: 16; Epstein 1977: 30). Contemporary black Creole dance styles associated with zydeco are often considered suggestive, to say the least, by Cajun and Anglo-American observers. Zydeco lyrics are often more than suggestive. It does not take blues scholars long to figure out the sexual metaphors in such songs as Clifton Chenier's version of the Blind Lemon Jefferson classic, "Black Snake Blues." Nor is there much doubt about the meaning of Canray Fontenot's "Joe Pitre a deux femmes" ("Joe Pitre Has Two Women"), Buckwheat Zydeco's "Give Me a Good Time Woman," Boozoo Chavis's "I'm Going to Dog Hill" (". . . where the pretty women're at . . ."), and Clifton Chenier's version of "I'm a Hog for You, Baby" (". . . rooting, rooting, rooting around your door . . ."). Much of African-American expressive culture features double-entendre and sexual imagery, often using foods as euphemisms for female sexual organs (e.g., cabbage, cookie, cake, candy, jelly roll, shortening bread) (Levine 1977: 242–43). More recent zydeco hits are even more obvious: "I Want a Big Butt Woman" and "Take Off Your Clothes, Throw 'em in the Corner."

There is an unmistakable tendency toward soul and rhythm and blues among contemporary Louisiana Creole musicians. Yet, the same band leaders who insist on singing English lyrics and adding saxophones, trumpets, and electric guitars in their groups demonstrate their deep understanding of the essential tradition when they play what they sometimes call "du vrai zydeco" (real zydeco). After receiving a Grammy Award in 1984 for his album *I'm Here,* Clifton Chenier commented, "Soul didn't get me that Grammy. Rock-and-roll didn't get me that Grammy. Zydeco got me that Grammy" (1984). Ironically, producer Chris Strachwitz had a hard time convincing Chenier to record zydeco for his first Arhoolie Records releases in the 1960s and 1970s (Strachwitz 1980). Chenier wanted to record rock and blues. He was quick to notice, however, that zydeco was what distinguished him from the rest of the crowd of musicians. Whether he was in a local dance hall or on the main stage of a major festival, he never failed to include some of the "real stuff," which featured his brother Cleveland on frottoir (ruboard) and Robert St. Judy on drums. The rest of the Red Hot Louisiana Band would drop out while Clifton and the percussionists beat out a jumping rhythm. Clifton transformed his piano accordion into a melodic drum, using it almost like a complicated version of an African thumb piano. The "real stuff" was also marked by exclusively French vocals and a percussive frenzy that clearly reveal that the style originated in the cultural creolization of Afro-Caribbean and Franco-American traditions.

Whatever its linguistic origins, zydeco, like the blues and rock and roll, is a product of the American blending process with a strong African base. But, like its fellow Louisiana product, jazz, zydeco has an important French element. A few years ago, anthropologist Alan Lomax predicted that zydeco could become as big as reggae, another product of the creolization process. At the time, that prediction was hard to believe because of the language barrier of hard-core zydeco. Yet, what had been a gradual drift toward English lyrics accelerated during the 1980s as young Creoles were less and less capable of performing in French. Beyond south Louisiana, Queen Ida's 1982 Grammy, Clifton Chenier's 1984 Grammy for "I'm Here!" (one of the most English-oriented albums of his career) and Rockin' Sidney's 1986 Grammy for "Don't Mess with My Toot Toot" have lots of musicians, from Patti LaBelle and Fats Domino to John Fogarty and Paul Simon, interested in zydeco.

Of course, what pop zydeco for national consumption gains in understandability, it loses in some other important areas, including contact with its French elements and intangibles that might be attributed to the social warmth (and even heat) of south Louisiana Creole dance halls. But the form is undeniably enjoying national attention. In south Louisiana, a veritable army of young Creole bands have become interested in the music of their heritage, and it is clear that zydeco has taken its place as part of the national music scene.

If there is a problem with today's zydeco, it is, ironically, rooted in the success of its major figure. To understand zydeco today, one must understand Clifton Chenier. Born in the country near Opelousas in 1925, Clifton and his brother Cleveland left Louisiana in 1946 to work in the postwar boom in east Texas. Later, they moved back to Louisiana, though Clifton never completely gave up his foothold in the Houston area.

The Chenier brothers were among the first to popularize their adaptation of the older juré tradition. They turned what had been an unaccompanied group singing tradition into instrumental dance music, performed on an accordion and frottoir. They may not have invented zydeco, but they certainly defined it with every performance. At first, they played for neighborhood house dances while holding down regular jobs. They decided to devote themselves to music full time when Clifton was fired from his job in an east Texas oil refinery because he could not and would not climb a tower. When he went back the next day to ask for his job, he played his accordion around the sandwich wagon while waiting for the foreman and picked up more money during the lunch hour than he had made working hard all week (Chenier 1984). Clifton and Cleveland quickly became very popular on the weekend dance hall circuit. Former owners of abandoned dance halls throughout southwest Louisiana speak proudly of the times that they played at their place.

Clifton's zydeco was culturally between Houston and New Orleans, between the blues and jazz, between the Delta and the Gulf. It was an ideal illustration of anthropologist C. Paige Gutierrez's notion that French Louisiana is actually south of the South (Gutierrez 1992: 4). In the 1950s, the influence of rock and roll and rhythm and blues imposed changes, and Clifton succeeded in translating his percussive zydeco sound into modern terms. The group grew to include electric guitars, a bass, drums, a saxophone, and even a trumpet, as Clifton carefully built what he perceptively named the Red Hot Louisiana Band. Together, the band members strained the floor joists under most of the area's dance halls during the straight four-hour sets that are still common (even necessary) among performers who play real music for real people in south Louisiana. There is little time for star gazing when folks want to dance.

The principles of the local zydeco music scene will tell the observer that the recipe for success was (and still is) to make a record and get it played on local radio and jukeboxes. It's not clear whether Clifton had a plan for getting ahead, but he had the goods, and people beat a path to his door. After recording a couple of tunes for Specialty Records in 1955, he drifted from one regional company to another. He finally returned to the national scene in 1964 with Chris Strachwitz's Arhoolie label, where he made his most memorable recordings. The Arhoolie releases also attracted the attention of young, hip whites in south Louisiana's urban, college-town center, Lafayette. Some overcame their nervousness at being the only whites for blocks to hear the master in his own element, in black clubs such as the Blue Angel and the old Bon Ton Rouley. Clifton's growing popularity soon sped past racial barriers, and he became a mainstay of unairconditioned student hangouts such as Willie Purple's and the legendary Jay's Lounge and Cockpit.

Clifton believed that his hot zydeco sound could also transcend regional and cultural barriers, and he made annual forays to the edges of America. He recorded for numerous labels, including Tomato, Blue Star, Jinn, and Free Bird, and was the subject of several films, including Les Blank's *Hot Pepper.* The fears of those who expected Lawrence Welk–style music from his piano accordion were invariably and immediately laid to rest. The list of musicians Clifton played with during those years reads like a who's who of American bluesmen and women, old and new, from Big Joe Turner to Big Mama Thornton, B. B. King to Johnny Winter, Ray Charles to Elvin Bishop, Lightnin' Hopkins to Gatemouth Brown. Aware of Europe's long fascination with American jazz and blues, Clifton arranged tours of France, England, Germany, Scandinavia, and Switzerland.

Throughout all of this, Clifton managed to blend success with real life, playing concerts for concert audiences and dances for dance hall audiences. He was keenly aware of his status as a culture hero. In 1971, the King of Zydeco first delighted audiences by appearing with a very conspicuous, rhinestone-studded crown (e.g., Gould 1992: xix). By the 1975 Tribute to Cajun Music festival in Lafayette, all the members of his Red Hot Louisiana Band had smaller, prince-sized crowns as well. Yet, the King of Zydeco maintained a warm closeness with his bread-and-butter constituency on the local zydeco circuit, regularly holding court over the bandstand rail in little dance halls throughout south Louisiana.

Clifton Chenier dominated the world of zydeco, as his title implies. He was such a creative genius that he transformed anything he played into his own, including pure blues, country, rock, western swing, and big band tunes. He was so important to the tradition that he helped to define that, after his death in 1987, the zydeco community fell into disarray. There was a power vacuum at the top. A well-intentioned attempt to stabilize the situation by one of Clifton's heirs, Alton "Rockin' Dopsie"

Rubin, only made things worse because of the volatile cultural politics of the times. Eventually, several musicians emerged to provide some much needed leadership. Musicians such as Delton Broussard, John Delafose, and Preston Frank brought forward a renewed rural style, featuring the simpler, single-row diatonic accordion. Wilson "Boozoo" Chavis, one of Clifton's colleagues from the 1950s, came out of retirement to assume the position of elder statesman with a few new hard-driving, old-style zydeco recordings. A new generation of musicians, such as Stanley "Buckwheat" Dural and his protégé Nathan Williams, as well as the Sam Brothers and Clifton's own son, C. J. Chenier, have distinguished themselves with excellent musicianship in the urban tradition developed by Chenier, characterized by the use of a chromatic piano-key accordion. An even younger generation, led by the creative forces of musicians such as Terrance Simien, Zydeco Force, and Beau Jocque, is exploring new trends, using a variety of instruments, including a chromatic three-row button accordion.

Yet, it is sometimes difficult to tell the difference between what passes for contemporary zydeco and the rock, soul, and blues it imitates. Clifton was such a huge presence that it was difficult to see past him to explore the sources he used and the styles that had influenced him. Unlike the young Cajun musicians, such as Michael Doucet and Steve Riley, who are reviving Cajun music with a strong sense of history and language, exploring the unaccompanied ballads and instrumental dance tunes of centuries past, it seems that most young Creole musicians see only as far back as the King of Zydeco. And when these young musicians look back for inspiration from his recordings, they assume that everything he did was zydeco, though he knew the difference. So their own music goes off in as many directions as his experiments, but often without a clear sense of what the "real stuff" is. Furthermore, the tradition's poetic quality has suffered in the shift from French to English lyrics. The state of contemporary zydeco is a good barometer for contemporary black Creole society, which has only recently begun to explore the complex and specific nature of its history, culture, and language. During the decades following World War II, when the Cajuns became interested in preserving their culture and language, the black Creoles were preoccupied with the Civil Rights struggle, and rightly so. Though there is still work to be done in this area, today no one really notices who's drinking out of the water fountain and where people are sitting on the bus. Some members of the black Creole community have begun to explore their community's special nature, apparently feeling that it can now afford such "luxuries" as culture and language. As organizations like Creole, Inc., have emerged to lead this effort, so too are there musicians who reflect its early results.

Lynn August, for example, who grew up with zydeco, turned to rock and popular music and has recently returned to the music of his heritage. He has released several recordings which include jurés he learned while exploring the historical music Alan Lomax recorded (e.g., *Creole Cruiser, Black Top 1074*).

Zydeco may be tempted by its brush with national appeal and move into the fast lane, developing in new directions that distance it from the traditions that gave it birth. Old-time French zydeco might then be relegated to a few south Louisiana versions of jazz's Preservation Hall where only a handful of nostalgia groups play the old stuff, while contemporary groups produce wave after wave of experimental new sounds. Or the tradition may preserve itself and develop in its own terms enough to continue stirring its pot of "unsalted beans." The current generation will, as it always does, determine the future.

References

August, Lynn. *Creole Cruiser*. Black Top 1074.

Bernard, Shane, and Julia Girouard. 1992. "'Colinda': Mysterious Origins of a Cajun Folksong." *Journal of Folklore Research* 29: 37–52.

Broussard, Delton, and the Lawtell Playboys. *Zodico*. Swallow 6009.

Charters, Samuel. 1982. *The Roots of the Blues: An African Search*. New York: Perigree/Putnam.

Chase, Gilbert. 1966. *America's Music, from the Pilgrims to the Present*. New York: McGraw-Hill.

Chenier, Clifton. 1984. Field recording, Barry Jean Ancelet collection, Center for Acadian and Creole Folklore Archive, Univ. of Southwestern Louisiana.

Chenier, Clifton. *Classic Clifton*. Arhoolie 1082.

Epstein, Dena J. 1977. *Sinful Tunes and Spirituals: Black Folk Music to the Civil War*. Urbana: Univ. of Illinois Press.

Fontenot, Canray. Field recording, Barry Jean Ancelet collection, Center for Acadian and Creole Folklore Archive, Univ. of Southwestern Louisiana, 1977.

Fontenot, Canray, and Alphonse "Bois-sec" Ardoin. *Boisec: La musique créole*. Arhoolie 1070.

Gilmore, Robert, Jeanne Gilmore, and Terry Clay Girouard. 1970. *Chantez la Louisiane: Louisiana French Folk Songs*. Lafayette: Acadiana Music.

Gould, Philip. 1992. *Cajun Music and Zydeco*. Baton Rouge: Louisiana State Univ. Press.

Gutierrez, C. Paige. 1992. *Cajun Foodways*. Jackson: Univ. Press of Mississippi.

Levine, Lawrence. 1977. *Black Culture and Black Consciousness: Afro-American Folk Thought from Slavery to Freedom*. Oxford: Oxford Univ. Press.

Lomax, Alan. 1934. Field recordings released as *Louisiana Cajun and Creole Music, 1934: The Lomax Recordings*. Swallow 8003–2.

Sigismund, Wilhelm Koelle. 1963. *Polyglotta Africana*. Graz, Austria: Academische Druck.

Strachwitz, Chris. 1980. Personal communication.

Whitfield, Irene Thérèse. 1939. *Louisiana French Folk Songs*. Baton Rouge: Louisiana State Univ. Press. Reprint, New York: Dover, 1969.

SEVEN

Albert Valdman

The Place of Louisiana Creole among New World French Creoles

Arguably, Louisiana offers the most complex linguistic situation found in the Caribbean rim. In the so-called Francophone Triangle one finds a finely meshed continuum in which it is possible to identify clearly only two idealized speech norms: Standard French (SF) and Louisiana Creole (LC). During particular speech events, speakers modify their linguistic behavior according to various factors in the communicative situation: participants, location, topic, etc., and it is difficult for the observer to assign particular features to any of the three traditional speech varieties in contact: Louisiana French (LF), Cajun French (CF), and LC. The re-introduction of SF through CODOFIL's French revival program has complicated the linguistic situation. Moreover, English, which has already eliminated Louisiana French from its main focal centers in New Orleans and along the Mississippi coasts, is exercising strong pressures on the two varieties, CF and LC, that show any signs of vitality.

The fact that there remain few monolingual speakers of these two varieties and the continuum situation that exists between them render the description of LC fraught with great difficulties. This explains the paucity of descriptions of the language; at present, there exist only two major studies, both of them limited to a geographically restricted variety of LC: Ingrid Neumann's study of the grammar of Breaux Bridge speech (1985) and Thomas Klingler's description of the lexicon of New Roads LC (1992).[1] This article presents some remarks about the sociolinguistic situation of the language; it offers a brief sketch of its structure; it deals with the destabilizing effect of English and the problem of the French <—> LC continuum; it proposes a scenario for its origin and development; it ends by addressing the issue of its African features.

1. The Distribution and Sociolinguistic Status of LC

Compared to CF, which is spoken throughout the Francophone Triangle, LC is found in three relatively isolated areas: to the east, in the former Acadian and German Coasts (Saint James and Saint John Parishes) between New Orleans and Baton Rouge (Marshall 1982, 1987, 1990); to the north, around New Roads in Pointe Coupee Parish (Jarreau 1931, Klingler 1992); in the center in the Bayou Teche region in Saint Martin Parish (Morgan 1959, 1960, 1972, 1976; Neumann 1984, 1985). The language is reported in use to the west, in the Lake Charles area (Calcacieu Parish), but no descriptive studies exist.

Ingrid Neumann (1985) estimates that the number of speakers of LC ranges between 60,000 and 80,000 persons, of whom about a quarter are whites. These figures seem rather optimistic. Thomas Klingler, who has conducted extensive fieldwork in New Roads has failed to discover a single monolingual speaker in that area. He cites a study undertaken by CODOFIL: in a group of 1,020 respondents 25 percent declared to speak CF at home, 14.3 percent spoke SF, but only 8.9 percent spoke LC (1992).

The attrition of LC results from its position at the bottom of the range of language varieties in use in francophone Louisiana. From the perspective of power and prestige the top position is occupied by English and SF, the latter reintroduced through the various revitalization actions launched by CODOFIL and the bilingual education programs of the 1970s. Louisiana French (LF) and CF are located at the middle. The devalorization of LC, reflected by the pejorative terms that even some of its speaker use to refer to it—*nèg, français nèg, Nigger French, couri vini,* etc.—stems in large part from its association with slavery. The low esteem in which it is held by white speakers explains why they are reluctant to use it in front of strangers and why they will often deny their habitual use of it. However, in the last half-dozen years an attempt has been made by the African-Louisianan middle-class group centered in Lafayette, Creole Inc., to revalorize it. This movement, which may be viewed as the counterpart of the consciousness-raising in the Cajun community under the aegis of CODOFIL and young Cajun intellectuals, has led to the creation of an English-language monthly, *Creole Magazine.* This periodical contains a regular section, *"La leson kreyòl,"* in which Herbert Wiltz provides sample conversations in LC and grammatical statements, and an occasional column, "Creole Linguistics," written by Albert Valdman, Margaret Marshall, and Thomas Klingler. One of the interesting aspects of Creole Magazine is the large place it gives to zydeco music. It seems that this Africanized version of Cajun folk music serves as a vector for a limited revitalization of the speech variety that symbolizes membership in the African-Louisianan community. Nonetheless, the term "Creole" when used to refer to language has not lost its stigma, nor does it refer only to LC. On numerous occasions this writer has heard African Louisianans claim that they spoke "Creole," whereas in fact they were using a form of CF containing occasional features of what will be referred to here as basilectal LC.

As will be pointed out later in this chapter, LC is probably the French-based creole that is closest to French structurally. In addition, because it is spoken by whites, many of whom have competence in CF, and enjoys low prestige even among its speakers, LC is often perceived as a deviant, corrupted, and mongrelized form of French. The dwindling number of habitual speakers of the language will tend to "move up" to CF, LF, or SF to the extent that their mastery of these other varieties permits it. As a result there exists no clear line of demarcation between CF and French, nor between LC and the more prestigious French varieties. This problem will be discussed in Section 3.

The pressure exercised by English, which stands at the apex of the sociolinguistic pyramid, also tends to blur the lines between that language and the French-related languages. English, or *American* in local usage, invaded Louisiana long before the official cession of the territory to the United States. Many of the large plantations along the Mississippi were taken over or established by American owners who came from the Carolinas or Georgia with their English or English-based creole-speaking slaves. For example Hall (1992: 181–83) mentions that a certain Dr. Benjamin Farar, a native of South Carolina, moved to New Roads with 153 slaves, of whom 72 adults were natives of South Carolina or Virginia. Most likely, on the large riverine plantations these "American" slaves adopted the local vernacular, LC, as a *lingua franca* but also retained their version of the speech of their masters.

Today the pressure of English manifests itself, as it does in the case of CF, by massive borrowing, calques, and code switching. The following is a short sample of discourse which shows the high level of lexical borrowing from English:[2]

> je te kŏnẽ prã ẽ bari, avɛk ẽ but lapo, e je te gẽ ʃofe lapo pu li vini "stiff". Kã li vini "stiff, then" je "bang" li. Mo pãs se de zafɛ je mẽnẽ isi dã "slavery".

> They used to take a barrel with a piece of skin, and they used to heat the skin until it became stiff. When it had become stiff, then banged on it. I think these are things that were brought over here [from Africa] with slavery.

Current research on code mixing and switching suggest that borrowing or code switching cannot be explained only in terms of filling needs. Bilinguals dip into the respective lexical inventories of the languages they speak and alternate between them on the basis of a variety of sociolinguistic and pragmatic factors: to express a change of attitude toward the message or the interlocutor; to respond to a change in the situation—for example, the arrival of another person who might not understand one of the languages; to stress a certain part of the message. Code switching constitutes one of the linguistic resources at the disposal of bilinguals, and they switch between speech varieties the same way and for the same reasons monolinguals alternate among styles of speech. Nonetheless, in explaining code switching one should not discount the effect of memory gaps and the pressures from the dominant language, which alone provides terms for many of the realities of everyday life. It is accordingly inappropriate to label as borrowing or code switching the use of terms or expressions for which the base language—here LC—provides no corresponding equivalents. This fact makes it difficult to classify apparent English forms as loans or code switches. Sometimes, pronunciation can provide an indication, as in the cases of *tivi*, pronounced [tivi] with short and non-glided [i], which marks the item as part of LC. On the other hand, the retention of English phonological features in the code switches: *Li te good looking* "He was good looking" or *Li ẽ school board president* "She is president of the school board" favor the code-switch interpretation.[3] The identification of English code switches is facilitated by the retention of the syntactic structure from that language, as in *Je se hang li up* "They could hang him", which contains the discontinuous structure verb + adverb, or of discourse shifters such as *boy* in *Boy mo te gẽ hõt!* "Boy, was I ashamed!" The most insidious Anglicisms, though, are calques in which English concepts are dressed up in LC forms. In *Li galɔp ẽ ʃɔp* "He runs a store", the word *shop* represents an integrated loan but, more importantly, the LC verb *galɔp* "to run", mirrors the English idiomatic expression "to run a shop." Similarly in *Mo va wa komõ sa va travaje* "I'll see how it works" the meaning of the verb travaje is extended from its basic meaning "to work" to include the sense "to operate" that is contained in the corresponding English verb.

2. The Structure of LC

2.1. Pronunciation

As the examples cited heretofore show, LC differs little from CF at the lexical level; there are few words which cannot be traced either to some dialect of French or which are traceable to English loanwords. The close relationship with French also surfaces at the phonological level.[4] As is the case for CF there are several variable features; for example, "to learn" is heard as [aprã], [aprãn], [aprõn], [aprɔn]. LC also has affricates [tʃ] and [dʒ] generally absent from French: [tʃõmbo] "to hold firmly", [motʃɛn] "mine"; [dʒab] "devil", [ladʒɛl] "mouth". Again, like CF there is a [h] phoneme, which alternates with [ʒ], e.g., [hale] "to pull", [hardẽ] or [ʒardẽ] "garden". Dental stops are slightly palatalized: [pitˢi] "child", [dᶻife] "fire". The velar nasal [ŋ], which correspond to [g] preceded by a nasal vowel of SF, functions as an autonomous phoneme: [lalãŋ] "language", [zepẽŋ] "pin". Finally, *r* is realized by a wide array of variants ranging from the apico-dental trill [r] to the velar fricative [ʁ] of SF. It is weakened after a vowel and lengthens the preceding vowel: [paʳle] or [pa:le] "to speak", [sɛr] or [sɛ:] "sister".

Like other New World French-based creoles LC shows the alternation between front rounded and unrounded vowels. Stated differently, words which in SF are pronounced with the front rounded vowels [y], [ø], and [œ] are produced with the corresponding unrounded vowel: [siʳ] or [syʳ] "sure", [pe] or [pø] "little", [sɛʳ] or [sœʳ] "sister". As is the case in SF, the distinction between high-mid and low-mid vowels tends to be neutralized: SF *pauvre* "poor" is pronounced: [pov], [pɔv], or [pɔ:v], bo*euf* "cow" [bef] or [bɛf] . Corresponding to SF [a] is a vowel ranging from [a] to [ɔ], although the vowels tend to be produced with retraction before [r], [l], and t [s]: [mɒl] "mail", [pɒʳl] "to speak", [pjɒs] "dollar (pia*stre*)". There are basically only two nasal vowels: a front vowel [ẽ] contrasting with a back vowel produced variably as [ã] or [õ].

A salient feature of LC, as compared to Haitian Creole, for example, is the large proportion of nouns containing an agglutinated etymological article or the last consonant of the latter; for example, [ẽ la mẽ] <— *la main* "a hand", [ẽ defig] <— *des figues* "a banana", [ẽ gro lefej] <— *les feuilles* "a large leaf", [so dezo] <— *des os* "his bone", [lẽ bã divã] <— *du vent* "a strong wind", [vu nepol] <— *(u)ne épaule* "your shoulder", [zorɛj] <— *(les)s oreilles* "ear". For nouns that begin with [la], [le], [de], or [di], the initial constituent is ambiguous because in Frenchified forms of LC, it may represent articles occurring before a noun. It is only when this constituent occurs after a determiner (articles or possessive adjectives) that they can be unambiguously analyzed as agglutinations. Compare [ẽ mal de tɛt] "a head ache" vs. [so latɛt] "his/her head", [ave la mẽ] "by hand" vs. [so lamẽ] "his/her hand".

2.2. Grammar

Because of the continuum relationship between LC and the various varieties of French with which it coexists, the generally accepted practice is to select forms from the pole most distant from French in describing its grammar. The term *basilectal* is used to describe these forms.

Basilectal varieties of LC that are spoken by blacks in Pointe Coupee, for example, do not show any gender distinction, and the definite article and plural marker occur after the noun[5]:

(1) *Sʃẽ la trape lɔdɛ lapẽ la.*   The dog picked up the scent
                                     of the rabbit.

     Mo sukuje dibwa je.   I shook the trees.

Strictly speaking the post-posed element la is not equivalent to the French
or English definite article. Its meaning is intermediate between that of the
definite article and the demonstrative adjectives of these languages. Also,
its domain of reference is the entire noun phrase rather than the noun itself:

(2) *Mo frɛ ki muri la.* . . .   This brother of mine who is
                                    dead . . .

In Pointe Coupee, T. Klingler has noted variation in the form of the definite
determiner conditioned by the nature of the last sound of the word it follows that reflects the complexity found in Haitian creole: *chat la* "the cat",
dolo a "the water", *vje mũn nã* "the old people", *lakrɛm lã/nã* "the cream".
As is the case for all Caribbean French-based creoles the demonstrative and
definite determiners co-occur postposed. In the plural there are *two* variants, both of which involve pre-posing the plural marker *le* but one of which
shows the post-posed plural *je* replacing the definite determiner:

(3) *gõbo sa la*   this gombo
    le kokodri sa la/le kokodri sa je   these alligators

One salient difference between LC and its Caribbean congeners is
the use pre-posed to the noun of a distinct set of possessive determiners.
These alternate with emphatic forms containing *-kɛn* (also realized as
-kẽn, -tʃẽn or -tʃɛn). There also exist analytical constructions employing
the prepositions *a* and *pu*:

(4) *Li leve so lamẽ aprɛ mwẽ.*   He signaled to me with his
                                     hand.

    Mo fe mokẽn rekɔt.   I made my harvest.
    Sa se vokẽn ku!   It's your neck!
    Mo te gẽ bõ lẽʒa mõ.   I had my own good clothing.
    Kabãn la se **pu mwẽ.**   That's my house.

In its pronominal system LC belongs to the conservative group of
French-based creoles which includes also French Guyana (Cayenne)

Creole and the varieties spoken in the Indian Ocean. This system is more complex than that of the Caribbean varieties (see section 3) in that it shows a three-way distinction between a subject set, a pre-posed possessive set, and a post-posed set functioning as direct object and object of prepositions. See Table 7.1.

Creole languages derived from European languages are characterized by the analytical character of their grammar: grammatical relationships are expressed by word order and by the use of function words rather than by inflectional endings. This typological feature is particularly salient in the verb system. In French-based creoles, temporal, aspectual, and modal distinctions are expressed by a set of functions words or markers occurring before an invariable verb base. LC differs from its Caribbean congeners by its richer set of markers and by generally showing in addition a distinction between two verb bases. For verbs that correspond to French *-er* verbs, the bases differ by the presence versus the absence of the final vowel: *mõʒe/mõʒ* "to eat", *blije/blij* "to forget". For other types of verbs the two bases may differ significantly, for example, *repõn/repõ* "to answer"; *uvɛr/uv* "to open", *sɔrtir/sɔr* "to leave", *vini/vjĕ* "to come". In general the short base expresses the imperative and the present, and it is used with the expression *i fo* "it is necessary." The long base occurs in all other cases.

(5) *Vu lav li.*   You wash it.
    Mo lave mo figi ave dolo fre.   I washed my face with cold
                                                         water

There are seven verb markers, many of which show elided forms: *ape* "progressive", *te* "anterior", *ale* "definite future", *va, sa* "indefinite future", *se* " conditional", *bin* "present perfect". The variation in form and the meaning of these markers are illustrated by the sample sentences in (6) below.

(6) ape:
    M ap repõn.   I'm answering.
    M e kuri travaj apremidi la.   I'm going to work this afternoon.
    te:

    Li te gẽ ẽ ʃar.   He had a car.
    Li mete sa ave medikamõ   He put that with the
    li t a aʃte.   that he had bought
    Apre li te vini, nu bwa kafe.   After he had arrived, we drank
                                                        coffee.

    Si mo te kõnẽ l te la, mo se   If I had known she was there, I
    pa vini.   would not have come.

Table 7.1

The Pronominal System of LC

	SUBJECT	POSSESSIVE	OBJECT
SINGULAR			
1	**mo** vini "I'm coming" **m** ole "I want"	**mo** pitit je "my children"	li tãn **mwa/mõ/mwɛ̃** "he/she is waiting for me"
2 familiar	**to** di sa "you say that" **t** a kõnẽ "you'll know"	**to** labuʃ "your mouth"	nu gete **twa/to** "we're looking at you"
formal	**vu/ou** se vini "you would come" **v** ote lekaj je "you removed the scales"	**vu/vo** fij "your daughter"	mo wa **vu** "I've seen you"
3	**li/i** mõde "he/she asked" **l** a vini bɛk "he/she returned"	**so** mun je "his/her people"	to di **li** "you told him/her"
PLURAL			
1	**nu/no/nuzɔt** isit "we're here" **n** e grene defɛv "we're shelling lima beans"	**nu** lamezõ "our house"	je te prõn **nu/nuzot/no** "they took us"
2 inf.	**zot/zo/uzot/ vuzot** galope "you went"	**zo** lalõg "your langue"	mo don **zot/uzot** sa "I gave you that"
for.	**vu/vuzɔt** di "you said"	**vu** pitit "your children"	m a don **vu/vuzɔt** "I'm giving you"
3	**je** te pron nuzot "they took us" **j** ole "they want"	**je** nõk je "their uncles"	mo kone **je** "I know them"

ale:
> *Nom la di: "Sa k ale mõʒe*   The man said: "Who is going to
> *le ʃat?" E Vø Dʒab di:*   eat the cat". And the Old Devil
> *"T ale mõʒe li, nɛg!"*   said: "You're going to eat it, man!"

va:
> *Vu pa kwa l a ʃinẽ?*   You don't think he'll win?
> *Nu va fe la rekɔl, mwẽ e twa.*   We'll do the harvest, you and I.

sa:
> *Kõ t a vini demẽ mo sa deʒa*   When you'll arrive, I'll already
> *parti.*   be gone.

se:
> *Mo se kõtõ kone sa.*   I would like to know that.
> *Si vu se vini apepre dø se mɛn*   If you had come two weeks ago,
> *pase nave de bõ budẽ.*   there would have been some
>   good boudin.
>
> *Li s ape peʃe astɛr, si la pli*   He would be fishing now were
> *se pa tõbe.*   the rain not falling.

bin:
> *Mo bin ap travaj isi dø smɛn.*   I've been working
>   here for two weeks.

A generic feature erroneously attributed to creole languages is the absence of a copula in equational sentences. There is indeed a zero copula in equational constructions containing an adjective or a complement of place:

(7) *Li fɛ́b.*   S/he is weak.
    Je deɔr.   They're outside.

But LC has three overt copulas: *se, je, dɛt*. The first occurs with noun phrases, but in this type of construction it is optionally deleted when the verb phrase contains the anterior marker *te*:

(8) *Mo pɛr se te ẽ Brusar.*   My father was a Broussard.
    Nu te sɛt frɛr.   We were seven brothers.

In interrogative sentences when the copula finds itself in final position, it is realized as *je*:

> *Au to je?*   Where are you?
> *Ki nasjõ to je? —Mo se frãse.*   What's your nationality?—I'm
>   French

LC is the only French-based creole to show the copula form *dɛt* (alternating with *ɛt*) in limited syntactic contexts, for example, with modal verbs of obligation, with the imperative, and in passive constructions:

> (9) *Le piti sipoze ɛt deɔr.*   The children are supposed to be
>   outside.
> *Sa gẽ dɛt fe.*   That has to be done.
> *Mo va ɛt la.*   I'll be there.
> *Dɛt la a siz ɛr!*   Be there at six o'clock!
> *La le pralin je pare*   Then the pralines were ready
> *pu ɛt wete õndo to*   to be removed from the pot.
> *ʃodjɛr.*

With regard to sentence structure, three features are noteworthy: the position of the negative marker pa, interrogative sentences, and the passive construction. In French-based creoles *pa* generally occurs before the verb, but in LC its position is subject to various factors. First, it occurs after the short base of verbs but before the long base:

> (10) *Mo mãʒ pa diri.*   I don't eat rice.
> *Sa mo pa sɛrvi , mo*   What I don't use, I put it in a jar.
> *mɛt li dã ẽdʒal.*

In stative, single-base verbs the position of the negative marker allows a differentiation between the completive and the present:

> (11) *Mo m pa wa "slavery".*   I didn't see (experience) slavery.
> *Li wa pa.*   He doesn't see.

Except in the case of the progressive marker *ape,* the negative marker is placed after verb markers.

> (12) *Sa se pa arive.*   That wouldn't happen.
> *Mo te pa fe arjẽ.*   I didn't do anything.
> *Mo va pa fe sa.*   I won't do that.

Li te **p** *ape garde ke kote l t ale.*	She wasn't looking where she went.
Li te **pa** *kõte kõt.*	He didn't tell stories.
Li te pal **pa** *krejɔl.*	She didn't speak Creole.

Interestingly *pa*, although it appears before modal verbs, its position shifts when the frenchified variation of these forms is used:

(13) *No* **p** *ole li.*	We don't want.
To ve (<— veut) *pa?*	Don't you want to?

Global (yes/no) questions, where the interrogation bears on the full predicate, are formed by the use of a final rise in pitch or the use of the interrogative marker *eske*. In partial questions, bearing on adverbial complements or objects, the interrogative element always occurs in initial position:

(14) *Ena ẽ lɔt mãjɛ?*	Is there another way?
Eske *to mõde de to tãt?*	Did you ask your aunt?
Sa ki *pa konẽ mo?*	Who doesn't know me?
Kofe *to vini?*	Why did you come?

Interrogative adverbs include *kote, au, eu* "where"; *ekã* "when", *kofɛ* "why", *kɔmã/kɔmõ/kõmõ* "how to", *kõbjẽ/komje* "how many, how much". The form *ki* serves both as subject interrogative pronoun and as interrogative adjective: *ki mũn* "who", *ki kalite* "what sort", *ki lɛ* "what time".

Like its congeners LC doesn't have *any* passive construction:

(15) *Mo rekõny par blã e nwa.*	I am well *considered* by blacks and whites.

However, the modal verbs *truve* "to happen" and *soti* "immediate past", as well as other verbal elements, can also be used to convey the passive meaning:

(16) *Li truve tʃuwe.*	He was killed (in an accident).
Li soti tʃwe.	She was killed (murdered).
Tu kiʃo se aʃte astɛ la.	Everything is bought now.
Li bøzõ lave.	It needs washing.

3. The LC–French Continuum

According to the classical model for the genesis and development of creoles when a creole language coexists with its base or lexifier language, because of the greater prestige and power that the latter possesses, the creole language will adopt its structural features and lexicon. This process, termed decreolization, leads to the creation of a continuum of variation in which it becomes impossible to neatly mark off the two varieties in contact from each other. One can only abstract two idealized poles, the *basilect* (the creole forms most different from the base language) and the *acrolect*, the base language itself. Between these pole lies the continuum of variation, the *mesolect,* which in Louisiana contains Frenchified variants of LC.

Mesolectal forms appear in particular in the nominal system. Frenchification takes the form of gender differentiation and the use of pre-posed determiners. The examples in (17) compare the mesolectal distinction between masculine and feminine nouns effected by pre-posed definite article forms with corresponding basilectal structures consisting of undifferentiated nouns accompanied by post-posed forms:

(17) Mo te **pø** kupe **le** ʃvø dẽ	I knew how to cut a man's
nõm prɔp. (. . . ʃvø **je**)	hair clean
Me ʃvø te ape grizõne.	My hair was turning grey.
(. . . **mo** ʃvø **je**)	
Mo se rãtre dã **la** ʃɔp.	I used to go into the shop.
(. . . ʃɔp **la**)	
Mo te lese dã **l** klo . . .	I used to leave the field . . .
(. . . klo **la**)	

It is not *rare* to find mesolectal forms that reflect the co-occurrence of the basilectal and acrolectal system:

(18) Eske **l** kuto **la** se pu twa?	Is that knife yours?

Example (13) from section 3.2. shows the combination of a mesolectal verb form, *vø,* instead of basilectal *ole* with the placement of the negative marker *pa* after the verb. The latter appears to be a mesolectal syntactic feature triggered by the use of the frenchified verb *form.* Other putative mesolectal features with which *pa* post-position seem *associated* are the use of the copulate *dɛt* and of short verb stems.

According to the classical model, decreolization develops gradually over time and follows a stage when the creole is maximally differentiated from its base language. In the case of LC this implies that decreolization resulted from close contact between that language and French varieties after a stage when the creole developed independently. In the next section, it will be argued that this view is not supported by historical evidence, and it will be concluded that variation between the basilectal and acrolectal pole was present from the beginning, although the use of LC and CF by bilinguals may account for some of the present day mesolectal forms.

4. The Origin of LC

Between 1790 and 1804, at the time when its population numbered 20,673 slaves and 18,737 free persons (whites and freed slaves), about 9,000 refugees from Saint-Domingue accompanied by their slaves landed in colonial Louisiana (Hall 1992). This has led some to assume a strong influence of Saint-Domingue Creole on LC. But there existed in Louisiana a slave population going back to 1710, and it is highly probable that a local French-based creole developed between that date and the massive influx of speakers of Saint-Domingue Creole. Unfortunately, early written attestations of early LC are scant. The earliest texts, written down by the director of the Company of the Indies, Le Page Du Pratz (1758; cited by Hall 1992), between 1718 and 1743 take the form of depositions of a certain Samba Bambara during a 1732 interrogation following a slave conspiracy. They reflect a pidginized form of French rather than a proper creole:

> (18) M. Le Page li diabe li sabai tout.   M. Le Page is a devil; he
> knows everything.
>
> Monsu, nègre Mian Mian   Sir, when a Negro is well fed,
> boucou trabail boucou, quand   he works well; when a Negro
> Nègre tenire bon Maître, Nègre   has a good master, a Negro
> veni bon.   becomes good.
> Qui cila qui dire cila à toi?   Who told you that?

A 1748 text, also in the form of depositions at a criminal inquiry, offers a sample revealing a more elaborated version of the developing creole. In that inquiry Charlot, a slave accused of murdering a soldier, quotes his remarks to the victim who had been shooting at birds caught in traps set by the slave (Hall 1992: 177–78)[6]:

> (19) Vu! laisser la notre trapes.   Hey you, leave our traps
> Pourqoui tirer vois sous   alone. Why are you firing
> notre trapes? [*sic*]   under our traps?

Other slaves made the following depositions:

(20) Ou toy courir Charlot pendants   Where did you go while we
que nous diner?   had dinner?
Qui toy tuer, Charlot?   Whom did you kill, Charlot?
—Moy na rien tué.   —I haven't killed anyone.

Still, these fragments differ widely from a sample of what might be termed fully developed, classical nineteenth-century LC, as illustrated by the following song collected by Lafacadio Hearn (1885, 1960)[7]:

(21) Ah! Suzette, Suzette to veux   Ah, Suzette, dear, you don't
pas chère?   want to?
Ah! Suzette, Chère amie, to pas   Ah, Suzette, my dear friend,
l'aimin moin.   you don't love me.
M'allé dans montagne, zamie,   I'll go to the mountains, dear,
M'allé coupé canne, chère amie,   I'll cut cane, dear friend,
M'allé fait l'argent, mo trésor,   I'll go make money, my treasure,
Pour porter donné toi.   To bring to you.

Ah! Suzette, Suzette to veux   Ah, Suzette, dear, you don't
pas chère?   want to?
Ah! Suzette, Chère amie, to pas   Ah, Suzette, my dear friend,
l'aimin moin   you don't love me.
Mo couri dans bois, zamie,   I went into the woods, dear,
Mo toué zozo, chère amie,   I killed birds, dear friend,
Mo fé plain l'argent, mo trésor,   I made a lot of money, my
    treasure,
Pour porter donné toi.   To bring to you.

This song is typical of the relatively stable version of LC reflected by a considerable body of nineteenth-century texts (Neumann 1987) that resemble the present-day basilectal variety. More importantly, the song differs markedly from an equally large body of texts illustrating late-eighteenth-century Saint-Domingue Creole. From that material the text that reflects the most basilectal form of that creole is a one-act play written by Henri Christophe's court poet and secretary, Juste Chanlatte (1818), to celebrate the sovereign's visit to Cap Haitian that year. In this scene, Valentin, an ironsmith, and Marguerite, a servant, are represented speaking in Creole. The excerpt in (22) shows that, by the late colonial period, Saint-Domingue creole distinguished between a pre-posed subject form of pronouns and a post-posed form functioning as both a direct object and a prepositional complement. As is still the case in present-day northern Haitian Creole, the latter, preceded by the connective a, served as possessive determiner (compare the pre-posed possessive determiners of nineteenth-century and current LC that are much closer to corresponding French forms).

(22)... **mo** va trenné bel rechange la, bel mouchoir la et bel chapeau la cé pou cila **m** a metté toute dehors. . . . Mais, Valentin, toute monde après présenté bouquette aqué couplettes chanson **a io**, est-ce **mo** pas le gangné quienne **à moé, to** pas songé Marguerite encore, **t'**aprés négligé **li**.

I'll wear the beautiful outfit, the beautiful handkerchief and the beautiful hat; it's for that occasion that I'll be putting everything out. .. But, Valentin, everybody is presenting bouquets and their stanzas of songs. Won't I have my own? You're not thinking of Marguerite. You're neglecting her.

In terms of complexity, specifically the number of functionally differentiated sets, and in terms of structural distance from French, the pronominal system of Saint Domingue Creole occupies an intermediate position between LC (more precisely, the conservative French-based Creoles) and present-day Caribbean varieties, as illustrated by Haitian Creole. Table 7.2, which offers a comparison of these three system, is designed to mirror the historical development: CREOLE 1 reflects the older stage and CREOLE 3 the most advanced and innovative one. Not only does it have an undifferentiated set of pronouns, but it also differs widely from French pronouns at the semantic level in merging the first- and second-person plural. It offers crucial evidence for the following scenario for the development of New World French-based creole (Valdman 1992).

The earliest form of French-based creole originated in the central Caribbean island of Saint-Kitts where, in 1627, the French established their first settlement. This French-based creole was exported first to Guadeloupe and Martinique, and then, perhaps from secondary disseminating points, to Saint-Domingue. Finally, it was introduced in the later-established French colonies of Cayenne, Louisiana, and the Indian Ocean islands (Bourbon, present-day Reunion, and Isle de France, present-day Mauritius). Invoking Bartoli's stratigraphic dialectological model to New World Creole French, the late G. Hazaël-Massieux (1991) postulates that Martinique, Guadeloupe, and Saint-Domingue formed the central zone in the formation and diffusion of the language. Accordingly, it is in these islands that one would expect to find today the most innovative or advanced form of Creole French.[8] Older forms would be found in isolated zones, such as Grenada, or lateral zones, such as Guyana and Louisiana.

The close relationship between LC and CF is explainable not only in terms of the phenomenon of decreolization resulting from contact between the two languages after the emergence of the former, but also in terms of LC's origin in vernacular and dialectal varieties of French. Surely, the slaves were not exposed to the uniform SF of the Versailles court, but to the highly varied speech of the common folk. Another reason for the reduced distance between CF and LC is the low level of demographic and economic development in colonial Louisiana. Unlike Saint-Domingue, where by the end of the eighteenth century the slaves constituted 90 percent of the colony's population of more than 500,000, in Louisiana the proportions of the servile and free groups remained equal. There existed in colonial Louisiana what Robert Chaudenson

Table 7.2
Postulated Development of the Pronominal System of French-based Creoles

	CREOLE 1		CREOLE 2		CREOLE 3
	LC, Guyana, Indian		Saint-Domingue		Caribbean
	Ocean creoles (Haitian)		Creole		creole
			PRE-	POST-	
SUBJECT	OBJECT	POSS	POSED	POSED	
mo	mwe	mo	mo	mwẽ	mwẽ/m[a]
to	twe	to	to	twe	—
vu	vu	vu	vu	vu	u/w
li	li	so	li	li	li/l—li/i
nu	nu	nu	nu	nu	nū/n
zot	zot	zot	zot	zot	—
jø(—>je/jo)	jø	jø	jo	jo	jo/j

NOTE: [a]In present-day Haitian Creole, personal pronouns are subject to complex morphophonological variation. Strictly speaking the forms separated by the slash line, e.g., *u/w*, are not always in free variation. See Valdman (1978).

(1992) labels the *habitation* system, which is characterized by a relatively egalitarian relationship between slaves and the various European groups (Hall 1992). The *plantation,* or agro-industrial, phase was not put in place until the end of the eighteenth and the beginning of the nineteenth century. By that time an infrastructure was put in place adequate to support the intensive cultivation of sugar and cotton in the nineteenth century. During the *habitation* phase, French remained accessible to the slaves, and this prevented the radical internal restructuring exhibited by LC's more innovative Caribbean congeners. Moreover, the reduced social distance between the slaves and the lower strata of the European population characteristic of that developmental phase of plantocratic society helps accounts for the large proportion of white speakers of LC.

5. The African Element in LC

Gwendolyn Midlo Hall (1992) offers solid evidence for an unusually cohesive and heavily Africanized culture in lower Louisiana. She claims that it was, in fact, the most Africanized culture in the United States in the nineteenth century (1992: 161). Because of the heavy African cultural influence, primarily from Bambara in the early years of colonial French Louisiana according to Hall, one would expect the language devised by the slaves to also be Africanized. This is, in fact, the conclusion drawn by the author: "The vocabulary of Louisiana Creole is overwhelmingly French in origin, but its grammatical structure is largely African" (1992: 188). This is not a novel point of view. More than fifty years ago Suzanne Comhaire Sylvain (1936), a Haitian linguist, characterized Haitian Creole as French vocabulary shaped by the mold of African syntax, specifically that of Ewe, a Kwa language spoken in present-day Benin (formerly Dahomey). More recently, Claire Lefebvre from the University of Quebec in Montreal, views Haitian Creole as being composed of the grammar of Fongbe, another Kwa language, clothed in French vocabulary. In Louisiana, however, only toward the end of the eighteenth century did a large part of the servile population originate from Kwa-speaking areas in the Gulf of Benin (Hall 1992).

All specialists of creole linguistics agree that the vocabulary of French-based creole languages is derived mainly from French. Even in Haitian Creole, which contains many African-based words associated with voodoo, more than 90 percent of the vocabulary can be traced to present-day French or regional dialects. There is, however, considerable debate about the source of the grammar. So far, no scholar has demonstrated, with support from carefully documented studies comparing the various French creoles and various African languages, a clear link between the grammar of a specific African language or groups of African languages and a particular French-based creole language or the entire group. In judicial terms, we would say that the evidence for the African origin of creole grammar is mainly circumstantial: the languages were created mainly by African slaves, and it stands to reason that it should show the influence of their various native languages.

Three structural features of LC might be attributable to grammatical calquing from African languages: the post-position of the definite determiner *la* and of the plural marker *ye;* serial verbs; and the interrogative adverb kofé Haitian Creole (HC), which appears to be the most Africanized, provides the best starting point for building a case for direct African influence. In that language, all determiners occur after the noun; we also find this feature in Ewe and various western African languages, such as Igbo and Yoruba. For the sake of convenience, we provide, in addition to English and French equivalents, the interlinear translation which gives the meaning of each constituent element:

> (23) HC   kay-*sa-a* "that house"; *cette* maison
>   Ewe   afe *a*
>   Yoruba   ile *yen*
>   house *that*
>   HC   moun *sila yo* "these people"; *ces* gens *(*là*)*
>   Ewe   ame *sia wo*
>   people *that* PLURAL

Interestingly, in both Haitian Creole and Ewe the article appears at some distance from the noun it modifies, for example, at the end of a relative clause:

> (24) HC   oto li vann mouen *an* "the car which he sold me"
>   car he sold me DEFINITE
>   Fr. *la* voiture (l'auto) qu'il m'a vendue
>   Ewe   evu si wòdra *la*
>   vehicle which he sold to me DEFINITE

But if we compare HC to everyday conversational French, improperly labeled *Français populaire* "Plebian French", the post-position of the definite determiner is not particularly surprising. In that type of French "that house" would be *cette maison-là*. The use of *là* to emphasize definiteness is even more frequent in Quebec French and in CF. For example, we find in Revon Reed's *Lâche pas la patate:*

On avait beaucoup plus d'ouragons dans <u>ces jours-là</u> qu'aujourd'hui.
"There were many more hurricanes in those days than today." (73)

Thus, the placement of the determiner is probably best accounted for as
a *convergence* between a feature found in the French the slaves heard
and that of their native languages or some other African languages with
which they may have been acquainted.

Another feature of French-based creoles traced to African languages
are *serial verbs*. This feature, illustrated by one of the names for LC,
kouri vini, involves combinations of two or more verbs. Compared to
HC the frequency of serial verbs is relatively rare in LC. In the latter
language the meaning of the combination cannot be derived by the individual meaning of the constituent parts. One of the verbs, usually a verb
of motion, adds a nuance to the main verb. For example, in the combinations *mennen ale* "[to lead + to go] = take someone away", *pote ale* [to
carry] + [to go] = "to carry away", *pote vire* "[to carry] + [to turn] = to
bring back" the second verb, a verb of motion, functions as an adverb: it
indicates the directionality of the action. In other types of serial verbs
combinations the verb *ba* "to give" carries the benefactive meaning and
functions like the prepositions "for" of English or *pour* of French:

(25) HC	M kuit manje **ba** ou.	"I cooked the food for you"
	"I cook food give you"	J'ai cuit la nourriture (le manger) pour toi
Ewe	meda nu **na** wo	

Serial verbs are relatively rare in LC, but they also consist of a verb of
motion plus another that carries the central meaning of the combination
(Neumann 1985):

(26) Je te **kuri kupe** diri.   "They were going to cut rice."
     "They PAST run cut rice"   Ils allaient couper du riz.

     Mo pa wɒ lœr li **vini rive**.   "I didn't see at what time he
                                         came."
     "I not see time he came arrive"   Je n'ai pas vu l'heure à laquelle il
                                         est arrivé.

The third putative African feature is the interrogative adverb kofɛ
"why". M. Roy Harris (1973) traces the semantic model of that form in
the combinations "why" + "make" of the Kwa languages and of Yoruba,

which is also reflected in Atlantic English-based creoles—*wa mek* in Jamaican Creole and *mek* in Gullah. However, he also finds the combination *quoi* "why" + *faire* "make" in the western French dialect, Saintongeais. Finally, that combination also surfaces in CF *Quoi faire vous dit ça?* "Why do you say that?" Again, this is best explained as a case of convergence between the vernacular and dialectal varieties of French spoken by the white settlers of colonial Louisiana and the languages spoken by the African slaves.

Although language and culture are closely linked, the relationship is not direct. While many aspects of Louisiana culture such as music, folklore and food have their roots in the slaves' native cultures, there is little evidence that the grammar of the new language that developed in colonial French Louisiana was shaped by the languages they spoke. But this is not to deny any African influence on Louisiana Creole. A dozen years ago, when talking about the creole of his island, the great Martinican writer Aimé Césaire gave in French what stands as the most profound statement about the African element in Creole: *Le créole est une langue dont le corps est français mais l'âme africaine.* "Creole is a language whose body is French but whose soul is African." The mistake many linguists have made is to equate the soul of a language with its grammar. Gwendolyn M. Hall comes closer to the truth when she points out that members of the Louisiana Creole community, which includes whites as well as blacks, share speech rhythms and intonation and ways of using language, including, for example, the use of proverbs (188). It is perhaps these aspects of language and language use, which have received scant attention from linguists, that constitute the soul of Louisiana Creole and where the permanence of African modes of expression and communication might be sought.

Notes

The research underlying this article has been funded in part by grants from the Lurcy Charitable Trust and Indiana University.

1. A dictionary of LC is currently in preparation under the direction of Albert Valdman based on material gathered in the field by Thomas Klingler, Margaret Marshall, and Amanda Lafleur and compiled from a representative set of written texts.
2. For the sake of convenience a notation differing slightly from that of the International Phonetics Association has been adopted to represent the nasal vowels: [ɛ̃] for [ɛ̃], [õ] for [ɔ̃], and [ã] for [ũ].
3. The examples cited are from Neumann (1985), who treats this issue in great detail.
4. That there exists a close structural relationship between French and LC does not imply that the latter is viewed as a dialect of the former. There is a clear structural break between any variety of French, including CF and LC, as will be shown particularly in the verbal system (Valdman 1978).

5. Henceforth LC forms will be represented in italics with a phonological transcription; for variable features, such as the choice between [ã] or [õ] or between members of mid vowel pairs, we will list the variant provided by our sources, mostly Morgan (1959, 1960), Neumann (1985), Marshall (1990, 1991), Klingler (1992), or noted by the field interviewer of our lexicographic project without the present author making any attempt at phonemic interpretation.

6. These texts are reproduced as they appear in Hall (1992). That author does not indicate whether the obvious spelling errors appear in the original court transcripts.

7. This lover's complaint evokes the celebrated song "Lisette a quitté la plaine" composed in Saint-Domingue around 1760 which has been preserved in several versions (Moreau de Saint-Méry 1797, Valdman 1978:99).

8. As is pointed out in Valdman (1992) this generalization is somewhat reductionist because it considers each French colony as a single monolithic entity. In fact there existed significant differences in economic development and demographics within each individual colony. For example, in Saint-Domingue there was a greater proportion of large sugar plantations—exhibiting all the features of the agro-industrial system—in the northern plains, where the 1991 slave revolt first broke out. In Louisiana, the *plantation* system was first established in the fluvial areas and hardly penetrated the bayou regions where the Acadians settled.

References

Chanlatte (Juste, Comte de Rosiers). 1818. *L'entrée du Roi en sa capitale en Janvier 1818.* Cap Haïtien.

Chaudenson, Robert. 1992. *Des îles, des hommes, des langues: Langues créoles, cultures créoles.* Paris: l'Harmattan.

Combaire-Sylvain, Suzanne. 1936. *Le créole haïtien: morphologie et syntaxe.* Port-au-Prince: chez l'auteur et Wetteren, Belgique: De Meester.

Du Pratz, A. Le Page. 1758. *Histoire de la Louisiane.* Paris: DeBure.

Faine, Jules. 1936. *Philologie créole.* Port-au-Prince: Imprimerie de l'Etat.

Hall, Gwendolyn M. 1992. *Africans in Colonial Louisiana: The Development of Afro-Creole Culture in the Eighteenth Century.* Baton Rouge: Louisiana State Univ. Press.

Harris, M. Roy. 1973. "Kofè 'Pourquoi', un africanisme parmi d'autres en créole louisianais." *Revue de Louisiane/Louisiana Review* 2 (2): 88–102.

Hearn, Lafcadio. 1885. Gombo Zhèbes: *Little Dictionary of Creole Proverbs, Selected from Six Creole Dialects.* New York: Coleman (Réimpr. 1960).

Jarreau, Lafayette. 1931. *Creole Folklore of Pointe Coupée Parish,* mémoire de maîtrise inédite, Louisiana State Univ., Baton Rouge.

Klingler, Thomas A. 1992. "A Descriptive Study of the Creole Speech of Pointe Coupée Parish, Louisiana," Ph.D. diss., Indiana University.

Lefebvre, Claire et al. 1982. *Syntaxe de l'haïtien.* Ann Arbor, Michigan: Karoma.

Marshall, Margaret M. 1982. "Bilingualism in Southern Louisiana: A Linguistic Analysis." *Anthropological Linguistics* 24(3): 308–24.

Marshall, Margaret M. 1987. "A Louisiana Creole Speech Continuum." *Regional Dimensions* 5: 71–94.

Marshall, Margaret M. 1990. The Origins of French Creole in Louisiana. *Regional Dimensions:* 23–40.

Marshall, Margaret M. 1991. "The Creole of Mon Louis Island, Alabama, and the Louisiana Connection." *Journal of Pidgin and Creole Languages* 6 (1): 73–87.

Morgan, Raleigh J. 1959. "Structural Sketch of Saint Martin Creole." *Anthropological Linguistics* 1: 7–29.

Morgan, Raleigh J. 1960. "The Lexicon of Saint Martin Creole." *Anthropological Linguistics* 2: 7–29.

Morgan, Raleigh J. 1972. "L'ordre des mots dans la syntaxe du créole de Saint Martin." *Revue de Louisiane* 1(1): 65–81.

Morgan, Raleigh J. 1976. "The Saint Martin Copula in Relation to Verbal Categories." *Identité culturelle et francophonie dans les Amériques,*. Emile Synder and Albert Valdman, eds., 147–65. Québec: Presses de l'Université Laval.

Neumann, Ingrid. 1984. "Le créole des Blancs en Louisiane." *Etudes Créoles* 6 (2): 63–78.

Neumann, Ingrid. 1985. *Le créole de Breaux Bridge, Louisiane: Etude morphosyntaxique, textes, vocabulaire.* Hamburg: Helmut Buske.

Neumann-Holzschuh, Ingrid, ed. 1987. *Textes anciens en créole louisianais: avec introduction, notes, remarques sur la langue et glossaire.* Hamburg: Helmut Buske.

Valdman, Albert. 1978. Le créole: structure, statat et origine. Paris: Klinksieck.

———. 1992. "On the Socio-historical Context in the Development of Louisiana and Saint-Domingue Creoles," *Journal of French Language Studies* 2: 75–96.

EIGHT

James H. Dormon

Ethnicity and Identity: Creoles of Color in Twentieth-Century South Louisiana

It would seem appropriate for the concluding essay in this collection—a collection that has, in some respects, and necessarily, begged hard questions of definition—to begin by returning to the basics, first by offering a brief reconsideration of terminology, thence to other matters pertaining to the ethnic identity of the "Creoles of Color." In choosing "Creoles of Color" as the descriptive terminology the contributors to the collection selected the term that was from the antebellum years until quite recently the designation most commonly utilized by the Creoles themselves to describe their group—the members of which still, in the words of a recent interviewee, "know who we are."[1] Over the last few years, however, the term "black Creole" has come into more common, and less precise, usage. From whence and why the shift in terminology?

At first glance it would appear to be nothing more than a harmless concession to the cult of the politically correct—"people of color" sounds not only antiquated but also condescending. Further reflection, however, may suggest the possibility of a more significant reason for the shift. "Black" is clearly a more *inclusive* terminology. And if indeed the more recent usage reflects a shift in attitude from exclusivity to inclusivity on the part of the Creole population (or its spokespersons), one of the former defining qualities of Creole ethnicity—its differentiation of the group from the generalized black population by virtue of its historically favored position in the social order—has tacitly been rendered inoperative.

Whether such is the actual case is not, in fact, the most significant problem inherent in this possible paradox. More important is the matter of the implications of the shift for personal ethnic identity formation, the central factor in assessing ethnicity. If indeed "we know who we are," and if who we are is to be defined in such inclusive terminology as to include the entire African-American ("black") population of south Louisiana, does the term "Creole" itself have substantive meaning in establishing basic group identity?[2] It is with the question of individual and group identity within the context of this apparently insignificant shift in terminology that my assessment of the Creole experience of the latter part of the twentieth century will commence.

It will be useful to begin by reiterating some of the central aspects of Creole ethnic identity as they had developed by the mid-nineteenth century. First, there was the matter of genetic makeup: Creoles of Color were by definition Afro-European (with the possibility of the presence of Native American genes in some cases). They were not "blacks," i.e., Africans. Second, they were also normally free persons, not slaves, nor had they descended from slaves. As the historian David Rankin has noted, so-called "mulattoes" in antebellum Louisiana enjoyed something of a *prima facie* claim to free status, while blackness raised a presumption of slavery (Rankin 1978: 381–82; Spitzer 1977: 155). Moreover, such free persons of color, often enough "Creoles of Color," were deemed equal to whites in law. There was, in this regard, a substantive, defining distinction between such Creoles and blacks and a clear value attachment to the status "Creole of Color" among the members of the group.

There were other defining qualities as well: Language was important, of course—true antebellum Creoles spoke French; Standard French in the case of those who were especially advantaged, but surely French in some form (LaChance 1992: 115–20).[3] At the very least the recent forebears of antebellum Creoles claimed French as their mother-tongue language, and they took pride in the fact. By way of religion, Creoles were of course Catholic; in New Orleans they were likely to be members of a predominantly Creole parish and very much part of a special community, membership in which was a source of considerable personal pride. Indeed, pride of group; personal attachments to group values (including values associated with their elevated status), education, a kind of bourgeois propriety—all were factors that characterized Creoles of Color and rendered them very much a self-aware ethnic community that took considerable satisfaction in their identity as a people who assuredly knew who they were (Domínguez 1986: 205–61).

One clear sign of the sense of their "we-ness"—of their group identity and self-awareness—was the fact of endogamy within the group: They married one another and, to a remarkable degree, *only* one another. Marriages were frequently arranged between families, but in any case individuals chose mates from within the community; so much so that a close student of Louisiana genealogy has argued that the Creole population "virtually constitute[d] a series of large, interlocked families. . . ." (DeVille 1989: 298; Mills 1977: 78). Family property was often a consideration in marriage arrangements; in that the Creoles constituted an economically advantaged group, there was a clear necessity to maintain property by marrying *within* the group. To do otherwise was to risk loss of property, and with such a loss came the threat of loss of status (Schweninger 1990: 37). Little wonder, then, that special dispensations for consanguinity were often required by the church for numerous Creole marriages.

A final defining quality of Creole status might be sought in the very matter of their relative prosperity and in their value commitment to work and its rewards. This feature of their culture was described with considerable clarity in a *New Orleans Picayune* editorial on July 16, 1859: "As a general rule," the editorialist asserted, "the free colored people of Louisiana, and especially of New Orleans—the 'creole colored people,' as they style themselves—are a sober, industrious and moral class, far advanced in education and civilization" (quoted in Rankin 1978: 381). And there could be little doubt that this was the prevailing attitude with regard to a "class" of people who provided (according to Rankin) a substantial percentage of "the city's finest masons, carpenters, tailors, shoemakers, jewelers, tradesmen, and merchants" (Rankin 1978: 382). They also owned substantial property, real and personal, including slaves. And, as previous essays in this collection have suggested, in general the defining qualities of the Creoles of Color prevailed not only in New Orleans but also elsewhere among the various Gulf coastal communities in which Creoles formed significant population elements. Such was the case at least until the coming of the Civil War.

The American Civil War provided a major watershed in the continuity of Creole ethnohistory. As Professor Schweninger has argued, Creole property owners were devastated by the war (Schweninger 1990: 37). Moreover, during Reconstruction Creoles began to lose their special legal status, and, despite their monumental struggle to preserve what they had won, they were doomed to further loss in both property and status as the Reconstruction process concluded. It was with a palpable sorrow that the New Orleans Creole intellectual Armand Lanusse notified his people of their abandonment by the white power structure. The Creoles, he lamented, had been left "in the shadow and in oblivion," while former slaves "have gained liberty, and have been made . . . [our] equals" (Rankin 1978: 389–90).

But despite the loss of status and property, the Creoles maintained their sense of identity and belonging, their basic group identity, as well as their conviction of their own superiority over the mass of the black population (Rankin 1978: 409; Anthony 1978: 163). While in many respects their circumstances did not differ radically from those of black freedpersons, their sense of group identity within their various communities gained strength from their very need to seek solace within the group. With the advent of systematic Jim Crow segregation in the 1890s and the removal of all vestiges of their "in-between" social status, the

Creoles were left with nothing but their sense of group identity and a nostalgia for halcyon times (Domínguez 1986: 137–48; Haskins 1975: 55; Mills 1977: 170). In the accurate assessment of one of the Creole dispossessed, the group had now come to constitute "a forgotten people" (Mills 1977: xxv; see also Anthony 1978: 93–118).

It is within this "nadir" of the black American experience (as Rayford Logan termed it)—this period of Jim Crow segregation that constituted the American version of apartheid—that the Creoles were forced into a sometimes uneasy alliance with their black counterparts (Logan 1954). As a generally better educated and more articulate group, Creoles naturally assumed the leadership roles in the fight against segregation, discrimination, and subordination, for themselves and for the "Negro" population as a whole. Beginning with the struggle against the imposition of Jim Crow, Creoles had formed the first line of resistance (Logsdon and Bell 1992). Over time, and despite many setbacks, as the twentieth century advanced, the "Negro" leadership managed some significant victories, frequently in the courts in cases brought by the NAACP. But the culmination of the struggle came with the onset of the great Civil Rights movement of the 1950s and 1960s; a movement that carried in its wake the "Black Pride" element that promised black solidarity in the quest for black rights.

It was in the crucible of the Black Revolution that Creoles of Color encountered the central paradox of their ethnohistorical experience. Were they to join fully with their black peers in the struggle, seeking their identity within the larger black community as they fought for black equality? Or were they to enter the struggle for black rights while maintaining their sense of ethnic identity as Creoles? The response would in fact be ambivalent. Surely there were those, more often than not the younger generation, who joined the movement and identified completely with the black community. Others made all the public gestures necessary to suggest that the black community was indeed bound by unqualified solidarity. And yet, others, largely the older, more traditional Creoles, were committed overtly to the movement while maintaining a clear sense of their identity as Creoles of Color—still a very special people (Woods 1989: 5, 8, 120).

Evidence of the paradox, and the ambivalence of the response thereto, may be sought in several forms, all of them elusive but suggestive. Clearly, the demographic evidence suggests a continuation of Creole determination to remain distinctive. The process of "enclavement" (a term suggested by sociologist Sr. Frances Woods, a specialist in Creole social organization) persisted over the decades of the late nineteenth and early twentieth centuries (Woods 1989: 5). Distinctive Creole communities with fairly clear boundaries, recognized by members of the group as well as by outsiders, managed to maintain their existence over time. Endogamy also continued to reinforce the enclavement process by providing family networks as the basis of community formation and maintenance. Even after the Civil Rights and Voting Rights Acts of 1964 and 1965 marked the culmination of the first phase of the Civil Rights movement, the Creole communities persisted in their relative isolation. As one observer of the Isle Brevelle community reported, "They [the Creoles] just live to themselves. They don't have anything to do with others. It's just like a colony of people that live for themselves" (Woods 1972: 10). This opinion was confirmed by another contemporary observer, who noted: "These people are a self-contained unit. They are different from the ordinary Negro. They look different with their thin lips, long narrow noses, and long faces. . ." (Woods 1972: 10).

Such observations from outside the boundary serve to confirm the continuation of Creole exclusivity, as did the evidence from within the boundary: "Even though we are considered colored," observed one Cane River Creole, "we look about ourselves, and see such a striking physical difference between ourselves and Negroes, that we cannot quite accept the story that we, too, are Negroes" (Woods 1972: 370). It was an opinion shared, though not always articulated, by many of the older members of the group.

But not all of the younger Creoles were comfortable with their special status that differentiated them from the larger black community, especially as the later 1960s produced the fully developed Black Pride phenomenon. One such disaffiliate from her Creole identity spoke forthrightly to this point. Despite the fact that her parents insisted to her that her family was not "Negro," she claimed otherwise. "We are Negro and just like the other Negroes here [Isle Brevelle] even though most of us are lighter." One of her contemporaries agreed: "We don't like the idea of your distinguishing Creoles and Negroes like some of our people do, since we are all the same. We are all colored people even though some of us are lighter" (Woods 1972: 370). Notably, the informant's use of the phrase "our people" suggests the persistence of identification with the group despite the disclaimer.

And what of the view of Creoles from the perspective of the non-Creole blacks? The evidence suggests that the 1970s produced something of a reaction against Creole exclusivity. Creoles, according to one black informant of the period, lack "the soul that all Negroes have." Nonetheless, she continued to note that if the Creole will "act as a Negro then he's accepted [by blacks] . . ." But any evidence of Creole exclusivity would surely result in the rejection of the pretentious offender by ordinary blacks (Woods 1972: 367). One of Woods's informants was especially forthcoming on this point: "The mulatto [read "Creole"] is not your pure race, but yet he will try to style himself above me, and I am pure. Now there are a few of those mulattoes . . . that put themselves on the same quality with me, but most of them try to class up with the whites. If I was mulatto, I would be looking for the darker race to try to get with them" (Woods 1972: 10).

And the Creoles clearly understood the implications of this injunction. They had fallen into a classic form of social marginality, and the result was frequently confusion and even distress with their circumstances. In a series of interviews conducted with a group of Creole college students in the summer of 1974, I found such distress to be palpable. One female student was near tears when she reported that "Whites think we're black, and blacks think we're stuck-up." A male student was also clearly distressed in commenting on the difficulties Creoles experienced in dating. "We can't go with white girls *or* black girls," he observed (interviews Feb. 2, 1974; Feb. 5, 1974). Of necessity, then, such young people were confined to relationships within the Creole group, or with more tolerant members among the whites and/or blacks. Even so, in the mid-1970s there still persisted a determination to maintain Creole identity among many if not most of the older generation (Domínguez 1986: 163).

Yet another dimension of the Creole paradox of the 1970s has been noted by a close observer of Creole culture, anthropologist Nick Spitzer. In a suggestive article published in 1977, Spitzer contended that the rural/urban distinction between the ethno-racial attitudes of Creoles and blacks bears further exploration. He noted that those most closely identified with Creole traditions, at least in the Prairie region, tended to be rural folk, who "still live traditionally," as opposed to the urban dwellers, "lured by black American culture" (Spitzer 1977: 150). The rural Creole night clubs, he argues, tend to be upper class and color conscious, while the urban clubs attracted a black clientele that perceived itself as sophisticated and "hip." Spitzer was actually warned away from a "Soul Club" by country Creoles, who informed him that the club in question was "full of 'town niggers and hoodlums'" (Spitzer 1977: 150).

Since the Spitzer article was published, however, Creole clubs featuring zydeco entertainment have become quite popular in such urban, sophisticated communities as Lafayette, Louisiana, and blacks are surely welcomed as patrons. These clubs are not "Soul Clubs" featuring the latest in soul, blues, and rap stylings, so the Spitzer distinction may still be valid. It bears mention that another of my interviewees from the mid-1970s, in noting that she was "raised Creole" in a rural community outside Lafayette, clearly believed that the concept of Creole culture was identified with essentially rural life. In that she was at that time living in the city and identified herself as "black," her account would tend to confirm the Spitzer distinction (interview Aug. 23, 1972). In any case, the confusion of class status, ethnicity, and identity that beset the Creoles of the mid-1970s would appear to have seriously threatened the continued existence of Creole culture.

It has been said that the decade of the 1970s constituted an "Age of Ethnicity" following in the wake of the aborted "Age of Aquarius" (Hershberg 1973). In reality, the Age of Ethnicity was the patent result of the successes of the black Civil Rights movement and the advent of black political and economic power. Group after group—Native Americans, Hispanic Americans, Asian Americans, and innumerable "neo-ethnic" groups representing Americans descended from European ancestors—followed the African Americans in their quest for ethnic identity and group power (Dormon 1980). It was thus to be expected that Creoles would begin to re-examine their own ethnicity. But the actual onset of the Creole revitalization movement came as the result of the efforts of yet another ethnic group to re-establish its identity: the Acadians (or "Cajuns") of south Louisiana.

While the effort to re-establish the sense of Louisiana Acadian identity (and to associate a positive value with that identity) looked all the way back to the 1930s, the more recent efforts in that direction may be dated from the mid-1960s and the desire to preserve the spoken French of the region now known as "Acadiana" (Dormon 1983: 79–87). The current, ongoing revitalization movement may be said to have begun with the efforts of a Louisiana lawyer/politician by the name of James Domengeaux, who determined that something must be done to stimulate interest in preserving spoken French. Domengeaux and his supporters launched a movement to bring state political and financial support to the preservation of the language. In 1968 their efforts culminated in the formation of the Council for the Development of French in Louisiana (CODOFIL), which provided an institutional framework for the movement.

While CODOFIL focused its efforts primarily on restoring spoken French to the region, other ethnic Cajuns took the lead in developing another, more popular, dimension of ethnic revitalization. Their thrust was in the direction of preserving a broader spectrum of Cajun culture, most notably Cajun music and other forms of folklife. And their efforts met with unqualified success. Beginning in the early 1970s, annual Cajun music festivals quickly established their popularity. (Notably, young ethnic Cajun activists insisted that Creole zydeco performers be included in all festival performances, despite Domengeaux's distaste for Creole culture.) Cajun and Creole food and crafts came to be featured in the festival showcases. Over the years, Cajun culture (or some popular approximation thereof) gained tremendous exposure, and things Cajun (or claiming to be Cajun) established an international vogue. To a degree, the Cajun French language came into increasingly popular public use, and, in the Acadiana region itself, popular use of the "Cajun" label assumed ubiquitous proportions.

Everything from the local university (Southwestern Louisiana—the "University des Acadiens") to its athletic teams ("Ragin' Cajuns") to the Lafayette public transit system assumed the Cajun label—much to the distress of certain groups within the region who could not and did not claim Acadian ancestry. Most notable among these non-affiliators was the black population in general and the Creoles of Color in particular. In the words of one insistent interviewee: "I can't be Cajun. I'm *black*" (interview Aug. 23, 1972).

The first actual protest of the ubiquitous Cajun label came with the appearance of an organization calling itself the "UnCajun Committee," a loose-knit group of young black activists who couched their program almost exclusively in terms of their non-Cajun status. Relatively unstructured, the committee did little other than to object publicly to the term "Cajun" and to protest especially the Ragin' Cajun label for the University of Southwestern athletic teams, which had a substantial number of black personnel.[4] And, while the protest did attract considerable interest and support among the black population, there was little in the way of a positive program of ethnic self-assertion. The committee was simply "non-Cajun."

A second organization soon emerged, however, that was specifically designed not only to protest the Cajunification of the entire region, but also to provided a more substantial, positive program of ethnic revitalization among "non-Cajun" blacks. Its founders called it "Creole, Inc." (The name of the organization is technically C.R.E.O.L.E., Inc.—an acronym for "Cultural Resourceful Educational Opportunities towards Linguistic Enrichment.") In reality, Creole, Inc., had a second, earlier, predecessor that harked back to 1982; a small group of Creole spokespersons who had come to fear the demise of their culture and most especially the music most identified with that culture: the definitive Creole music called zydeco. The result of their efforts was the first of the now annual Southwest Louisiana Zydeco Festivals held in Plaisance, Louisiana, in St.

Landry Parish north of Opelousas. The festival was designed specifically to promote Creole culture, again in part as a response to similar promotions of Cajun culture. And it was an immediate success, drawing large, enthusiastic crowds despite the heat and humidity of the region in early September (Foote 1990: 18).

Five years later, in 1987, the founders of Creole, Inc., launched the next, and to date the most ambitious, program of Creole ethnic revitalization. The immediate background for the formation of the organization was actually another major festival, the "Festival Internationale de Louisiane," held annually in Lafayette and also inaugurated in 1987. Several of the leading spokespersons of the Creole community served as facilitators and translators for the first international festival, and during the festival they discussed the possibility of organizing a new group, one calculated to reinvigorate Creole culture and to reach out to other francophone nations with Creole populations, most notably Haiti and Guadeloupe (Drake 1990: 14). The group met, designed a charter, a program, and a flag. The flag purported to represent the origins of the Creole population and featured the national symbols of Africa, Spain, France, and the United States. The founding members identified themselves as "[a] group of individuals interested in preserving the Creole culture as it exists in the State of Louisiana." The slogan for the new organization read "L'Union Fait la Force": "Unity Makes Power" (publicity brochure, Creole, Inc.). The group also stated its governing purposes:

> 1) To develop, preserve and perpetuate the Creole culture in Louisiana by:
> a) identifying its rich resources b) encouraging its appreciation
> 2) To provide opportunities for establishing ties between Creole communities world-wide by:
> a) fostering an awareness of similar cultures
> b) improving communication between these different communities
> c) encouraging exchanges at all levels.

Scheduling monthly meetings and a membership campaign—membership was open "to anyone who is Creole or anyone having an interest in the Creole culture"—the founding group had launched a major revitalization program. Over the following years, Creole, Inc., emerged as a major force guiding the Creole ethnic renaissance.

In 1990, another of the leading Creole publicists, Ruth Foote of Lafayette, provided a journalistic outlet for expressions of Creole ethnicity when she founded *Creole Magazine* (she served as editor and publisher). December 1990 saw the initial appearance of the journal, one in which Foote stated editorially the purpose of her venture: To promote and preserve Creole culture, a culture "that has made significant contributions to the music, cuisine, and language of this region" (*Creole Magazine,* Dec. 1990: 3). In successive issues, the magazine was to feature an assortment of articles and features pertinent to the concerns of Creoles or those interested in Creole culture. Regular features included items on Creole folklore, music, cuisine, cultural affairs, leisure activities, and language. Indeed, Herbert Wiltz, a local language teacher and another key publicist of Creole affairs, offered a monthly lesson in the spoken Creole language—a language he identified with that of the Creoles of Haiti and Guadeloupe as well as Louisiana. A second contributor to the Creole language column was Professor Albert Valdman—who prepared the essay on language for this volume.

Other features included biographical treatment of individuals from the Creole community whose accomplishments were deemed of interest to the readership. Civil Rights and black-oriented politics got good coverage in feature articles and regular columns. Finally, the social activities of the Creole community received full treatment. Accounts of zydeco dances, outings, festivals, and the enormously popular Creole trail rides—weekend excursions on horseback involving hundreds of riders, accompanied by refreshment vans and live musical entertainment—received extensive coverage.[5]

In the initial issue of the magazine, two key supporters of the Creole revitalization movement, local businessmen/politicians Charles and Donald Cravins, pointed to the need to assert Creole unity and cultural pride in the interest of enhancing *economic* gain for the population. "The city of Lafayette and the state have spent hundreds of thousands of dollars," they asserted, "to promote the Cajun culture. . . . That expenditure has paid off for Cajuns. Tourists come to the area and seek out Cajun establishments. . . . [But] Creole people pay taxes too. Our culture should be promoted also so that businesses owned by Creole people can benefit" (Cravins and Cravins 1990: 9). The Cravinses, along with Herbert Wiltz, also began offering weekly radio and television shows featuring zydeco and Creole cultural material more generally, thus providing media outlets for information, events, meetings, and the like.

Such energy and action designed to promote Creole causes proved effective indeed. Wilbert Guillory, a key figure in the zydeco festival promotion, claimed in *Creole Magazine* in 1990 that he no longer feared the demise of Creole ethnicity. "I think there's a rebirth of the Creole culture. It's coming back. . . . More and more black people from this area realize that we have a culture out there that we were losing that we are trying to capture" (Foote 1990: 19). Within the context of Creole identity, Guillory's next phrase bears particular note: "We lost the identity of blackness of Afro-Americans. It's through the *black Creoles* that we capture that—through unity" (emphasis mine). And (in a similar vein) Foote adds editorially that the Creole "way of life" was "deeply rooted in African tradition, . . . one we should be proud of . . . whether you consider yourself Creole or not" (Foote 1990: 21).

Clearly, the spokespersons for the Creole cultural rebirth were in the process of shifting the basis of Creole identity to a more inclusive kind of dual ethnic identity: They were Creoles, but they shared a secondary identity with the larger African-American population. And, in a later interview, Foote re-emphasized the shift, even as she expressed something of the ambivalence of contemporary Creole identity formation. When asked whether she called herself a Creole, she hesitated. "Well, I would qualify," she observed. "But no, I am an African American, and African Americans do not need anything that would divide them any further" (interview July 13, 1993). It was a viewpoint shared by many of the younger Creoles, whose collective consciousness had been raised and whose political commitments were primarily to the causes of black unity and the promotion of African-American interests. For persons of her generation and ethno-racial sensibilities, this commitment to a shared, multivalent identity was essential. It would appear that their primary purpose was to offer to the Creole population some sense of their cultural particularity, but only as a variant of black culture, even as it was a variant of francophone Louisiana culture. Nonetheless, Creoles were still, as it were, special and different.

And for some of the Creole population, generally the older Creoles, who are closer to their historical origins as a genetically mixed, Catholic, francophone "third caste," the sense of their status and special place in the social order remains strong. A recent study of the Creole community of Parks, Louisiana, for example, supports this conclusion. "Even today [1989]," claims the author, the Creoles "form a separate group . . . and strive to maintain a separate identity" (Maguire 1989: 431). Another recent investigation of the Cane River/Isle Brevelle community came to a similar conclusion, though there was evidence of considerable identity confusion among some interviewees. For example, a participant at a large Creole family reunion confessed: "[B]eing a [member of the family] is a confusing identity. Some people in the family consider themselves Black, because they married Black and they have gone in that direction, but there are some that consider themselves white and don't want to be included in the Blacks, and some consider themselves white because they are Creole" (quoted in Woods 1989: 9).

Another interviewee recounted the case of a prairie Creole family with two daughters, one of whom married "well," i.e., married another Creole, while the other married a black New Orleanian. The latter union was not popular with the family, despite the fact that the new husband was a young attorney with real career potential. He was simply not "one of us" (interview Nov. 20, 1991). And, in an extreme example of persistent Creole commitment to the elevated status of their people, a recent interviewee admitted that he looked down on blacks—he termed them "Niggers"—and claimed that he avoided associating with "them" whenever possible (interview Feb. 21, 1992). He further implied that many of his Creole associates shared his distaste for blacks, but were reluctant to admit this to "outsiders." In any case, there can be no doubt about the continuing prevalence of Creole self-awareness in southwest Louisiana, despite the fact of varying value attachments to Creole identity.

Such would appear to be the case in New Orleans as well. Recent studies have documented both the contemporary commitment to Creole particularity as well as ambivalence regarding the status of Creoles. Haskins, whose research came largely out of the early 1970s, found the Creoles of the city committed to black pride and black consciousness. Domínguez, whose research derived from the 1980s, found that members of the city's Creole population "regard themselves, and are generally regarded in the New Orleans black community at large, as pretentious and elitist." And, while one wonders whether they actually regarded themselves as pretentious, Domínguez's work surely confirms a persistent Creole ethnic identity (Haskins 1975: 74; Domínguez 1986: 166; Gehman 1994: 110–12). More recently, Hirsch has argued that the "peculiar history of the creoles"—i.e., their relatively advantaged position in the social order—"may have made them key agents" in the political struggle for dominance in New Orleans, "but it also rendered them anachronistic" (Hirsch 1992: 319). No doubt this has been the case. Creoles everywhere may be expected to join fully with black political interests in contests divided along black and white lines.

But hear, on the other hand, a contemporary Creole woman living in Harahan, a river community on New Orleans's West Bank: "Why can't we be whatever we want to be? Cajuns can be Cajuns. African-Americans can be African-Americans. Why can't I be Creole, in terms of being a different kind of culture? . . . Black people get upset when you call yourself a Creole. It's OK to say I'm African-American. But yet I can't say without feeling uncomfortable . . . that I'm Creole, because first thing is like, she thinks she's better than us" (*New Orleans Times-Picayune*, Aug. 18, 1993). Once again, the boundary between black and Creole seems clearly demarcated in the words and sentiments of this heartfelt plea.

If the current Creole ethnic revitalization process is to persist, it will be because Creoles do indeed believe that they are the recipients of a culture and a set of traditions worth preserving. If, at the same time, they—or at least some of them—want to partake of the larger dimension of the African-American experience, there is a likelihood that they may do that too, though not always comfortably. There is still the possibility of tension between the (exclusive) Creole identity and the (inclusive) African-American identity when value attachments clash. Do Creoles exist because they are in fact *not* black, as was assuredly the case until Jim Crow segregation rendered the distinction politically and socially inoperative? Or is ethnic identity a protean concept, sufficiently malleable to meet the psychological, ego-forming needs of a given moment and set of circumstances? One suspects that it may be so; but in any case it remains clear that the concept "Creole of Color" endures as a meaningful social/historical reality, even if the dictates of contemporary sensibilities demand that "black Creole," however defined, becomes the acceptable (and accepted) descriptive terminology.

Notes

1. In that many of the individuals interviewed as sources for this essay requested anonymity, I have determined to cite *all* interview sources by date of interview only. All interview notes and tapes are on file.
2. The concept of "basic group identity" holds that personal affiliation and identification with an ethnic group provide the identifiers with one important element of their manifest sense of self; i.e., it is one of the many defining elements that make up the individual's personal sense of identity. For an extended treatment of the concept, see Isaacs (1975). See also Dormon (1980).
3. Paradoxically, "Plantation Creole" (the Franco–West African linguistic hybrid) was normally spoken by francophone slaves and their descendants. I am indebted to Carl Brasseaux for pointing to this important distinction.
4. The arguments of the "UnCajun" activists took an absurd turn when they came to include the position that the whole Cajun movement was an anti-black conspiracy, pointing to the fact (for example) that "Ragin'" spelled backwards was "Nigar."
5. The popularity of the trail rides suggests the historic association of the Prairie Creoles with cattle ranching. Many of their forebears were, in fact, cowboys.

References

Anthony, Arthé A. 1978. "The Negro Creole Community of New Orleans, 1880–1920: An Oral History." Ph.D. diss., Univ. of California, Irvine.

Cravins, Donald, and Charles Cravins. 1990. "Jambalaya." *Creole Magazine* 1: 9–10.

DeVille, Winston. 1989. "White by Definition: A Critique." *Plantation Society* 2: 295–300.

Domínguez, Virginia. 1986. *White by Definition: Social Classification in Creole Louisiana.* New Brunswick, N.J.: Rutgers Univ. Press.

Dormon, James H. 1980. "Ethnic Groups and 'Ethnicity': Some Theoretical Considerations." *Journal of Ethnic Studies* 7: 23–36.

———. 1983. *The People Called Cajuns: An Introduction to an Ethnohistory.* Lafayette, La.: USL Center for Louisiana Studies.

Drake, Mary Alice. 1990. "C.R.E.O.L.E." *Creole Magazine* 1: 14, 17.

Foote, Ruth. 1990. "Zydeco Festival '90: The Creole Players Behind the Scenes." *Creole Magazine* 1: 18–19, 21.

Gehman, Mary. 1994. *The Free People of Color of New Orleans: An Introduction*. New Orleans: Margaret Media.

Haskins, James. 1975. *Creoles of Color in New Orleans*. New York: Thomas Y. Crowell.

Hirsch, Arnold R., and Joseph Logsdon. 1992. *Creole New Orleans: Race and Americanization*. Baton Rouge: Louisiana State Univ. Press.

Hirsch, Arnold R. 1992. "Simply a Matter of Black and White: The Transformation of Race and Politics in Twentieth Century New Orleans." In Hirsch and Logsdon (1992).

Hershberg, Theodore. 1973. "Toward the Historical Study of Ethnicity." *Journal of Ethnic Studies* 1: 1–5.

Isaacs, Harold. 1975. *Idols of the Tribe: Group Identity and Political Change*. New York: Harper and Row.

LaChance, Paul F. 1992. "The Foreign French." In Hirsch and Logsdon (1992).

Logan, Rayford W. 1954. *The Negro in American Life and Thought: The Nadir, 1877–1901*. New York: Collier Books.

Logsdon, Joseph, and Caryn Cossé Bell. 1992. "The Americanization of Black New Orleans, 1850–1900." In Hirsch and Logsdon (1992).

Maguire, Robert E. 1989. "'Hustling to Survive': Social and Economic Change in a South Louisiana Black Creole Community." Ph.D. diss., McGill Univ.

Mills, Gary B. 1977. *The Forgotten People: Cane River's Creoles of Color*. Baton Rouge: Louisiana State Univ. Press.

Rankin, David. 1977–78. "The Impact of the Civil War on the Free Colored Community of New Orleans." *Perspectives in American History* 11: 379–416.

Schweninger, Loren. 1990. "Prosperous Blacks in the South, 1790–1880." *American Historical Review* 95: 31–56.

Spitzer, Nicholas R. 1977. "Cajuns and Creoles: The French Gulf Coast." *Southern Exposure* 5: 140–55.

Woods, Sr. Frances Jerome. 1972. *Marginality and Identity: A Colored Creole Family Through Ten Generations*. Baton Rouge: Louisiana State Univ. Press.

———. 1989. *Value Retention among Young Creoles: Attitudes and Commitment of Contemporary Youth*. Mellen Studies in Sociology, Vol. 5. Lewiston, N.Y.: Edwin Mellen Press.

Selected Bibliography

Ancelet, Barry J., et al. 1991. *Cajun Country*. Jackson: Univ. Press of Mississippi.

Berlin, Ira. 1974. *Slaves without Masters: The Free Negro in the Antebellum South*. New York: Oxford Univ. Press.

Blassingame, John. 1973. *Black New Orleans, 1860–1880*. Chicago: Univ. of Chicago Press.

Brasseaux, Carl A. 1987. *The Founding of New Acadia: Beginnings of Acadian Life in Louisiana*. Baton Rouge: Louisiana State Univ. Press.

———. 1990. *Acadian to Cajun: Transformation of a People, 1803–1877*. Jackson: Univ. Press of Mississippi.

———. 1994. *Creoles of Color in the Bayou Country*. Jackson: Univ. Press of Mississippi.

Brathwaite, Edward. 1971. *The Development of Creole Society in Jamaica*. Oxford: Clarendon Press.

Cohen, David W., and Jack P. Greene, eds. 1972. *Neither Slave Nor Free: The Freedmen of African Descent in the Slave Societies of the Free World*. Baltimore: Johns Hopkins Univ. Press.

Domínguez, Virginia. 1986. *White by Definition: Social Classification in Creole Louisiana*. New Brunswick, N.J.: Rutgers Univ. Press.

Gehman, Mary. 1994. *The Free People of Color of New Orleans: An Introduction*. New Orleans, La.: Margaret Media.

Gould, Philip. 1992. *Cajun Music and Zydeco*. Baton Rouge: Louisiana State Univ. Press.

Hall, Gwendolyn Midlo. 1992. *Africans in Colonial Louisiana: The Development of Afro-Creole Culture in the Eighteenth Century*. Baton Rouge: Louisiana State Univ. Press.

Haskins, James. 1975. *Creoles of Color in New Orleans*. New York: Crowell.

Hirsch, Arnold R., and Joseph Logsdon. 1992. *Creole New Orleans: Race and Americanization*. Baton Rouge: Louisiana State Univ. Press.

Johnson, Michael P., and James L. Roark. 1984. *Black Masters: A Free Family of Color in the Old South*. New York: W. W. Norton.

McDonald, Robert R., et al., eds. 1979. *Louisiana's Black Heritage*. New Orleans: The Louisiana State Museum.

Mills, Gary B. 1977. *The Forgotten People: Cane River's Creoles of Color*. Baton Rouge: Louisiana State Univ. Press.

Morner, Magnus. 1976. *Race Mixture in the History of Latin America*. Boston: Little, Brown and Co.

Rankin, David. 1977–78. "The Impact of the Civil War on the Free Colored Community of New Orleans." *Perspectives in American History* 11: 379–416.

Roussève, Charles B. 1937. *The Negro in Louisiana: Aspects of His History and His Literature*. New Orleans: Xavier Univ. Press.

Schweninger, Loren. 1990. *Black Property Owners in the South, 1790–1915.* Urbana: Univ. of Illinois Press.

Spitzer, Nicholas R., ed. 1985. *Louisiana Folklife: A Guide to the State.* Baton Rouge: Louisiana Folklife Program.

Sterkx, Herbert. 1972. *The Free Negro in Antebellum Louisiana.* Rutherford, N.J. Fairleigh Dickinson Univ. Press.

Valdman, Albert. 1978. *Le Créole: Structure, Statut et Origine.* Paris: Klinsieck.

Vincent, Charles. 1976. *Black Legislators in Louisiana During Reconstruction.* Baton Rouge: Louisiana State Univ. Press.

Weber, David. 1992. *The Spanish Frontier in North America.* New Haven: Yale Univ. Press.

Williamson, Joel. 1980. *New People: Miscegenation and Mulattoes in the United States.* New York: Free Press.

Woods, Sr. Frances Jerome. 1972. *Marginality and Identity: A Colored Creole Family through Ten Generations.* Baton Rouge: Louisiana State Univ. Press.

————. 1989. "Value Retention among Young Creoles: Attitudes and Commitment of Contemporary Youth." *Mellen Studies in Sociology* 5. Lewiston, N.Y.: Edwin Mellen Press.

Contributors

BARRY JEAN ANCELET, Professor of French and currently Chairperson of the department of modern languages at the University of Southwestern Louisiana, is a linguist and folklorist who has published widely in the area of Francophone studies and Creole and Acadian music and folklore.

CARL A. BRASSEAUX, Associate Professor of history and Assistant Director of the Center for Louisiana Studies at the University of Southwestern Louisiana, serves as managing editor of *Louisiana History*, the journal of the Louisiana Historical Association. His extensive publications have dealt primarily with the Louisiana Acadian and Creole populations.

JAMES H. DORMON, Professor of history, University of Southwestern Louisiana, is a specialist in American culture and ethnic studies. He has published books on African-American culture and Louisiana Acadians as well as American popular culture and the painter and naturalist John J. Audubon.

VIRGINIA MEACHAM GOULD received her Ph.D. from Emory University in 1991 and is presently Adjunct Professor of history at DeKalb College in Atlanta. Her major academic interests, in addition to Creoles of Color, include urban slave women in the Gulf port cities of New Orleans, Mobile, and Pensacola.

KIMBERLY S. HANGER, Assistant Professor of Latin American history at the University of Tulsa, formerly served as Historian for the Louisiana State Museum. The author of several important articles, she currently has a book in press on the free people of African descent in Spanish New Orleans.

LOREN SCHWENINGER is a Professor of history at the University of North Carolina at Greensboro. He has published major articles on free persons of color in antebellum America and is author of *Black Property Owners in the South, 1790-1915* (1990).

NICHOLAS R. SPITZER is Research Associate and Artistic Director of the Folk Masters series at the Smithsonian Institution. His Ph.D. is in anthropology, and he has significant publications on Zydeco as well as on other aspects of Creole and Acadian folklore. He also directed the PBS broadcast film *Zydeco* in 1986.

ALBERT VALDMAN holds the title of Rudy Professor of French and Italian and Linguistics at Indiana University. A specialist in Creole languages and language acquisition, he has been internationally recognized for his contributions to the study of Creole linguistics.

Index